THE INVESTOR'S PARADOX

THE INVESTOR'S PARADOX

THE POWER OF SIMPLICITY IN A WORLD OF OVERWHELMING CHOICE

BRIAN PORTNOY

palgrave
macmillan

First published in 2014 by PALGRAVE MACMILLAN® in the United States—a division of
St. Martin's Press LLC, 175 Fifth Avenue, New York, NY 10010.

Where this book is distributed in the UK, Europe and the rest of the world, this is by
Palgrave Macmillan, a division of Macmillan Publishers Limited, registered in England,
company number 785998, of Houndmills, Basingstoke, Hampshire RG21 6XS.

Palgrave Macmillan is the global academic imprint of the above companies and has
companies and representatives throughout the world.

Palgrave® and Macmillan® are registered trademarks in the United States, the United
Kingdom, Europe and other countries.

ISBN: 978-1-137-27848-7

Library of Congress Cataloging-in-Publication Data
Portnoy, Brian.
    The investor's paradox : the power of simplicity in a world of overwhelming choice /
Brian Portnoy.
        pages   cm
    Includes index.
    Summary: "We're all familiar with "choice overload," whether on a trip to the grocery
store, or while flipping through satellite TV channels. And while it's human to want all of
the options, the surprising truth is that the more choice we have, the less satisfied we are.
And nowhere is this more true--or more dangerous--than in our investments. Despite
the troubled global economy, there are tens of thousands of mutual funds, hedge funds,
exchange-traded funds, and other vehicles waiting to take your money. For help, individual
and institutional investors alike turn to financial managers, though they are often no better
equipped than the average person to assess and manage risk. In The Investor's Paradox,
hedge fund expert Brian Portnoy explains how to sift through today's diverse investment
choices and solve even the most daunting portfolio problems. Drawing on cutting-edge
research in behavioral economics, social psychology and choice theory, Portnoy lays bare
the biases that interfere with good decision-making, and gives readers a set of basic tools
they can use to tell the good from the bad. Along the way, he demystifies hedge funds, cuts
through the labyrinth of the modern financial supermarket, and debunks popular myths,
including the idea that mutual funds can "beat the market."" —Provided by publisher.
    ISBN 978-1-137-27848-7 (hardback)
    1. Portfolio management. 2. Investment analysis. 3. Investments. I. Title.
HG4529.5.P678   2014
    332.6—dc23

                                                                        2013027032

A catalogue record of the book is available from the British Library.

Design by Letra Libre Inc.

First edition: January 2014

10 9 8 7 6 5 4 3 2 1

Printed in the United States of America.

Out of clutter, find simplicity.

—Albert Einstein

CONTENTS

Acknowledgments   ix

Foreword by Ted Seides   xi

INTRODUCTION   The Trillion-Dollar Job That No One
                Talks About   1

PART I
CHALLENGE

CHAPTER 1   More   13

CHAPTER 2   Picking ~~Winners~~ Losers   25

CHAPTER 3   Alternative States   55

PART II
SOLUTION

CHAPTER 4   Adaptation   97

CHAPTER 5   Madoff's Hobgoblins   125

CHAPTER 6   The Devil(s) You Know   155

CHAPTER 7   Parsing Lake Wobegon   183

CHAPTER 8   Less   209

Notes   219

Index   235

About the Author   241

ACKNOWLEDGMENTS

ONE OF THE JOYS OF THIS PROJECT WAS RECOGNIZING THAT WRITING is an exercise of discovery as much as it is one of expression. You sort of don't know what the book is really going to be about until you've actually written it; the process of figuring it out vacillates between being terrifying and being exhilarating. A primary reason for feeling the latter was the opportunity to share this journey with so many friends and colleagues who offered help and encouragement along the way.

It's a no-brainer to put my agent, Leah Spiro, at the front of the line for thanks. Without her direction, my nub of an idea wouldn't have become realized. She has been a steadfast advocate from the get-go, offering calm, measured advice when a certain author might not have been especially calm or measured. I owe thanks to the entire team at Palgrave Macmillan, especially my editor, Emily Carleton. From our first meeting in the Flatiron Building in New York, they embraced the project and provided the needed resources for its fruition.

Several friends generously read the entire manuscript and offered valuable criticisms and suggestions. First among them is Ben Happ, who read countless drafts of various chapters, deftly tore up the original full manuscript, and offered sage advice on many things. Paul Musgrave quickly reminded me of the best that academia has to offer in terms of collegiality and rigor. Mark Carhart, Eric Jacobson, Meredith Jones, Cem Karsan, John Kenny, and Gil Ottensoser also made major contributions. Erin Arvedlund's guidance throughout the process has been indispensible. Many others have shown support along the way by providing edits, helping talk through some sticky issue or another, or just giving positive encouragement. Thanks to Laura Abendschein, Dave Adams, Rob Bloomberg, Pat Burke, Trish Halper, Matt Edwards, Bill Friend, Rich Geller, Greg Hall, Jim Cahn, Thomas Kim, Anthony Lawler, Joe Nicholas, Ed O'Reilly, Laura Payne, Gabriel Presler, Paul Pryor, Josh Rogers, Jake Rossof, Greg Schwieder, Marci Sepulveda, Eric Slaim, Richard Webley, and Leon Yi. Over many years, I learned much from numerous colleagues at Morningstar and Mesirow, institutions filled with professionals dedicated to doing right by their clients. I owe a big thanks to Pat Lynch and the team at Chicago Equity Partners, who could not have created a more collegial environment to work through the day and still feel motivated to write at night.

And, finally, my family. As with most things in my life, this book owes the deepest gratitude to my wife, Tracy. We learn at some point, I believe, that life is defined less by getting knocked down and more by the determination and grace by which one gets back up. I couldn't be more blessed to have her as my best friend and partner to traverse all that comes our way, and as a role model for our children in knowing what really matters. To Ben, Zach, and Sarah: We often talk about the adventure of it all, of the promise and the opportunity. Mine would be a hollow journey without you. I cherish our adventure together, which only seems to get better and better over time. I love you each dearly.

FOREWORD

By Ted Seides

Co-Chief Investment Officer and
President, Protégé Partners

THE INVESTOR'S PARADOX COMES AT A CRITICAL MOMENT FOR INVESTORS. Scrutiny of hedge funds in the mass media is at an apex, yet allocators simultaneously have chosen to invest in hedge funds more than ever before. What gives?

Students of market history need not stretch to understand the dilemma. With interest rates historically low, bonds are very rich. After a healthy run beginning in 2009, stocks are not cheap, either. Considering these factors, many conclude that the traditional way of making a buck may have a tough slog ahead.

Investors of all stripes realize that picking the right money managers may matter a lot more going forward than it has in the past, when passively owning a diverse array of assets achieved their long-term objectives. This search for something different has led many to alternative investments, but how to proceed from there remains puzzling. In addition to choosing among thousands of different stocks, bonds, or traditional mutual funds, we now have an entirely new category of options. Liquid alternatives are abundantly available to anyone with a brokerage account.

The challenge of choosing the right money managers has defined my career for the last twenty years. I had the great fortune to spend the nascent years of my career under the tutelage of David Swensen, the chief investment officer at Yale University's endowment. Many readers of his terrific book, *Pioneering Portfolio Management,* came away with the idea that the "Yale Model" of generously allocating to alternatives was the root of the endowment's success. The truth, however, is that Yale's asset allocation had hardly benefited from moving out of equities and bonds when Swensen wrote his book.

Instead, from behind the curtain, what I saw on a daily basis was the consistent skill with which Swensen and his team sourced, researched, and chose managers to include in Yale's portfolio. Throughout Swensen's illustrious career at the university, the endowment has benefited substantially from outperformance of carefully selected active managers across every asset class and investment style. Indeed, skill in manager selection matters to achieve long-term investment success.

Since leaving Yale some time ago, I have continued a career investing through managers. Just after the dot.com bubble popped, I helped launch Protégé Partners, a business focused on the inefficient area of small and emerging hedge fund managers. Along the way, I made a well-publicized wager with Warren Buffett about the long-term prospects of hedge funds relative to the market. Yet in my continuous study of the art and science of manager selection, I don't recall a body of work specifically addressing the increasingly important issue of how to improve the chance of investment success through manager selection.

The Investor's Paradox has arrived at just the right time. We face an unprecedented amount of choice in implementing investment strategies, and this insightful book helps filter out the noise to home in on what matters when making these critical decisions, whether you're a sophisticated allocator or an individual investor. I can't think of a better book on how to choose the best investment experts. Portnoy's application of the current insights of behavioral finance raises the bar for those grappling with manager selection.

Knowing Brian over the last decade, I consider him one of the most thoughtful and creative researchers I have come across. Teaching what he has learned through years in the trenches, he leverages key lessons of history and taps into the best practices demonstrated by the world's top investment managers. For individual and professional investors alike, *The*

THE TRILLION-DOLLAR JOB
THAT NO ONE TALKS ABOUT

An expert is a person who has made all the mistakes that can be made in a very narrow field.

—Neils Bohr

FEW VISITORS TO CLIFFORD STREET IN LONDON'S TONY MAYFAIR neighborhood would find much to remember. It is narrow and short, with an uninterrupted row of stately but unremarkable low-rise buildings, perhaps most relevant for cabbies ferrying wealthy shoppers between the jewelers on Bond Street and the clothiers of Savile Row.

Once mostly residential, Mayfair has seen many of its homes converted into offices, and even centuries-old structures demand some of the highest rents in the world. Art, commerce, and cuisine are welcome endeavors in Mayfair, but it is the power of finance that courses through the labyrinthine district. Behind these nondescript doors are some of the world's most secretive and prosperous wealth managers, private banks, and hedge funds.

Clifford Street's lack of noteworthiness stands in contrast to the gravity of wealth resting on the other side of pale-brown stone facades and weathered white porticos. When I first turned the corner onto Clifford Street in the fall of 2005, my job was a combination of talent scout and financial analyst, charged to find good portfolio managers to whom my firm could allocate capital on behalf of our clients, which were mostly conservative pension funds and other large institutions. Because our average investment was very large, we held the skeleton key to enter every locked door in Mayfair and beyond.

On that particular day, I was responsible for leading the due diligence on a so-called event-driven hedge fund, meaning that they took bets on the likelihood of mergers, acquisitions, and other corporate restructurings. We had already vetted the firm's New York–based associates, and it had gone well, so my boss and I flew to London to meet the other key principals. Upon arriving, we were escorted into a room that looked suited for a law school seminar, with wainscoted mahogany walls and a large, worn conference table.

Over the past fourteen years, I have conducted something like 4,000 interviews with portfolio managers and other investment professionals. Sometimes we meet in person, sometimes over the phone; sometimes it's one conversation with a single person that lasts less than an hour, other times meetings with an entire team fill a whole day; sometimes hundreds of millions of dollars are on the line, other times it's a casual coffee to get to know someone better. This particular session in Mayfair was to be nothing out of the ordinary. We would review the background of the principals, the market opportunity, and the details of their investment process.

Instead, it was a train wreck—the worst due diligence session I have ever conducted. The meeting started harmlessly enough. The lead portfolio manager arrived in his Mayfair uniform: fitted dark suit, understated tie, posh accent. But after some opening pleasantries, the conversation went awry. It turned out he was less interested in a dialogue than in regaling us with heroic stories of trading conquests. Even at that early stage in my career, I could usually corral an egotistic fund manager back on track, but for some reason that day, I was inept. My questions were indirect and open-ended, which only let him bloviate more. My feeble attempts to redirect the conversation failed. After a certain point, it felt like a conversation with Charlie Brown's teacher, all intonation and no words. My boss opted not to intervene. As things went steadily south, I sensed him sliding lower in his chair. Finally he just left; I can't recall if he actually needed to be somewhere else or just needed to not be there.

I'm still not sure why things went so poorly. Perhaps I was unprepared; overly deferential to a glib professional; intimidated by the watchful proximity of my boss; or just jet-lagged. Whatever the reason, this failing wasn't trivial. We had flown thousands of miles at great expense to vet this investment. Our firm was in steep competition with other global allocators to source great talent. Wasted meetings weren't an option, especially overseas.

When it was finally over, I stepped back out onto Clifford Street, thankful for some fresh air and oddly in good spirits, just knowing it was over. The rush was short-lived. In reviewing my notes, I realized I had barely any of the answers we needed in order to decide whether we should invest. This was an enormous waste of resources. And there are no do-overs in this game. Shortly thereafter, at a coffee shop down the block, I reconnected with my boss. At first, no words were spoken. Just a look. "That was a disaster," I muttered. After a pause, he responded, "Yes. Yes it was."

NO ONE GROWS UP WANTING to do fund manager research. Of all the lofty and interesting career aspirations that I recall from my youth and that I now see with my young children—fireman, astronaut, comic book illustrator, Pittsburgh Steeler, princess—the vocation of outsourcing investment discretion to professional money managers never figured. There are plenty of tales about young folks who developed an early passion for picking stocks. But this is something different. I suspect that no child has ever dreamed of doing the task to which I've devoted my career.

Fund managers—like those from firms like Fidelity, JPMorgan, Bridgewater, Fortress, and thousands of others—manage money on behalf of their clients. Fund managers pick securities, mainly stocks and bonds. How they do so is the stuff of conventional finance.

By contrast, fund investors pick people, not securities. How to buy and sell people is a square peg in the round world of finance because people aren't tickers. They lack audited financial statements, and they don't vary in price from moment to moment (which isn't to say they're not volatile). People are riddled with behavioral biases, and they often don't act in ways that would be objectively considered rational. In finance, quantitative metrics might be open to interpretation, but they don't lie. People can and sometimes do.

This is a book about making good investment decisions—of a particular kind. Few of us actually build our portfolios by directly selecting individual stocks, bonds, commodities, currencies, or other securities. Instead we turn to experts—to fund managers—to help us navigate complex markets. But even choosing those experts is fraught with difficulty. There are countless books and seminars on how to pick stocks and bonds; not so for choosing the right experts.

I have now spent a good majority of my career trying to pick winning fund managers. As a researcher at firms in both the "traditional" (mutual fund) and "alternative" (hedge fund) industries, I have vetted thousands of managers, overseen multibillion-dollar portfolios of underlying fund investments, published dozens of articles praising or panning specific managers, and collaborated with scores of talented analysts. The job has taken me to every corner of the globe, from tiny outposts in Mumbai and Oslo to the tallest skyscrapers in New York, Hong Kong, and Tokyo. There have been plenty of successes and plenty of setbacks along the way; I have made many mistakes. Both disappointing and edifying, the episode on Clifford Street was one of many exercises in the peculiar art of fund manager selection that informs my perspective today. Indeed, we all know how to get to Carnegie Hall.

Based on my experience, the genesis of this book was an attempt to make sense of what I believe to be two big shifts in the world around us. First, in the aftermath of the 2008 global financial crisis, markets appear to have changed. My and my parents' generations benefited greatly from a nearly thirty-year bull market that kicked off in the early 1980s. Many serious analysts now suggest that the future won't resemble the past. I agree. While it was never easy, the strong headwinds now facing the investor class are arguably unprecedented. Second, the playbook has changed. Investors have an increasingly broad and complex set of investment choices before them—including the explosion of accessible hedge funds onto the scene—in order to succeed in this new world order of money management. We might think that serious challenges call for new and powerful tools, but as the old saying goes, be careful what you wish for.

It is this intersection of dangerous markets and overwhelming choices for which I aim to provide some useful guidance. To do so, I leverage a concept I've coined called the "investor's paradox," which speaks to how difficult it is to actually choose the right investments in light of the broader forces at play. In particular, we desire an abundance of choice—but often find it defeating. As well, we feel compelled to tackle complex challenges with sophisticated solutions—but frequently find them disappointing.

Unlike many treatments of investing, the source of my guidance stems less from the strictures of finance than from the insights of behavioral psychology. The modern paradox facing investors—ranging from big institutions overseeing billion-dollar portfolios to the everyman tending to his nest egg—is part of a broader challenge on how to make good decisions. Indeed, one of the most important insights of the behavioral and cognitive sciences is that happiness occurs when outcomes meet our expectations. Likewise, much of investing success is about appropriately managing expectations, yet this is informed by adaptive human behavior more than by technical treatments of stocks or bonds. Square pegs don't fit round holes.

AN ODDBALL CAREER

My nonlinear career path strongly influences the forthcoming narrative. In retrospect, it seems that I entered the financial markets at the beginning of the end. In early 2000, as I moved from academia to Morningstar, the shop that basically invented the field of manager research, the stock market experienced the start of a prolonged decline. Arriving at the end of a party is rarely fun; I was able to cut my teeth by analyzing managers and fund complexes just as many of them fell into steep decline. It was not only the highfliers of the period such as Janus, Putnam, and AIM that took it on the chin; even the most respected firms struggled to protect their clients' investments. Many investors not only lost their nest eggs; they grew anxious and confused about what to expect next. It was the beginning of a lost decade for many investors, when stock markets returned just about nothing.

I was too far immersed in the weeds of interviewing portfolio managers day in and day out to truly appreciate some of the broader forces at play. Within the context of the traditional mutual fund—long-only, fully invested, narrowly focused, and mandated to beat a benchmark rather than make money—I tried to assess whether a fund manager was good at picking stocks, managing risk, and delivering good performance. In retrospect, my task amounted to dancing on the head of a pin, exploring issues of fo-cus, skill, and returns, when in fact the imposed constraints of traditional structures largely predetermined the results.

Meanwhile, in the same decade, those investors who experimented with so-called alternatives generally survived well, even earning big profits during the 2000–2002 bear market. By coincidence—pure luck, really, since I hadn't yet caught on to the emerging paradigm shift—I left Morningstar to become a hedge fund analyst with Mesirow Advanced Strategies, a well-regarded "fund of hedge funds." Funds of funds specialize in identifying good hedge fund managers, building portfolios of them (hence the literal name, fund of funds), and monitoring their activities, all with the aim of delivering clients good returns. That firm, along with other sizable peers (e.g., Grosvenor, Harris Alternatives, Glenwood), established Chicago as one of the premier global hubs for hedge fund investing. At peak, there was probably around $60 billion of funds-of-funds capital parked within a few blocks of Lake Shore Drive.

At that time, hedge fund strategies were just beginning to attract massive amounts of capital from serious institutions like pension funds, insurance companies, and foundations. Teachers' unions, hospital endowments, and corporate pensioners became increasingly reliant on investing in the right hedge funds (whether their constituents knew it or not). As a result, high-quality groups like Mesirow grew exponentially in just a matter of years.

I was not alone in my accidental vocation. There are hundreds of thousands of professional investors and financial advisors worldwide who spend a good chunk of their time researching, selecting, and monitoring money managers—from traditional mutual funds to more complex hedge funds. Massive sums of capital get allocated and reallocated by profes-sional fund pickers. At present, roughly one-third of the investments in the $2 trillion hedge fund industry flow through the fund-of-funds vehicles ex-ecuted by a profession that until recently few had ever heard of. Meanwhile, investment consultants now advise on trillions of dollars of manager allo-cations. And more recently, many end investors—pensions, endowments, insurance companies, sovereign wealth funds, and so forth—are now look-ing to bypass these intermediaries and "go direct." They are bringing pro-fessional fund picking in-house.

Yet manager research remains a curious and largely unknown profession. There are virtually no college or MBA courses on the topic, in stark contrast to the endless seminars on equities, fixed income, or portfolio theory. There are few good books on the topic, but many compelling texts on securities analysis. Though there are many skilled talent scouts, it's hard to point to industry "stars." On the annual registration form for the prestigious Chartered Financial Analyst (CFA) certification, there is no box to check to indicate that you pick managers for a living. And the profession certainly does not pass the cocktail party test; ever try telling a stranger in a noisy room you work at a fund of funds?

This book illuminates this practice of manager selection, a task both important and obscure. And because the challenge is not reserved to professional advisors but is for anyone serious about their financial future, I believe the investor class is under assault by an overwhelming, sometimes intimidating, set of choices. When you add up the available mutual funds, hedge funds, exchange-traded funds (ETFs), and other managed risk pools, we are confronted by tens of thousands of potential opportunities. The investments business is a consumer products business like any other. Many of its design labs and factories are churning at full capacity.

This journey from academia to Morningstar to the world of alternatives directly informs the argument and themes inside *The Investor's Paradox*.

ONE APPROACH

"Convergence" is upon us. The once-distinct traditional and alternative investment worlds are colliding rapidly. Traditional asset-management firms, fighting shrinking margins on their core businesses, are building new forms of investment risk that can be packaged and sold at premium margins. Meanwhile, hedge fund shops, generally tiny in comparison, see massive yet untouched markets that can be potentially accessed by delivering more investor-friendly structures. Alternatives are going mainstream, and fast.

This convergence means more choice for everyone in the investment community. That's not necessarily a good thing. In response, *The Investor's Paradox* offers a singular framework for choosing the right investment experts, independent of labels or investment styles. Indeed, my gigs at

Morningstar and Mesirow were analytically identical, despite the appearance of being quite different. Both involved researching money managers in order to distinguish winners from losers. The only difference was the breadth and complexity of the strategies under scrutiny, not the general process of due diligence. In addition to simplifying our investment decisions, this unified approach allows us to calmly demystify hedge funds, which are largely misunderstood, not only by the popular media but also through much of the financial community.

SUCCESS THROUGH SIMPLIFICATION

Attempting to pick funds that consistently outperform others is futile. Just as there's little evidence that even seasoned stock pickers can "beat the market," there is no evidence that fund pickers can regularly pick winners. While outperforming other well-informed talent scouts is unlikely, finding and selecting the right fund managers for a particular purpose is quite possible. This is accomplished by recognizing that out of the seemingly countless items that clutter investment decisions, there are actually just four core issues that should drive our quest for the right experts:

- ✓ Trust
- ✓ Risk
- ✓ Skill
- ✓ Fit

The Investor's Paradox is built around unpacking these items, especially the first three. It is then incumbent upon us to establish and adapt our expectations across these dimensions. Finding simplicity isn't necessarily easy, but the effort will be rewarding. This is a message of empowerment in a daunting age.

METHOD MATTERS

In an attempt to make systematically rigorous choices, method matters more than content. Prior to my markets career, I earned a PhD from the University of Chicago, where *what* I researched and taught was less relevant than *how* I was taught to pose questions and answer them. Endless information gathering without a method to structure it is akin to drinking from a fire hose: you are much more likely to end up a sopping-wet mess than slake your thirst. In the world of investments, the fire hose of data is inexhaustible, which is why storytelling often passes for real insight.

As such, this book is about method, not content. It won't—and can't— be a primer on the many technical features of finance and investments. Those are the necessary but insufficient inputs to making sound choices. But ultimately, due diligence is a method, not a checklist. It is a means of adapting to uncertainty; a path not linear, but circular. Like the plight of Sisyphus, the task is never fully complete; those interested in analysis that produces tidy, final answers should likely avoid the vocation of manager research.

ORGANIZATION

Investing is as informed by choice theory as it is by finance; investment satisfaction stems from fulfilled expectations, not great performance; there is just one set of tools to analyze any type of investment fund; even the smartest among us cannot pick winners; four basic questions produce good investment decisions; method trumps storytelling. These are the themes of *The Investor's Paradox*. None of them match conventional wisdom.

Here's how the book is organized. In part I, I articulate the challenge before us. Chapter 1 is about choice. I highlight some of the generic challenges to effective decision making and elaborate on the specific nature of the investor's paradox. Chapter 2 is about experts. In light of the difficulties involved in choosing, we often delegate to others. However, experts are often prone to error. I make an important distinction between decision makers who abide by rigid, unitary worldviews and those who engage in flexible, adaptive thinking. The latter tend to be much better experts. Chapter 3 is about history. I detail the evolution of the investment choices from the early bull market of the 1980s through today, concluding that the breadth and complexity of our options have grown massively. The rise of the hedge fund and ETF industries has driven that change.

In part II, I offer my road map for resolving the investor's paradox. Chapter 4 is about method. Contrary to the storytelling that characterizes much investment decision making, I detail a framework that allows us to adapt to changing times. How we manage and update expectations in light of new information is its centerpiece. My experience suggests that this approach is amenable to any sort of investment, ranging from the simplest of mutual funds to the most complex of hedge funds. This unified approach to investment decision making is the crux of the book's effort at simplification.

I then follow with three chapters on the main topics of inquiry that should define any effort at choosing the right expert. Chapter 5 is about trust. Based on a behavioral interpretation of the Madoff debacle, I suggest that the confidence we place in our experts can also be a source of betrayal. Ultimately, robust institutions and a proper alignment of incentives will create happy outcomes. Chapter 6 is about risk. I offer a novel "risk prism" that allows us to efficiently think through the bets that our managers make on our behalf. This prism simplifies and unifies the discussion of all investments, ranging from traditional to alternative. Chapter 7 is about skill. While almost all treatments of skill center on the narrow idea of outperformance, I suggest something different, broader, and more robust. Ultimately, an expert's skill is the ability to meet expectations. But because the source of those expectations is the result of a qualitative dialogue more than a quantitative algorithm, the achievement of skill is both more complex and more attainable than most investors suspect. Finally, chapter 8 is about ourselves. Much of investing success starts with a look in the mirror. What we want from our investments is driven by what we expect of ourselves.

So where to begin our journey? In the world of high finance, a conventional journey starts in places like Manhattan or Mayfair. But our unconventional tale is more about choice than money. Our compass is method, not content. So we'll start somewhere more immediately relevant to how we make complex decisions, somewhere much closer to home: your local grocery store.

PART I

CHALLENGE

1

MORE

The "success" of modernity turns out to be bittersweet, and everywhere we look it appears that a significant contributing factor is the overabundance of choice.

—Barry Schwartz[1]

THE LESSONS OF STRAWBERRY JAM

It's Saturday morning. After your coffee, you head over to your local supermarket to pick up a few items. As is common these days, especially with fancier stores like Whole Foods or warehouse stores like Costco, there are numerous stations set up where you can sample different foods for free. On this particular day, there's a table set out in the condiments section with a large variety of gourmet jams, ranging from classic strawberry to unrecognizable blends of wild berry and spice. This tantalizing rainbow of alternatives—maybe a couple dozen or so—draws you in, and you spend a few minutes sampling the jams, despite an overcrowded store and a day full of errands ahead. When you're done sampling, the table attendant gives you a "dollar off" coupon good for any of the full-size jars, which are located mere steps away from where you're currently standing.

What do you do next? If you are the typical customer in this scenario, you walk away from the samples table, walk away from the jams aisle, and *buy nothing.*

Let's consider another scenario, exactly the same as the first—except in this case the samples table features only six jams, versus twenty-four.

What happens in this case? First, fewer customers are attracted to the booth. With just a few choices, it's not as appealing. But the outcome among the smaller set of samplers is vastly different. Those who do sample this limited menu of jams are more likely to walk down the aisle and then purchase the jam(s) they enjoyed most. How much more likely? In one of the more famous studies in the field of social psychology, *ten times* more likely.[2] What's more, customers reported afterwards a relatively high level of satisfaction with the experience. The limited number of customers who purchased jams from the larger choice set reported a lower level of satisfaction.

In sum, more was less. Experiments like this one have been repeated across a range of different types of choices, with similar results.[3]

How we make decisions has been a topic of intense inquiry since the earliest philosophers. Political views on liberty, economic views on utility, sociological and anthropological views on social outcomes, moral views on fairness and justice—these all take into consideration, implicitly or explicitly, how people and groups choose. There is now an abundance of scholarship about how our built-in cognitive and emotional biases influence the choices we make. So-called behaviorists explain the reality of how we choose, usually in stark contrast to what classical economists would call rational cost-benefit analysis.[4]

This school of thought has been increasingly undergirded not only by countless empirical studies, but by the study of the brain itself. Technology now allows us to literally see how we react to stimuli: how the brain instantaneously processes sensory information, associates reward or punishment with a particular experience, and takes action based on that risk assessment. In her powerful *The Art of Choosing*, Sheena Iyengar makes clear that the desire for choice is a biological imperative. Humans have a larger prefrontal cortex than animals, which is probably why choice is so important to us, and in turn to our place in the global pecking order. Humans dominate without claws, fur, or other physical adaptations. Instead, we are smarter: "The ability to choose well is arguably the most powerful tool for controlling our environment."[5]

But there's something more going on. The desire to choose, Iyengar writes, "often operates independently of any concrete benefits. In such cases, the power of choice is so great that it becomes not merely a means to an end but something intrinsically valuable and necessary."[6] Our satisfaction often stems from the *perception* of control (what behavioralists often refer to as the "illusion" of control) as much as if not more than control per se.[7]

To evidence the power of choice, consider a well-cited study of nursing homes.[8] Researchers set up an experiment with two groups of elderly residents. One group was encouraged to exercise their liberty. Among other empowering directives, an attendant told them: "If you are unsatisfied with anything here, you have the influence to change it." Each person was also given the choice of taking care of a small plant; those that did were allowed to choose one of several plants from a large box. Finally, the group was asked which movie they cared to watch the following weekend. The other group received a different message—that if they would like their environment to be different, they should inform the staff, who would make the changes for them. Each resident was also given a plant that would be watered by the staff, and they were told what movie they'd be watching on Friday night. Generally, the former group was given frequent reminders that they had the power to make changes to their rooms and their routines; the latter group was not.

The results were somewhat striking. Aging individuals who were given enhanced personal responsibility demonstrated much better outcomes in the following months. Those with more control registered a higher degree of mental alertness as well as higher reported happiness. They were more likely to participate in social activities, such as movies, mixers, and game night. Finally—strikingly—they were more likely to live longer. The mortality rate in the eighteen months following the original study was double for the group with less control (30 percent versus 15 percent). Choice and control matter.

The desire for choice is not itself a choice; we are hardwired that way. It is the reason that so many more customers in the supermarket were attracted to the table with many jam samples compared to just six. Indeed, there are a litany of positive outcomes we tend to associate with more choice, such as freedom, motivation, variety, and the chance of getting what we want.

Yet here's the fascinating modern twist to the choice paradigm. The availability of options ultimately becomes self-defeating. Barry Schwartz famously describes this "paradox of choice":

> When people have no choice, life is almost unbearable. As the number of available choices increases, as it has in our consumer culture, the autonomy, control, and liberation this variety brings are powerful and positive. But as the number of choices keeps growing, negative aspects of having a multitude of options begin to appear. As the number of choices grows further, the negatives escalate until we become overloaded. At this point, choice no longer liberates, but debilitates. It might even be said to tyrannize.[9]

We want more choice, but the more choice we have, the less satisfied we become. Hence the unwillingness of most overwhelmed jam customers to purchase anything, and for those that did, to report lower satisfaction with the experience. The labels "rational" or "irrational" are not relevant here. For better or worse, it is how we decide.

Why does more often produce less? There are a few reasons. With lots of choices, we sometimes find ourselves overwhelmed, unable to process the information, let alone take action. The menu at the Cheesecake Factory or a traditional Greek diner at first amuses, but then overwhelms. (That one daily special paper-clipped to the diner's menu is there to simplify your task by giving you one choice—which is likely to be a higher-margin item than the standard fare.) We begin to think that with more options, there will likely be a better choice that we don't make; this "anticipated regret" can be paralyzing. With more choices, we expect better results, but achieving them is uncertain, thus creating yet another form of regret. And when we do actually choose but don't achieve our hoped-for satisfaction, we are increasingly likely to blame ourselves, since we did, after all, have the "freedom" to choose a better option. We find ourselves less satisfied with more choice.

CHOICE REGIMES

We're all familiar with the consequences of "choice overload," whether we're walking through the grocery store, comparing mobile phone plans, flipping through satellite TV channels, or surfing the web to purchase a garden gnome (a Google search produces about 3.8 million results). Indeed, we live in a time of unprecedented availability. In other words, what I call "choice regimes" evolve.

Let's point to three primary qualities of choice regimes: volume, complexity, and breadth. The first is the *number of choices* themselves, a somewhat obvious feature (e.g., 6 versus 24 jams; 3 networks versus 300 satellite channels; 1 pension plan versus 20 choices in our 401(k); etc.). The second is the *dimensionality* of each choice. Objects might have fewer or more features that make the latter a more "complex" choice (e.g., bicycles versus cars; cell phones versus smartphones; mutual funds versus hedge funds, etc.). The third is the *number of choosers* themselves. How inclusive is the regime? It could pertain to just a few individuals, or most of the planet.

We are experiencing an inflection point in choice regimes across most areas of modern life. At home, the deregulation of utilities has exploded our choice set in how we receive power, gas, and telecommunications services. In health care, the medical industry now compels us to make unprecedented choices among procedures and doctors. We are pelted with print and broadcast advertisements for prescription drugs that we couldn't purchase for ourselves even if we wanted to, yet suddenly recognize as possible solutions for potential problems.[10] In education, the mandatory assignment to the neighborhood school has been replaced by a lattice of magnet, gifted, charter, parochial, and other private alternatives. And most obviously, in mass consumption, the number of immediately available goods is now countless, whether it be books, music, clothing, or garden gnomes. The Internet and other modern forms of communication don't just facilitate the trend; they help create it.

Most affluent societies have transformed into do-it-yourself cultures where more options are no longer just desirable—they're mandatory. It's no surprise that researchers refer to "decision fatigue," the physical and mental exhaustion many people report from having to make so many decisions so frequently.[11] Yet we would be disconcerted if our choice sets suddenly reverted to those available a generation ago. (Three TV networks, anyone?) Regardless of your personal feelings about whether "more is less" or "more is more," the left side of that equation is now fixed. There's no going back.

THE INVESTOR'S PARADOX

The choice regime for investments mirrors what we see in consumer goods, health, education, and elsewhere. Set aside the directly purchased securities—stocks and bonds, mostly. There are countless tickers to choose from, but only a small fraction of us are trained to choose at that level. Most of us buy funds, not securities. We hire experts who themselves can purchase and assemble these securities for us. But then screen for "five star" funds on Morningstar, shop on the platforms at Schwab or TD Ameritrade, or attend (if permitted) a hedge fund "capital introductions" conference in which hundreds of allocators mingle with hundreds of portfolio managers. You'll be quickly overwhelmed.

Hence what I call the *investor's paradox*: We crave abundant investment choices to meet daunting portfolio problems in a world of volatile markets, manic news flow, and shifting geopolitical rhythms. But the more choices we are afforded, the more overwhelmed, less empowered, and ultimately less successful investors we potentially become. More is less.

Unfortunately, it gets worse. A generational stretch of nearly uninterrupted prosperity has recently yielded to an era of heightened uncertainty and economic stress. Fixed-income securities are vulnerable in a low-interest-rate environment like our current one, and equities are unpredictable. Because complex times prompt us to seek complex solutions, investors have increasingly gravitated toward experts with extensive tool kits and flexible modes of thinking over those who are tightly constrained or who bet only that markets climb upwards over time. The deeper, more insidious level of our investor's paradox is that the more adaptable, creative experts are also the ones more likely to disappoint because we automatically expect more from them. In the theory of choice, unmet expectations trigger powerful emotions. When expectations and outcomes don't match, disappointment ensues. And because drawing clear expectations for flexible experts is much harder than it is for those with tighter constraints, the chance the former can satisfy is lower.

31 (THOUSAND) FLAVORS

While chapter 3 will detail the factors over the past thirty years that determined how we got into our current predicament, let's tee up its salient features. There are multiple examples. If there's any area in American finance where the do-it-yourself culture has been most profound in the last couple of decades, it is in the individual selection of one's own retirement funds. The shift away from defined benefit (pension) plans to defined contribution (401(k)) plans has forced investment novices (which is most of us) to become fund analysts, and in turn to direct our own financial futures.

The paradox of choice infuses the process of picking one's retirement options. In one study, researchers examined 401(k) participation rates among clients of the investment firm Vanguard, across more than 600 plans covering more than 800,000 employees.[12] Controlling for a large number of variables that might influence investor participation (e.g., compensation level, overall wealth, gender, tenure at the company), they found that the more funds offered, the lower the rate of participation. For every ten additional funds included in a plan, there was a 1.5 percent to 2 percent decline in the participation rate. Keep in mind that many of these plans offered matching contributions, meaning that more choice actually deterred individuals from accepting free money. Thus, for those employers who offer scores, even hundreds, of retirement plan options on the belief that more choices are better, the reality is actually the opposite.

Second, the advent of the market for exchange-traded funds (ETFs) is also emblematic of the modern investment choice regime. An ETF is a bundle of securities that aims to capture the profile and performance of a predefined market segment. The constituents of those baskets are mostly fixed, as distinct from actively managed funds in which portfolio managers buy and sell positions at their own discretion.

ETFs have grown into a multitrillion-dollar business in recent years on the back of the idea that stock pickers actually aren't very good at picking stocks. The popular but controversial efficient markets hypothesis, pioneered by economist Eugene Fama, suggests that no one can sustain an informational advantage in liquid markets (that is, markets with many buyers and sellers).[13] This idea first sparked the growth of passively managed index funds (most popularly through Vanguard Funds) and then ETFs, which are effectively the same as index funds but can be bought and sold throughout the trading day, rather than only at the end of the day, like mutual funds.

The original premise of exchange-traded funds was that if you can't beat the market, you might as well own the market. Thus, the most popular ETFs focus on the biggest markets, such as the S&P 500. But in recent years, asset management companies have manufactured a bewildering array of additional choices. There are now more than 1,000 ETFs that divide the market into increasingly microscopic slices. Recently created ETFs that allow you to buy the market for soybeans, aerospace stocks, and Australian bonds now sit on the shelf alongside vehicles for US mid-cap stocks, gold, global technology stocks, and Russian commodities. Ironically, investors are being empowered to access precisely the markets they desire, but then they have so many opportunities that they suddenly lack the necessary expertise to select the right markets—hence the impetus for the ETF "solution" in the first place.[14]

Third, the mainstreaming of hedge funds is the most foundational shift in our evolving universe of investment choice. In 1990, it was an industry with limited choices and less than $40 billion in assets under management (AUM). It now features an estimated 10,000 offerings (no one knows the exact number) that manage more than $2.4 trillion in client assets. That still pales in comparison to the approximately $26.8 trillion in mutual fund assets, but it's an astonishing growth trajectory in not only market share but also mindshare.[15] Mutual fund executives are considerably more concerned about the encroachment of the alternative investment business than vice versa.

The landscape is broadening and somewhat intimidating. We are increasingly confronted by secretive, muscular names like Fortress, King Street, Citadel, Brigade, Maverick, and Anchorage; comforting monikers such as Bridgewater, Lone Pine, Blue Ridge, Halcyon, and Highbridge; and the acronymic maze of firms such as GLG, AQR, GAM, CQS, GEM, COMAC, and HBK. Most of those firms have many billions of dollars in assets under management, yet the nonprofessional investor probably hasn't heard of a single one.

Like a precocious child in too-small clothing, the hedge fund industry is bursting at the seams, an awkward giant at this early stage in its development. Few, if any, hedge fund firms have the brand recognition of mature consumer products companies (including traditional asset managers), so customers in this space cannot rely on the typical mental shortcuts that brands provide. We recognize that with T. Rowe Price we can "invest with confidence" or that Fidelity's green arrow follows a path to success. What path are you on with Och-Ziff or Brevan Howard? As it appears increasingly likely that hedge fund firms will be allowed to advertise in the popular press as a result of forthcoming regulatory changes, this is something many of us will need to figure out.[16]

These "alternatives" are an increasingly visible allocation in public and private pension plans, endowments, foundations, wealth management platforms, and retirement plans. Investment consultants have strongly advocated for extra portions of hedge fund investments to help institutions meet their future obligations. Compared to traditional offerings, hedge funds charge premium prices and can be relatively complex and opaque. The *Wall Street Journal* and other establishment critics often portray hedge funds as esoteric, controversial, and risky. Meanwhile a new class of choices called "liquid alternatives" are offering complex hedge fund strategies, including the use of derivatives and leverage, in easy-to-access vehicles, such as mutual funds or ETFs. Hedged strategies are now sometimes included in 401(k) plans. For all intents and purposes, all of us can now purchase hedge fund strategies with a few clicks at our online brokers' sites.

TOO MANY CHOICES

From historical and behavioral vantage points, a primary reason hedge funds and "alternative" strategies have been the source of both fascination and consternation is not what we see in the papers every day—spectacular trades, newly minted billionaires, aggressive tactics—but something more fundamental: they represent *a further explosion in the size of the choice set* in a market already saturated with product. The rise of hedge funds per se, as well as the debate over what alternative strategies are all about, is intensely constitutive of something we all both crave and detest: more.

Let's be sure to grant that the abundance of choice is hardwired into modern finance as something desirable. Something called the fundamental law of active management (FLAM) posits that investment skill is best achieved in part through "breadth," or a high number of independent bets—we want to spread our bets across different securities as widely as possible.[17] Likewise, modern portfolio theory (MPT) is built on the principle of diversification, which suggests that the aggregation of lower-correlated investments will produce better portfolios. Thus, having more options provides the potential to move out farther on the "efficient frontier." While there is nothing in *The Investor's Paradox* that explicitly or implicitly disagrees with this underlying principle of diversification— it remains our most powerful tool to build good portfolios—our mission is different and does question the value of "more" as it relates to the conduct of investment decision making. We ask: More of what? A larger number of line items in one's portfolio is not the equivalent of diversification, but the opportunity to add those line items has never been easier. Whatever the threshold is for investment choice overload, we are surely already well past it—and the mainstreaming of the alternatives industry is only getting started.

Hand in glove with the number of choices in prompting overload is the complexity of those choices. This is important for the study and practice of choosing investment vehicles, and the reason that the entry of alternative investments into mainstream portfolio debates has been so disruptive and controversial. Bottom line: hedge funds are complex investment vehicles, with more moving parts than traditional investments, including leverage, derivatives, and esoteric asset classes. As we'll see in chapters 4 through 7, these features are ultimately matters of degree, not type—which is why it still makes sense to use one consistent method for all your investing decisions.

Complexity is not just a matter of supply, but also of demand. When we perceive a problem to be complex, we tend to search for solutions that are themselves complex. Take something basic, like jeans. Once upon a time, a trip to the store to buy jeans was uncomplicated. Given your waist size and inseam, you chose from a few prominent brand names—Lee, Wrangler, Levi-Strauss. Not so today. Straight, Skinny, Slouchy Slim, Boot,

Standard, Easy, Loose, Original, all in multiple colors: these are my current choices just on Gap.com. Whether you prefer Gap, Seven for all Mankind, True Religion, or Lucky; shop at Walmart, Nordstroms, or Jeans.com, not only is the choice set enormous, but your decision inevitably defines your body "type" and even more deeply (and perhaps insidiously) your own sense of body image and worth. Most people would agree it was a lot easier (and probably healthier) in the old days. Yet they likely wouldn't go back—because once we've defined the search for the appropriate blue jeans in increasingly granular terms, we internalize the "need" for the right solution.

Choice regimes evolve. We thus end up demanding variety we originally didn't know we needed (or didn't even know existed).[18] And, even more interestingly, our own definition of the problem becomes more complex when we are presented with an increasingly differentiated series of solutions. A self-perpetuating feedback loop ensues.[19] Investment options matter more than jeans, because there are graver consequences if you choose wrong. So it's no surprise that the complexity of the macroeconomic and geopolitical environment we now face sparks the urge for elaborate solutions; and when traditional solutions don't seem to be working, there is a quicker flight to alternative solutions. The mere fact of having these new alternatives inspires regret among potential buyers *even when they don't buy.* Just knowing that more is "out there" creates psychological turbulence.

Some of the standard methods for mitigating the paradox of choice cannot resolve the investor's paradox. Social psychologists suggest "preference articulation," which basically states that the clearer you are about what you want, the more that abundant choice is a good thing.[20] If you know exactly what you want prior to making a decision, then you can effectively rank order your choices, in which case having more choices helps maximize utility.[21]

But such certainty is rare. Even in the simple jams example, customers were introduced to flavors they weren't familiar with beforehand, thus triggering a re-articulation of preferences. With complex financial products, the ranking of preferences is as much an outcome of the process as it is at the start of the search. Fund managers typically sell a market opportunity as much as, if not more than, a skill set: *Invest in emerging markets! Short*

Treasuries! Buy stocks! Sell stocks! As we often source investments by the at-tractiveness of the market opportunity, preferences and their ordering are malleable. Especially with hedge funds that trade in esoteric markets, that discovery process is critical.

Another approach to alleviate choice overload is "alignable assort-ments."[22] This is the notion that the more one can compare choices along the same dimension, the easier it is to choose. My children recently got new scooters. My wife searched around and identified the make and model she liked based on certain features (e.g., three wheels instead of two, price, durability). Given that make and model, we gave our children one choice: color. Theirs was generally not a stressful experience. In fact, the more choices in this case, the better. My daughter opted for pink, but with only three other colors to choose from (blue, green, and yellow), my two boys fought over who got the blue. If other favorite colors like red and orange had been available, there would have been no fight at all (both prefer blue to green or yellow, but only one prefers orange or red to blue).

Can we align options when sorting through a menu of investment products? I don't think so. We might be able to theorize how that can be done, but as a practical matter it's too messy. There are far too many di-mensions, many of them known only through a resource-intensive discov-ery process. Solving the investor's paradox this way is a nonstarter.[23]

WHILE WE'VE JUST SET OUT some of the broad parameters of the chal-lenge of how to choose wisely, our jumping-off point to the next chapter is that in areas of complexity, we tend to rely more heavily on experts to help us choose. We value experts precisely because they have the status of "expert."[24] Regardless of the circularity of that logic, it's empirically true that this is the way we act. Unfortunately, as we are about to see, relying on purported experts is not necessarily the panacea that we would like it to be.

2

PICKING ~~WINNERS~~ LOSERS

The future ain't what it used to be.
—Yogi Berra

THE SKY'S THE LIMIT (OR NOT)

On March 30, 1998, James Glassman and Kevin Hassett, two relatively un-known researchers at the American Enterprise Institute, published an op-ed in the *Wall Street Journal* forecasting the steep acceleration of financial prosperity in an era already awash in riches. Having bottomed out at 776 on August 12, 1982, the Dow Jones Industrial Average (DJIA), an index of blue-chip US stocks, sat at 8,782 on the day the op-ed was published. At the end of 1999, the year the authors published a book-length treatment of their thesis, the index closed at 11,497.

Glassman and Hassett were hardly alone in their bullishness at the time.[1] However, the sheer boldness of their prediction—captured in their book's now-infamous title, *Dow 36,000*—was unprecedented. Far from a casual guess, the number was based on a detailed analysis of why qual-ity US large-cap stocks were poised to *triple* in price over the next few years. (The authors, to be fair, were not so sanguine about high-flying NASDAQ stocks.) Glassman, a Harvard graduate and prominent publisher and writer, and Hassett, who earned a PhD in economics from Penn and worked for years as an economist at the Federal Reserve Board, argued that the market had overestimated the risk of stocks. Stocks should not be as-signed the wide "risk premium" over bonds that they had been historically, they claimed; and despite the fact that the price-to-earnings and price-to-book ratios on many stocks were at astronomical levels at the end of 1999, stocks were still cheap and poised to rise. "Tomorrow, stock prices could immediately double, triple, or even quadruple and still not be too expensive."[2]

The book was sharply criticized by some economists, but the prediction captured the fancy of the general public and gained credence in the marketplace of ideas. And most importantly, investors voted with their pocketbooks. *Dow 36,000* was a best seller.

Of course, Glassman and Hassett were egregiously wrong. Not long after the book was published, the DJIA peaked at 11,723 on January 14, 2000, and then fell sharply, bottoming on October 9, 2002, at 7,286. Stocks then surged again, and the DJIA peaked at 14,164 on October 9, 2007, only to swoon again to 6,547 on March 9, 2009. In September 2013, it hovers around 15,000. Fourteen years after their forecast, Glassman and Hassett aren't even close. After claiming in a 2009 interview that there was still hope ("Q: Do you still think it will hit 36,000? A: I have no doubt about that. I think that is absolutely true. But I'm not going to tell you what date."), Glassman finally admitted in a 2011 op-ed, again in the *Wall Street Journal*: "I was wrong."

EXPERTS

The act of prediction is a cornerstone in the larger architecture of choice. As Sheena Iyengar elegantly states, "To choose means to turn ourselves to the future."[3] And the future is invariably uncertain, so to choose at all is to assert some control over the unknown, no matter how modest and ephemeral it may be. That we make mistakes when anticipating future outcomes is hardly controversial, or even all that distressing. In fields as trivial as sports betting and as nontrivial as medicine or marriage, we are lousy at predicting the future. Due to a lack of complete or accurate information, insufficient or incorrect analysis, and a slew of cognitive and emotional biases, we humans are prone to error.

In our increasingly complex society, where the division of labor is sliced ever thinner, each individual's expertise is necessarily limited, rendering him reliant on others in most areas. He can therefore navigate the many choice regimes before him either by giving it his best shot—despite his lack of knowledge—or by relying on others for help. We're more likely to do the latter for more complicated decisions, where the resources (including time) necessary to choose wisely are significant, and when the costs of being wrong are high.

One of the rarely noted features of choice in modernity is our frequent need to relinquish that choice to others who we feel could do a better job, or at least take the blame if things don't work out as planned. Paradoxically, the more individual liberty we achieve—the more choices we have— the more we rely on the expertise of others.[4] This can create an awkward, sometimes confusing balance between liberty and dependence. We simultaneously want to control and relinquish. We are sometimes too paralyzed to choose, but in other cases, we pass the buck to others we deem more skilled or more competent than ourselves. We are now freer to delegate, hence the rise of consultants, coaches, "subject matter experts," and the like. We now devote a lot of energy to choosing others to choose for us.

This increased reliance on experts raises the potential for disappointment. That's in part because we hold experts to a higher standard, as well we should: they should *know better*. A deliberately egregious example of failed expertise, *Dow 36,000* certainly prompted people to buy more stocks on the expectation that this forecast was at least reasonable, if not precisely correct. In other words, the use of legitimate, credible experts—in finance, meteorology, medicine, sports, engineering, and so forth—establishes legitimate, credible expectations for what the future holds.

The more we use experts, the higher our expectations are set, the larger the potential for disappointment. It is not accidental that our current era of overwhelming choice has produced so much public contemplation over how our decision making falls short and why, in turn, we seek expert advice. There is now a cottage industry in writing about experts, expertise, and forecasting.[5] Serious books with titles like *Wrong, Being Wrong,* and *Why We Make Mistakes* now line our bookshelves. The popularity of Malcolm Gladwell's *Blink* and Daniel Kahneman's *Thinking, Fast and Slow* reflects enormous interest in behavioral quirks—and their consequences.

THEY'RE JUST LIKE US!

So how do our experts fare in the long haul? Not well—and that's true beyond anecdotes such as the *Dow 36,000* example. The modern academic touchstone to thinking about expertise is Philip Tetlock's magisterial study, *Expert Political Judgment: How Good Is It? How Can We Know?* No one before Tetlock, then a professor of social psychology at UC-Berkeley and now on the faculty at the University of Pennsylvania, had taken such a systematic, methodologically sound approach to evaluating expert judgment.[6]

Oddly enough, the genesis of Tetlock's project corresponds to one of the more influential experiences early in my career. In the fall of 1989, as a sophomore at the University of Michigan, I was enrolled in an Eastern European politics class taught by Professor Roman Szporluk. Ukrainian by birth and a student of Isaiah Berlin at Oxford in the 1960s, Szporluk was a renowned scholar who published extensively on Marxism, the Soviet Union, and nationalism in Eastern and Central Europe.[7] Not long after the semester started, the world Professor Szporluk had been studying and teaching about for decades began to fall apart. In a cascade of peaceful revolutions, Poland, Czechoslovakia, Hungary, Romania, Bulgaria, and East Germany rejected their Soviet overlords and pushed for self-determination. The most powerful signifier of this period, of course, was the dismantling of the Berlin Wall in November 1989. The excitement of the time was one of my original motivations to pursue graduate studies in international affairs.

As these changes accelerated, the syllabus Professor Szporluk had put together for the class grew largely irrelevant. One morning, he arrived in class and instructed us to toss out the syllabus and just start reading the *New York Times* every day. There was no other publicly available source that could better illuminate what was transpiring. No one had expected these changes, so there was nothing in academic publication to help us make sense of them.

Two thousand miles west of Ann Arbor, in northern California, Philip Tetlock, like Szporluk, noted that virtually no one had anticipated these events, including the cadre of Sovietologists and other regional experts spawned by the Cold War. Tetlock had already begun research on our ability to forecast future events. The Velvet Revolution in Czechoslovakia and the subsequent fall of the Soviet Union two years later further reinforced his suspicion that what we called "expertise" might have major shortcomings when it came to understanding the world around us.

So Tetlock embarked on a massive study of hundreds of experts, people whose professions included "commenting or offering advice on political and economic trends." He asked these experts to forecast the probability of future events, not only within their own realm of expertise, but outside of it as well. He also asked many questions about how these experts made their decisions—their method of predicting—and how they reacted, if at all, to contrary evidence.

The types of forecasts Tetlock asked the experts to make were straightforward questions for individuals with decades of training and experience in a specific area of domestic politics, economics, and international security. Questions, for instance, focused on electoral outcomes, the likelihood of rebellions, the direction of interest rates or GDP growth, or future involvements in armed conflicts and in international alliances There were also questions on special topics at the time, such as the likelihood of a Persian Gulf War, the adoption of the euro as a regional currency, or the chance that the late 1990s bubble in technology stocks would burst.

By 2003, Tetlock had systematically accumulated 82,361 forecasts across all of these issues from his army of experts. He established a standardized probability scale that each expert used to estimate whether an outcome was more likely (the extreme case being "certainly"), less likely (the extreme case being "impossible"), or something approximating the status quo. Experts in a particular area were not asked exclusively about their area of expertise but about other fields as well. Thus, an expert in African politics might also be asked about the US economy or a Sovietologist might be asked to predict the end of the NASDAQ bubble. In addition to comparing experts to educated pedestrians as a baseline, Tetlock also established simple decision rules—effectively coin flipping or the colloquial chimpanzee throwing darts at a board—to predict outcomes in each category.

So how'd they do? Score one for the chimps.

Tetlock's marquee finding was that experts were not skilled in understanding what would come next in the fields to which they had dedicated their careers. Rather, Tetlock's simple, even random decision rules were nearly as accurate as the informed experts. "It is impossible to find any domain in which humans clearly outperformed crude extrapolation algorithms, less still sophisticated statistical ones."[8] The lack of skill was evident across regions and categories, as well as whether the forecasts were short- or long-term in nature. Nor did experts significantly outperform nonexperts. "People who devoted years of arduous study to a topic were as hard-pressed as colleagues casually dropping in from other fields to affix realistic probabilities to possible futures."[9] The expert on African politics predicted US unemployment rates about as well as an economist did, while the Japanologist was about as good at predicting rebellions in South America as was a regional specialist.

MARKET MAVENS

It's not hard to find evidence that corroborates Tetlock's findings. The track record of experts in markets and investing is unquestionably disappointing. First, there have been many globally important market events that very few people saw coming. The "big bang" that nearly everyone missed in politics was the disintegration of the Soviet Union. The analogous big bang in markets was the financial crisis of 2008. We can see now that there were *ex ante* signs that our financial institutions were rotting at their cores: highly leveraged consumers taking advantage of easy credit, overvalued homes, the proliferation of structured products by banks across the globe, and so forth. But even in the highest echelons of finance, there were few suspicions that anything was awry. A few select quotes from Federal Reserve Chairman Ben Bernanke:

- "The Federal Reserve is not currently forecasting a recession" (January 10, 2008).
- "The risk that the economy has entered a substantial downturn appears to have diminished over the past month or so" (June 10, 2008).
- "Housing markets are cooling a bit. Our expectation is that the decline in activity or the slowing in activity will be moderate,

that house prices will probably continue to rise" (February 15, 2006).

- "At this juncture, however, the impact on the broader economy and financial markets of the problems in the subprime market seems likely to be contained. In particular, mortgages to prime borrowers and fixed-rate mortgages to all classes of borrowers continue to perform well, with low rates of delinquency" (March 28, 2007).[10]

Bernanke was hardly the only one who had relatively little grasp of the impending meltdown. In testifying to Congress on October 23, 2008, Bernanke's predecessor, Alan Greenspan, attempted to evade most of the blame for the crisis but did haltingly admit: "This crisis has turned out to be much broader than anything I could have imagined."[11] More broadly, Wall Street analysts, corporate executives, and other market pundits generally missed the boat. To be sure, there were a handful of prescient bears who anticipated the crisis, but the capital allocated to being long on mortgage securities massively dwarfed that which was short. Those who caught the "Big Short" were, with limited exception, marginal investors largely disregarded by the broader investing public and the media.[12] In sum, we are lousy at anticipating big, material events for which there is little precedent, even when there is substantial evidence available, in hindsight, to have made the call—what author Nassim Nicholas Taleb famously calls "black swan" events.[13]

Moving from economics to investing, the evidence is also mixed. For instance, in the field of securities analysis, numerous studies demonstrate that Wall Street analysts in aggregate are wrong about near-term corporate profits. A study by David Dreman and Michael Berry compares 66,100 consensus analyst estimates with actual reported results, finding a significant gap between estimates and real outcomes, with analysts typically overoptimistic about next quarter's earnings. They also, interestingly, suggest that the size of the gap appears to be growing over time, even as finance supposedly grows more technically sophisticated—meaning that analysts are becoming worse at their jobs, not better.[14]

What about stock pickers? This question taps into the longstanding debate over "skill" versus "luck" among portfolio managers. Whether portfolio managers are skillful is basically the same question as whether experts can anticipate the future. Here the evidence is mixed. The acumen of traditional or "long-only" stock pickers—those who run standard investment vehicles like mutual funds—has been under assault since the 1960s, when a first wave of scholarship delivered evidence that they tend not to add value beyond what is gained by exposure to an index fund or some other passively managed basket of securities. Seminal research in the 1990s extended that argument further by pointing out that even where it appears that skill exists, it is mostly explained by the manager's style— such as exposure to small-cap or value stocks—rather than by his or her smarts.[15] Meanwhile, the question of skill found in hedge fund strategies remains fiercely debated. At a glance, the data appear more kind than they do for the long-only crowd. However, this is something we explore in detail in chapter 7.

Then there are the pickers of the pickers—what I've been doing most of my career in finance, and how most of us invest: by choosing experts to do it for us. It won't come as any shock that if the stock pickers themselves exhibit only modest skill, the pickers of the pickers rank about the same. One important finding is that professional investors chase good performance just like "regular" investors do. In a study of selecting long-only managers, researchers looked at 3,400 pension plans and other institutional investors over the course of the decade.[16] They found that plan sponsors were much more likely to choose managers with recent outperformance, only to find that those excess returns generally did not persist post-hire. The plan sponsors frequently fired underperforming managers, only to latch on to other outperforming ones, creating churn that added no value for the fund's beneficiaries—and often subtracted from it. The authors found that in a typical "round trip" of hiring and firing decisions, professional fund pickers would have been better off sticking with (or even adding more capital to) their original choice and exercising patience.

With alternative investments, more so than with long-only vehicles, institutional investors will often outsource their choice of managers to technical experts. Indeed, many institutions with their own professional investment staffs will further delegate to a fund of funds or rely on consultants. Institutions will often allocate to multiple funds of funds, sometimes more than ten. For example, the New Mexico State Investment Council, a prominent public pension plan, owned thirteen funds of funds until it recently decided to trim its portfolio.[17]

Because we want to know whether the *chooser of the choosers* adds value—independent of whether the choosers themselves add value—we need to be careful in distinguishing whatever value is added by the underlying hedge funds. Are professional fund pickers good at picking funds? A 2011 study by Benoit Dewaele, Hugues Pirotte, Nils Tuchschmid, and Erik Wallerstein offers a thoughtful examination.[18] Their research basically asked three questions. First, can funds of hedge funds choose managers that deliver alpha over time? This is a question about one-off fund picking. Second, can funds of funds deliver true alpha, independent of the aggregate alpha of the underlying selections? This is a question about portfolio construction. Third, would a random sampling of the same universe—another instance of chimpanzees throwing darts at a board—produce better or worse results than the professionals? This, ultimately, is a question about skill versus luck.

The answer to all three questions is a nuanced no. They conclude that only 21.2 percent of fund of funds managers channel alpha from managers after subtracting fees. And only 5.6 percent of them add value above the alpha created by the underlying managers. In other words, only one out of twenty professional hedge fund pickers exhibits the skill we would expect them to have. Finally, there is no significant difference between the average fund of funds and a random fund picker.[19] On top of it all, while these analyses are net of the fees of the underlying hedge funds, they are gross of the funds of funds fees, meaning the numbers would look even worse on a net basis: "[Funds of funds] managers do not exhibit hedge fund picking or strategy-timing skills even before controlling for the fees they charge."[20]

Although complex hedge fund analytics have a twenty-first-century ring to them, social psychologists offered at least a partial explanation for these disappointing findings just after World War II. In his classic 1954 study, *Clinical versus Statistical Prediction: A Theoretical Analysis and a Review of the Evidence,* Paul Meehl presented overwhelming evidence that relatively simple quantitative methods, such as linear regressions, are sturdier predictors of success than is subjective human judgment. Interviews or other formal interpersonal evaluations tend to be less effective than simple decision rules. Decades of follow-on research into Meehl's finding has largely corroborated his disheartening notion that our "clinical intuition"—our personal judgment, regardless of how sophisticated our interview methods or other forms of qualitative evaluation are—isn't very good. Nearly half a century after the original publication of this "disturbing little book," fewer than 5 percent the book's findings have been overturned.[21]

Furthermore, Robyn Dawes demonstrates that even very simple decision rules (compared to more elaborate statistical models) consistently outperform in scenarios such as the ability of clinical psychologists to accurately assess their clients' conditions, of bank loan officers to predict which borrowers would default, or of admission officers to know which students will succeed.[22] While experts might know which variables are keys to future success, they are still bad at two tasks. The first is accurately estimating which of those variables matter more than others in that particular circumstance (in other words, assigning relative weights to the variables). The second is appreciating how these variables interact with each other, and what perverse outcomes might result from that interaction.

TO ERR IS HUMAN . . .

We have thus far delved into one element in the challenge of choice, which is the attempt to anticipate the future. Tetlock doesn't pull punches: "We too easily convince ourselves that we knew all along what was going to happen when, in fact, we were clueless."[23] This applies not just to novices but to experts as well. In finance, the track record is pretty clear. Indeed, if the goal of investing were merely to pick the winners—fund managers, stocks, or otherwise—then we would fail. This is sobering news for those who aim to "beat the market" or find the next "hot" fund manager—practices that are unfortunately quite common.

Following a different path, there are in fact effective measures for making good decisions, revolving around our ability to adapt to the world around us and to take control of our expectations of others and ourselves. Yet we can't fully appreciate those measures before first delving into why we are so prone to making mistakes. So let's do that now and then reveal the sources of effectiveness.

These are natural qualities that impede good decision making:

✓ Overconfidence
✓ Pattern seeking
✓ Risk aversion
✓ Information mismanagement

We Are Overconfident

There are few things we think we're bad at, at least that we're willing to admit to. Countless studies evidence this disposition toward overconfidence. In a famous 1981 study, Ola Svenson polled a sample of both US and Swedish drivers and found that 93 percent of the Americans and 69 percent of the Swedes rated themselves as better than average.[24] Other studies show that students think they are more academically gifted, better leaders, and more likeable than they really are. Professionals from astronomy to zoology rate themselves highly versus their peers. Cognitive researchers David Dunning and Justin Kruger not only demonstrate that we overestimate our own skill in tasks ranging from test-taking ability to motor skills to playing games; they also show that the *least* capable are most likely to overestimate their skill.[25] These individuals are particularly weak at self-assessment, tending not to take cues for self-improvement.[26] It is only the truly skilled who tend to *under*estimate their acumen relative to others.

The illusion of superiority is endemic to the human condition. As a matter of simple math, we cannot all be above average. But as a matter of evolutionary biology, our overconfidence is part of who we are, though it's not entirely clear why. If overconfidence is associated with systematically overestimating our own abilities and underestimating those of others, then the net effect is to put ourselves in hazardous situations. So why would evolution permit such a trait to survive? Recent scholarship by Dominic Johnson and James Fowler suggests that it's not just confidence but *over-confidence* that spurs attributes like ambition, morale, resolve, persistence, and credible bluffing.[27] Specifically, they demonstrate how overconfidence can produce an advantage in the social competition for scarce resources. Overconfident individuals and groups may have been more likely to survive, thus passing that trait from one generation to the next. In a different study, Robert Trivers explains how overconfidence is a dangerous form of self-deception that helps us deceive ourselves, in turn fooling others.[28]

One consequence of this tendency is that we are too comfortable making bold predictions. The belief that we know more, or are better than we actually are, underwrites our willingness to forecast. Experts are particularly prone to this. Ironically, the more subject matter expertise one has, the more likely one is to engage in erroneous speculation. One of Tetlock's more interesting findings is that precisely because experts have so much confidence in their own insights—precisely because they know *so much* about a particular subject—they are more comfortable offering bold predictions.

Depth of knowledge undermines the accuracy of predictions. In fact, success in forecasting extraordinary events—market crashes, terrible storms, technological breakthroughs—is actually an indicator of *poor* forecasting ability, since such events are the exception, not the rule. Often the most confident seers are weak forecasters because they tend to adopt the boldest stances, which bring notoriety, for better or worse. Semiannually the *Wall Street Journal* asks fifty economists to predict the outcome on eight macroeconomic variables: GDP, the unemployment rate, the consumer price index, the three-month Treasury bill, the ten-year government note, federal funds, the yen, and the euro. Economists whose predictions were correct on extreme outcomes (i.e., those that deviated from the average by wide margins) were the most likely to be the *worst* forecasters in general.[29]

Glassman and Hassett's punt on *Dow 36,000* is a clear example of this flaw. Like Babe Ruth pointing toward one spot on the distant fence, a bold call sets you up to be either hero or goat, but not much in between. In reality, life and choice pivot on the margins; they mostly proceed incrementally. But we are generally not disposed to think conditionally, instead focusing on singular or point predictions. Thinking through contingent outcomes is much harder to execute.

We See Patterns Where None Exist

Nearly all of us have walked past the roulette table in a casino where there stands a vertical digital display of the recently spun numbers, usually sixteen numbers deep. We also know what our gut reaction is when we see a long streak of either red or black numbers tallied on the display: "it's time" for the opposite color to hit. On quick reflection, we realize of course that spins of the roulette wheel are truly independent of one another—that the "streak" is illusory or at least ephemeral—but that nagging feeling that a black number will follow after a spurt of reds is hard to shake.

This Gambler's Fallacy, in one form or another, is all around us. We see patterns that aren't actually there. With repeated flips of a balanced coin, we swear we can see streaks in either heads or tails and would bet, mentally or otherwise, on either the continued streak or its reversal. Statisticians call this the "law of small numbers": we take the probability properties of a long data series and assign them to a short, statistically insignificant series.

We are wired to see order where in fact there is only randomness. All else being equal, we prefer certainty over unpredictability, even when it is a certainty of danger. Under known situations, we at least have a better chance to adapt. One of the core arguments of Daniel Kahneman's *Thinking, Fast and Slow* is that the more active part of our brain is always seeking and often finding order, even when it doesn't exist. Coincidences and causality are commonly conflated. The well-documented phenomenon of performance chasing in investment returns demonstrates the strength of our belief in hot streaks. Traders on an apparent hot streak more easily attract new assets and are more likely to appear on CNBC. But the actual persistence of performance is seldom robust. Nonetheless, we flood recent outperformers with new moneys because we anticipate that the good times will continue. We want to ride along with a winner. Ever bet the "Don't Pass" line in craps? Me neither.

The "hot hand" in sports is another set of examples. When I watch LeBron James hit a couple of jump shots in a row, I reflexively believe that he's "in the zone" and that his teammates should feed him the ball as much as possible. Basketball fans believe that a player's chance of hitting his next shot is higher after hitting his previous shot than after missing it. (It's the same with hitting in baseball or serving in tennis.) The right question is: What is the *conditional probability* of making the next shot (or hit or ace) following a made shot? The instinct among players and fans alike is: higher.

Not so. Studies of the hot hand evidence the Gambler's Fallacy. Looking at real NBA shooting data from two teams (the Boston Celtics and Philadelphia 76ers), researchers found no evidence of a positive correlation between the outcomes of sequential shots relative to a player's baseline shooting percentage. "People's intuitive conceptions of randomness depart systematically from the laws of chance."[30] That classic study has been corroborated many times over. Studies by Avugos et al. and Bar-Eli et al. found little to no evidence of the hot hand in sports.[31] Nonetheless, we see patterns in random sequences because randomness is psychologically disorienting. Without those patterns, we feel less in control, so in order to settle ourselves, our brain identifies consistencies in our surroundings.[32]

We Incur More Pain from Losing Than Pleasure from Winning

One of the more fascinating human biases is that losses tend to weigh more heavily on our psyche than gains do. Known as "loss aversion," this particular bias is highly germane to investing. Following on research by Daniel Kahneman and Amos Tversky, let's look at a couple of simple examples to demonstrate the principle.[33] First, a coin toss. In the simplest scenario, we win $50 if we're right and lose $50 if we're wrong. Though it's even odds mathematically, most of us decline the wager because we don't think it's worth it. How about if we change the upside payoff to $55 but keep the loss at $50 if we're wrong? What if the upside is $60 or even $70? Most of us would still walk. Psychologically, we need enough of a gap between our upside winnings and downside losses to make the bet feel worthwhile. Social psychologists estimate that the threshold for that gap is a ratio somewhere between 1.5 and 2.5 winnings to losses. So if we say it's about double (i.e., 2.0), then that means we would want our potential gains to be about twice our potential losses to feel comfortable taking the bet. And on the flip side, a loss of $100 feels about twice as bad as a gain of $100 feels pleasurable.

These feelings are highly relevant for the real-world exercise of investing. Regardless of whether I'm talking to a traditional long-only stock picker or someone making complex relative value bets with derivatives, a portfolio manager will typically insist that the prospective return of a worthwhile trade has an "asymmetric" payoff. This means that the trade has more upside than downside. Traders of any stripe frequently seek a payoff of at least 2:1 or 3:1. Otherwise, it's not worth it. Not only do those standard ratios bake in the realistic chance of being wrong, they also correspond roughly to the risk-aversion threshold explored by social psychologists.[34]

There are some interesting corollaries to this tendency toward loss aversion. A major one is that we tend to be comfortable taking *more* risk when we have already encountered big losses. Take this example: Say you had a bad day at the track. You're already down $1,000, and your system for picking the ponies isn't working. If you were even for the day, you would have little trouble walking away. But when losses mount, there's something keeping you from doing so. From a pure rational choice perspective, the probability of a long-shot bet to get you back to scratch should not appeal. By definition, it's unlikely to happen.

But you stick around. Say you can still bet another $100 at 10:1 odds on the last race of the day, meaning that there's a 10 percent chance you'll end the day even and a 90 percent chance you'll be down $1,100. Most people will take the gamble. From a standing start, with nothing lost or gained as in the first coin flip example above, we are disproportionally afraid of losses. But once we've incurred them, our feelings change. Here, too, the implications for investing are plain to see. A stock or fund we had high hopes for didn't pan out. This is not only literally impoverishing, it's emotionally disappointing. Many of us then adopt the belief that if we are patient, it will "come back." Indeed, we might even add to the investment in order to prove our conviction—to ourselves, to others, or both.

We Misuse, Fabricate, or Ignore Important Information

Thus far, we've covered three of the four natural qualities that impede decision making. The fourth is as important as, if not more important than, the others: our ability to effectively process information. This topic is a deep well in the cognitive sciences, so let me point to three well-documented biases on how our brains work: availability bias, confirmation bias, and hindsight bias.

Availability bias.   The most easily accessible information is often the source of our beliefs. For instance, watching the local Chicago nightly news, a depressing exercise for numerous reasons, I could be led to believe that murder is the leading cause of death in my metropolitan area of 9 million people. Though most nights feature a top story about homicide, in fact it doesn't rank anywhere near the top causes of death, such as heart disease, cancer, and stroke.

What's most available in our memory is often the primary driver of how we see the world.[35] It is difficult and time-consuming to construct robust data sets about all the things we see. When I read of a shark attack off the coast of Florida, I'm less likely to vacation there for fear of attack. But in 2012 there were twenty-six shark attacks in Florida, none of which were fatal, while injury and death due to rip currents were far more prevalent.[36] In addition to the media focus on more sensational data, my personal memory aggravates the problem. I haven't watched *Jaws* in twenty-five years, but it remains a terrifying memory; I don't recall seeing any movies about menacing rip tides. A plurality of the car accidents with which I'm familiar involve a Honda Odyssey or Toyota Sienna, but that shouldn't lead me to believe those vehicles are less safe than others. It just so happens that most of our friends have children and many of them drive minivans, meaning that my sampling of car accident data is skewed.

More extreme and salacious details tend to dominate our memories. Outliers come to mind more quickly than the average. Although car-related deaths are far more numerous than airline disasters, the latter are so horrific that they're more memorable. In finance, what most people know comes from media headlines. The *Wall Street Journal,* the world's leading financial newspaper, will occasionally publish stories about hedge fund managers and bankers being alleged crooks. While each individual story might be accurate, it does not speak to the prevalence of fraud in our financial system. Nonetheless, we are prone to make judgments based on easily retrieved memories rather than on a more complete sweep of the pertinent information.

Confirmation bias.   We don't like to be wrong. It is personally upsetting and professionally dangerous. To say that we seek out evidence to confirm our beliefs and expectations is hardly new. The English philosopher Francis Bacon wrote in 1620:

> The human understanding when it has once adopted an opinion (either as being the received opinion or as being agreeable to itself) draws all things else to support and agree with it. And though there be a greater number and weight of instances to be found on the other side, yet these it either neglects and despises, or else by some distinction sets aside and rejects; in order that by this great and pernicious predetermination the authority of its former conclusions may remain inviolate. . . . The human understanding is moved by those things most which strike and enter the mind simultaneously and suddenly, and so fill the imagination; and then it feigns and supposes all other things to be somehow, though it cannot see how, similar to those few things by which it is surrounded.[37]

Finding ways to prove yourself right is a natural instinct. Psychologists have conducted countless studies that support the existence of confirmation bias.[38] In American politics, conservatives watch Fox News and liberals watch MSNBC. Very few sample both stations to "objectively" establish their viewpoint. Spouses suspicious of infidelity will likely weigh certain cues as confirmatory, no matter how inconclusive they might be.

Confirmation bias is strongly reflected in the questions we ask. Studies of criminal justice, for example, show that skeptical interrogators tend to pose guilt-presumptive questions, which in turn impact the rate of confessions.[39] (Do you still shoplift?) The quest for knowledge is often just a self-fulfilling prophecy. I speculate that that's true in investing as well. Many fund manager interviews are conducted by analysts with a preexisting hunch that the manager is potentially talented (understandably, since otherwise they likely wouldn't be bothering).

In the manager due diligence I have personally witnessed, the most common questions posed to managers are: "What's your best idea?" and "What's your edge?" These are leading questions, teeing up the portfolio manager to tell us how talented he is. My failure on Clifford Street stemmed in part from this. Inquiries into weaknesses or mistakes are rarely pursued with comparable vigor. Furthermore, studies show that confirmation bias is most pronounced when information is gathered sequentially (as in an unstructured interview) rather than simultaneously (as in a survey). So once we head down the path of "best ideas" and "edge," we tend to ask confirmatory follow-up questions.[40]

Hindsight bias.   Finally, once we see an outcome, we retroactively assign a much higher probability of that particular outcome's having occurred instead of others. It's the "Monday morning quarterback" effect. And when things don't work out as anticipated, we can see what the problem was going to be. Of course, *ex ante,* we had little idea what was going to happen. Otherwise, there would be far more fabulously wealthy pundits and sports bettors.

Hindsight bias is all around us. In the days leading up to the 2012 US presidential election, there was disagreement among serious pollsters on who would win. But after the landslide, both the Left and the Right immediately took to the theory that non-white support for Obama not only clinched victory but made for a durable political advantage for the Left. It's so clear now that Neville Chamberlain was a complete dupe for signing the 1938 Munich Agreement because Hitler was planning for world domination. There were so many red flags surrounding Bernie Madoff's operation that it was, in retrospect, obviously a fraud. After the 9/11 attacks, it was easy to second-guess politicians and intelligence officers who had access to several clues forecasting the event—among thousands of other relevant data points that did not. I always suspected that the scheme installed by the Steelers' newly appointed offensive coordinator, Todd Haley, was a mismatch for quarterback Ben Roethlisberger's dynamic style—a suspicion that peaked after their most lackluster season in years. Hindsight is always 20/20.

Hindsight bias powerfully influences how we evaluate expert decision makers. We believe experts should know better—that's why we employ them in the first place. Thus, we tend to be ungenerous when judging them. That's somewhat justified, given that they themselves have inaccurate memories. In his study, Philip Tetlock is struck by how commonly experts who made incontrovertibly false forecasts believed in retrospect that they were correct. In another way, it is not justified. Daniel Kahneman points out that hindsight bias "leads observers to assess the quality of a decision not by whether the process was sound but whether its outcome was good or bad."[41] If we delegate our decisions to others as infallible analysis machines, rather than as experts with sound processes, we set ourselves up for disappointment. What's more, we create perverse incentives for some experts to make unduly bold predictions, which, as we saw with the study of macroeconomists above, puts them in a position to be generally ineffective.

. . . TO ADAPT DIVINE

We are overconfident. We see patterns where they don't exist. We focus more on the negative than the positive. We mismanage information in numerous ways. Yet, somehow, we still get by. We figure things out.[42] There are several factors that elevate the art and science of choosing, factors that directly inform all of the substantive chapters on investing to come. These are:

- ✓ Adaptation
- ✓ Feedback
- ✓ Satisficing

The Disposition to Learn

The primary finding of Tetlock's *Expert Political Judgment* is that experts are bad at forecasting, even in their own professional realms. On average, they aren't much better than a chimp throwing darts at a board. But Tetlock makes a second, fascinating finding: some experts are much better than others at forecasting. The method by which different experts evaluated information made a statistically significant difference in the quality of forecasts. Those with a more flexible, adaptive, and humble approach performed better than those using more rigid, overarching worldviews.

Tetlock leans on legendary Oxford philosopher Isaiah Berlin to colorfully make his case. In 1953, Berlin wrote a now-famous essay that leveraged an analysis of Tolstoy's view of history as expressed in *War and Peace* into an elegant insight into human agency and the engine of history. To do so, Berlin resuscitated a line from the ancient Greek poet Archilochus, who wrote:

The fox knows many things but the hedgehog knows one big thing.

Foxes are cunning hunters, using many different tactics to survive. Hedgehogs are small creatures with limited tactics; under threat, they roll up into a ball. In the wild, foxes prey on hedgehogs.

Berlin wrote in *The Hedgehog and the Fox* that the distinction between the two creatures "can be made to yield the deepest differences which divide writers and thinkers, and, it may be, human beings in general." This "great chasm" divides those "who relate everything to a single central vision, one system, less or more coherent or articulate, in terms of which they understand, think and feel—a single, universal, organizing principle in terms of which alone all that they are and say has significance—and on the other side, those who pursue many ends, often unrelated and even contradictory . . . related by no moral or aesthetic principle."[43]

For Tetlock (and now for many following his scholarship), this metaphor captures two personality types that help to explain variable success among experts. The importance of method over content is paramount:

What experts think matters far less than how they think. If we want realistic odds on what will happen next, coupled to a willingness to admit mistakes, we are better off turning to experts who embody the intellectual traits of Isaiah Berlin's prototypical fox—those who "know many little things," draw from an eclectic array of traditions, and accept ambiguity and contradiction as inevitable features of life—than we are turning to Berlin's hedgehogs—those who "know one big thing," toil devotedly within one tradition, and reach for formulaic solutions to ill-defined problems.[44]

The foxes of Berlin's and Tetlock's paradigm are flexible, self-critical, doubting. They admit mistakes. They embrace complexity. They think about their process of thinking, engaging in "meta-cognition." They endeavor to understand their own biases and mitigate their impacts.

Based on quantitatively rigorous analysis, Tetlock's foxlike subjects were better forecasters in the statistically significant sense. "Good judges tend to be moderate foxes: eclectic thinkers who are tolerant of counterarguments, and prone to hedge their probabilistic bets and not stray too far from just-guessing and base-rate probabilities of events."[45] For instance, students of Eastern Europe and nationalism who deployed overarching, deductively formulated theories of ethnic and political violence far overpredicted the level of violence in the region after the fall of the Soviet Union. Those with more nimble theories were more accurate in anticipating where violence would erupt and where it wouldn't.

Hedgehogs are often unwitting victims of unarticulated biases. They are more likely to be closed-minded and to exhibit hubris. They are averse to admitting mistakes, correcting them, and updating their beliefs. Not that the fox is the perfect hunter. Foxes are overly comfortable with, even solicitous of, complexity. On the surface, and perhaps at a deeper level, a fox's nimble mind lacks conviction. And sometimes foxes just make no sense. They've got too much going on.

Ironically, therefore, while foxes are more likely to be right, we generally prefer to listen to hedgehogs. We value pundits precisely because they tend to know one big thing.[46] Right or wrong, we know where they're coming from, and we can judge them accordingly. Foxes can be tiresome, as well as wrong. Perhaps even more importantly, while we might accept that foxes are better performers, most of us individually aspire to be hedgehogs. This was the genius of Berlin's analysis of Tolstoy. A brilliant, complicated writer, Tolstoy aspired to identify a unifying worldview, even though his complex rendition of both character and history betrayed that very effort. For the rest of us, it's not so complicated: We want to make sense of it all with as few moving pieces as possible. Out of the clutter of life, we want to find simplicity.

An Investing Metaphor.   The implications of this metaphor for investing—and specifically, for choosing fund managers—are profound, if largely unexplored. In markets, there are foxes and there hedgehogs. More accurately, there is a spectrum of these qualities, and virtually all of us are hybrids of both.

If there is one universally acknowledged truth in investing—that one big thing—it is that markets go up "in the long run." Whether this is in fact true depends largely on how we define "long run," but that empirical question is not our primary concern. Instead, we want to look at *how* experts think about this paradigm, not *what* they think.

Traditional investors believe that markets appreciate over long stretches of time and that their portfolios should be positioned accordingly, meaning that they should always be bullish, or exclusively long the market. Regardless of their high intelligence and healthy skepticism, they have chosen to operate within constraints that mitigate the relevance of skeptical, adaptive thinking. To be sure, they may overweight or underweight certain benchmark-related risks. But they have relatively little ability to actively profit from their informed views, even when they are correct. Likewise, traditional managers must operate in the corner of the market to which they have inextricably committed themselves—benchmarked against a market index or style—regardless of what they see as the true opportunity. In late 1999, a traditional tech-focused manager had to keep owning technology stocks, even if he thought the sector was overvalued. In 2013, a traditional high-grade bond manager must stick to owning low-yielding issues, knowing full well how vulnerable his or her portfolio is to rising interest rates. Hedgehogs have few options.

Alternative investors operate differently. They may very well believe that markets appreciate over time. But that does not lead them to hew to a formal benchmark or some predefined style; these are of tangential relevance to their mission. This is a valuable distinction between hedgehogs and foxes in markets, the former tying their choices to that one big thing while the latter adapts their beliefs and approach to changing circumstances. As ideal types, alternative managers are foxes while traditional managers are hedgehogs. Of course, ideal types do not hold perfectly when measured against real-world examples. But fully granting that any money manager sits somewhere along a spectrum between the two idealized poles, the analogy simplifies the menu of tens of thousands of choices before us.

Fund managers who know "one big thing" are probably, all else equal, less likely to succeed in uncertain markets. Managers with more flexibility (and this doesn't have to be hedge funds per se, but could be "go anywhere" long investments), who know "many little things"—including that markets may move downwards or sideways for long periods of time or that their

preferred asset class may be out of favor—are more likely to get th
right in uncertain times. They are also harder to understand and pin do
Indeed, while we would like to rely on foxes as our experts, their very r
ture makes them difficult to work with.

Here's a critical point: *Setting expectations for a fox is far more difficult than setting expectations for a hedgehog.* That's why hedge fund due
diligence is so much more complex and resource intensive than mutual
fund research. It has little to do with either the inherent skill of the manager or the relevance of that particular mandate to an investor's portfolio,
and everything to do with the challenge of defining *ex ante* the skills our
hired expert brings to bear, as well as learning how to update our expectations through time as circumstances dictate. This is the deepest level of the
investor's paradox: the experts best equipped to navigate our investment
choice regime are the ones most likely to disappoint, precisely because setting expectations for foxlike investors is so difficult.

The Opportunity to Learn

A fox in the desert will be compelled to behave differently than a fox in
the mountains. Likewise, not only is it important to consider whether an
expert has foxlike qualities, but we must also understand the environment
in which he operates, particularly the quality and pace of information flow.
Some environments are rich with information that flows bountifully and
rapidly, while others are tinny.

The strength or weakness of the information feedback loop dictates
our ability to learn from experience. How fast we can recognize mistakes
is a key variable in being able to improve. In forecasting, knowing quickly
and credibly whether we are correct provides more opportunities to learn
than does a weak feedback loop. By the same token, weak loops embolden
our biases. When we don't receive comprehensive feedback on the quality
of our judgments, overconfidence persists.

We saw earlier that the evidence for whether experts deliver reliable
judgment is mixed, at best. Across different domains there are highly variable rates of skill, driven by the type of work and nature of information flow.
Researchers have found stronger performance in vocations as disparate as

weather forecasters, livestock judges, grain inspectors, test pilots, auditors, chess masters, physicists, accountants, mathematicians, and anesthesiologists. Bad performance manifests more frequently with clinical psychologists, psychiatrists, court judges, student admissions officers, personnel selectors, parole officers, stock brokers, and polygraph interpreters.[47]

Why the variance? One proposition is that in some areas there is more opportunity to learn from past decisions. In turn, experts have the opportunity to make adjustments to new information. Take a domain that impacts each of us every day and for which experts have continuous feedback: the weather. Meteorologists know quickly whether they are right or wrong. As a result, the science of meteorology has been able to make significant strides over the decades, and professional weathermen are outstanding at predicting the future.[48] Within professions, we see meaningful differences in forecasting ability. In medicine, for example, Kahneman cites studies proving that anesthesiologists and radiologists have markedly different success rates, in no small part because the former receive instant feedback on the status of their patients, while the latter do not.[49]

The feedback loop weighs heavily on the ability to build expertise. For the musician, a misplayed note is an instant opportunity for learning. So too with many athletes, airplane pilots, and chess players. In those cases, years of experience create a massive internal database to draw from, whereas for those in weak loops, a decade may not be long enough. My oldest son is ten, but whether I'm a skilled parent remains to be seen.

When does practice matter? Thanks to Malcolm Gladwell's popular *Blink,* much has been made of the "10,000 hours" it takes one to generate true expertise. In that book's memorable story, the art experts knew in an instant that a sculpture was a fake because after years of examining genuine art, their brains had become hardwired to issue immediately such summary judgments. I would amend this view to allow for consideration of the strength of the feedback loops in place. Ten thousand hours of practice for a musician or meteorologist is not the same as it is for someone who picks money managers for a living.

Now let's revisit the domain of choosing fund managers. The data presented earlier unequivocally show that professional fund pickers are, on average, unskilled. Now we have a solid hypothesis for this sobering finding, which is that there is little opportunity to learn how to be better. This is especially true with hedge fund vehicles, some of which are officially valued only on a monthly basis.[50] Thus, it's hard to know whether performance is living up to one's expectations. Despite the hedge fund's reputation as an aggressive, trading-oriented culture, I strain to think of many other professional domains with a weaker feedback loop than hedge fund investing. Precisely because it can take years to credibly evidence whether you were "right" or "wrong" about an investment (either alternative or traditional), the opportunity for learning and self-improvement is diminished. In weak loops, it is hard to learn.

Over what time frame should a decision be evaluated, then? That challenge plagues professional fund pickers and regular investors alike. A few years ago, I led the due diligence on a fund that invested in stocks and, over many years, had historically delivered performance that had a low, sometimes *negative*, correlation to other long/short equity funds. This is hard to find, so after getting comfortable with other key factors such as the team's integrity, business stability, and investment process, we chose to invest.

Shortly thereafter, this fund had a major performance hiccup due to an idiosyncratic bet on emerging market equities. While such exposure was within our expectations, a bad loss during generally good markets was unwelcome. First impressions are the most important. While the fund remained negatively correlated to others—though not in the good way at that moment—this early disappointment led to a quick termination. Fast-forward a couple of years, and the fund posted positive returns in 2008, a remarkable feat. We had already fired the manager by then, so we were not around to benefit from what we initially believed was a likely outcome. There is no algorithm to decide whether or not the shorter time frame or the longer time frame was the appropriate window for evaluation. But it is clear that the generally weak feedback loop on whether that manager was living up to our expectations influenced our decisions.

In sum, the difficulty of mastering one's domain varies considerably according to both the inherent nature of the expert and the environment in which he operates. Within any particular domain, there will be some individuals who are more inclined than others to seek multifaceted solutions, to admit mistakes, to be creative in ways to compress time (and thus

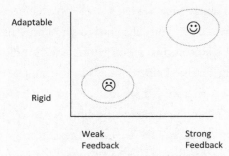

Figure 2.1: Happy and Sad Decision Domains

strengthen the feedback). In other words, among meteorologists and fund pickers there are both foxes and hedgehogs. Nonetheless, there are structural constraints we cannot avoid.

In figure 2.1, I've made a simple graph showing this dynamic. The vertical axis reflects the spectrum from hedgehogs to foxes. The horizontal axis reflects the strength of the feedback loop. Domains in the northeast are conducive to positive choice outcomes. In areas where there is rich, fast-flowing information and where choosers (or those to whom we delegate) have adaptable, foxlike qualities, we are much more likely to be satisfied. The southwest corner is a sad place. Narrow-minded experts exist in a slow, thin information environment. It's hard to imagine a lot of good outcomes under these circumstances.

The Beauty of Good Enough

Lastly, independent of the expert or the environment, we must face ourselves. Unmet expectations are a powerful human phenomenon. In his extensive analysis of the power and purpose of regret, Neal Roese writes that "the aching remorse of actions left undone, of better possibilities left unattained, is an emotion common to all people."[51] Regret impacts us deeply. While we have little to no control over most outcomes, we do, to some extent and in most scenarios, have a say over what we anticipate. We set the bar at a height of our own choosing.

Roese points to an interesting study of the happiness of Olympic athletes that showed that silver medal winners tended to be less satisfied with their accomplishment than bronze medal winners. This is a somewhat counterintuitive finding insofar as second place is by definition a better outcome than third place. However, the yardstick by which either group measured itself drove the level of happiness. The silver medalists were disappointed at not being able to attain the top prize. But the bronze medalists were pleased to earn a medal at all. In other words, the former set their expectations upwards, while the latter set them downwards. Thus, an objectively better outcome produced less satisfaction.[52]

When outcomes don't meet expectations, we are distressed in proportion to the magnitude and consequence of the miss. This is not merely a cold calculation; it's a built-in physiological response. As biologists have recognized, when stimuli meet or exceed our expectations, the brain releases dopamines, which are pleasurable.[53] After a pattern forms between stimulus and outcome, the brain is conditioned to expect this relationship, and, in turn, we adjust our behavior to drive further pleasurable outcomes. When expectations are met, dopamines are released. When the pattern is broken—or as scientists say, when "prediction error" occurs—the anticipated dopamines are not released. This is a demonstrably uncomfortable experience.[54]

One reason that abundant choice can make people miserable is that the wealth of options escalates our expectations.[55] The bar is raised when there is a wide variety of choice because we believe that, amid such abundance, the right choice must be available. More choices lead to the expectation of better outcomes. When events don't pan out, we blame ourselves more under conditions of abundance than of scarcity; with the latter we can at least say that our ability to choose was limited.

A solution to expectations management is simple and intuitive: lower the bar. It is a common, long-held sentiment. Eighteenth-century poet Alexander Pope wrote, "Blessed is he who expects nothing, for he shall never be disappointed." A standard assumption in classical economic theory is that all individuals are fully informed, rational decision makers who seek to maximize their utility. The truth is, while there's something pure and aspirational about the constant quest to maximize, it's also impractical. In the formal economic sense, this was first recognized by Herbert Simon, a prolific social scientist of the postwar era and an eventual Nobel Prize winner, who pointed out that humans lack the cognitive ability to engage in truly maximizing behavior. We are unable to collect, let alone process, complete information on the issues that matter to us.[56]

We are rational decision makers—within limits. This perspective, which has come to be known as "bounded rationality," underlies Simon's concept of "satisficing," which suggests that we will choose less-than-best options owing to inescapable cognitive constraints. The notion of satisficing gives credence to the practice of focusing on the *optimal,* versus the *maximum.*[57] Sometimes available low-cost solutions are *good enough.* The loose screw on my sons' bunk bed requires a Phillips-head screwdriver, which is out in the garage. My Swiss Army knife, in my desk drawer, has a flat-head screwdriver that gives me enough torque, even though it slips out of the thread frequently. The former would do the job twice as quickly, but it's not worth it when I consider having to walk to our detached garage on a cold day. Any of us could come up with dozens of these examples from our daily lives. Ultimately, it's not just a matter of what's best, but of what works. We'd rather be approximately right instead of precisely wrong. This is satisficing.

Situated at the intersection of formalized choice theory and common sense, this notion of satisficing—choosing what's good enough—helps to resolve the investor's paradox. We want the tastiest jam, the coolest pair of jeans, and the savviest money manager. We are unlikely to acquire them. Instead, we recognize that expectations management is central to the process of choice. Humming in the background of this book is a satisficing framework, built to constructively and positively dampen expectations.

GOOD CHOOSERS ADAPT to changing environments. They infuse current decisions with valuable feedback from previous mistakes. They recognize that the perfect is the enemy of the good. All three elements require a certain amount of humility. Acknowledging errors is emotionally disheartening and sometimes professionally jeopardizing.

Good investing is a function of making good choices. Central to understanding and resolving the investor's paradox is recognizing that investing is a problem of choice—behavioral, emotional, messy—as much as it is a problem of finance and statistics. Successful investing depends on building reasonable expectations of future outcomes and adapting those expectations in an informed, timely manner based on new information about our subjects as well as changes in our broader environment. Understanding the parameters of effective choices in general precedes a substantive understanding of the specific domain in which one is choosing. This book about navigating markets has barely discussed markets thus far, but that's okay. Method precedes content.

Having now teed up these behavioral matters, we next introduce the historical dimension of effective investment decision making. The combination of this chapter's evergreen issues with the context-specific challenges of our post-2008 world will prepare us to devote the balance of our narrative to a focused, simplifying solution for resolving the investor's paradox.

3

ALTERNATIVE STATES

As in political revolutions, so in paradigm choice—there is no standard higher than the assent of the relevant community . . . this issue of paradigm choice can never be unequivocally settled by logic and experiment alone.

—Thomas Kuhn[1]

OLD AND NEW NORMALS

How we make choices depends on the context in which we choose. This context—what I have referred to as a choice regime—has a historical quality, meaning that what we focus on today is largely driven by what we considered and decided yesterday and the days and years before that. It has sociological, anthropological, and political qualities insofar as institutional constraints, cultural factors, and power relationships shape our choice set.[2]

The choice regime for investment funds has evolved dramatically over the past few decades. First, there are many more choosers. As in other realms, finance has undergone a democratization in which a vast number of individuals now have liberties that they did not enjoy a couple of generations ago. Second, there are many more choices—there has been an explosion in the number of options. Third, the complexity of those choices has increased considerably.

The modern era of investment management, which began in the early 1980s, has had three phases (figure 3.1). In the early period, there was an extraordinary bull market in stocks and bonds during which simply being long the market was the smart move. The investment industry responded with a proliferation of traditional long-only products. Over time, fund companies divided up market segments with increasing granularity based on the ascendant influence of the Morningstar Style Box. Ultimately, though, being fully invested and long the market was in itself the winning strategy. During this stage, hedge funds were relatively small and obscure, thus of little relevance to the choice regime.

The second phase began with the bursting of the tech stock bubble in 2000 and continued through the 2008 crisis. As the bull run in stocks petered out, investors began to grapple with various models for the right way to allocate during a time of heightened uncertainty and anxiety. Institutional investors in particular began to experiment with alternative strategies that appeared more resilient than traditional long-only strategies. The modern hedge fund industry was born. It was also during this decade that the exchange-traded fund (ETF) industry exploded in size.

Post-meltdown, we entered a third phase, in which institutions and individuals alike are grappling with the right way to meet their objectives in light of heightened fear and a proliferation of choice. Alternative strategies have become available to the mainstream; the prevalence of so-called liquid alternatives is growing quickly. We have entered an era of *convergence* in which the traditional and alternative fund industries—previously distinct from one another—have begun to overlap, triggering

	The Great Moderation, 1982–2000	The Lost Decade, 2000–2009	The New Normal, 2009–Forward
Themes	Exuberance and Paradigm Supremacy: Bull markets, proliferation of choices, relative return investing, and style boxes	Volatility and Experimentation: Rise of hedge funds to institutional prominence	Uncertainty and Convergence: Multiple models of alpha generation and portfolio construction
Features	Broadening set of product offerings with limited complexity	Due to the legitimization of hedge funds for institutional investors, breadth and complexity both expanded; the ETF industry also grew massively	Breadth and complexity wider due to continued ETF boom and the main-streaming of alternatives

Figure 3.1: Evolution of the Investment Choice Regime

a period of industrial change that has just begun and whose outcome is uncertain.

In this period of uncertainty, investors are experimenting with different solutions. What's clear is that the exercise of picking the right managers—of outsourcing investment discretion to the experts—has grown more difficult. In a market environment that is generally trendless and choppy, the choice of fund manager matters more than it does when markets generally march upwards. Manager selection matters more during tough times.

Let's now walk through the history of the fund industry, to see where we came from and where we might be going. That will then tee up the balance of *The Investor's Paradox,* which offers a road map for navigating the path ahead.

THE GREAT MODERATION

The modern money management industry took off during the bull market in stocks and bonds that began in the early 1980s. Before then, for nearly two decades, markets had lurched through a long spell of up-and-down results. The Dow Jones Industrial Average closed 1964 at a value of 874; fifteen years later, at the end of 1979, the index sat at 838. It peaked in the early 1970s north of 1,000, but this fifteen-year stretch was hardly fruitful for most equity owners, especially those committed to investing "for the long run."

The investment management industry was small and fragmented prior to the 1980s. Choice was limited. According to the Investment Company Institute, there were only 170 mutual funds in 1965, with few assets under management.[3] Smaller local banks and advisors were the main source of supply. Nor was there much demand for broader choice. According to Peter Bernstein in *Capital Ideas,* institutional investors typically relied on one bank, which "had total responsibility for bonds as well as stocks, for determining the mix between the two, and for selecting the securities in each sector. After a time, it became common to have one manager for equities and another for fixed income securities, but in the early 1970s the idea of having a bevy of equity managers was still a novelty."[4]

Nor was there a broad equity culture or an investor class to speak of in the pre-modern era. During this period, bond investors could achieve high nominal yields from even the safest of instruments: the benchmark ten-year US Treasury bond yielded between 6.8 percent and 10.8 percent in the back half of the 1970s (ultimately peaking in 1981 at 15.6 percent). As this was also a period of rising, elevated inflation, the real return on fixed income was far less attractive than nominal returns.

It took a fundamental economic shift to launch the first phase of the modern investment choice regime. The 1980s witnessed the onset of the so-called Great Moderation, what then Federal Reserve governor Ben Bernanke described in 2004 as a "remarkable decline in the variability of output and inflation."[5] This was a profound breakpoint in how developed economies operated. Before this, the "normal" business cycle experienced bigger swings in output, employment, and inflation. Now the cycle dampened markedly.

In a seminal 2003 article, economists James Stock and Mark Watson presented comprehensive evidence of this new era.[6] Most important, they observed that the volatility in US GDP growth declined sharply into a persistently lower volatility era starting in early 1984. And it was more than just the trend in the growth of output that smoothed: "The decline in volatility has occurred broadly across the U.S. economy: since the mid-1980s, measures of employment growth, consumption growth, and sectoral output have had standard deviations 60% to 70% of their values during the 1970s and early 1980s. Fluctuations in wage and price inflation have also moderated considerably."[7] There is little academic disagreement over the occurrence of the Great Moderation, which lasted from roughly the mid-1980s to about 2007. Nor was this only a US phenomenon. Other wealthy economies, especially in Western Europe, also experienced similar patterns.

A variety of factors contributed to this sea change. The shift toward less cyclically sensitive service-based industries, "just-in-time" inventory management, and the lack of serious shocks to money supply, productivity, or oil prices—these all smoothed the business cycle. The most popular explanation for the Great Moderation is policy change. Specifically, the Volcker-Greenspan era ushered in new thinking for managing the money supply, with ideas and tools aimed toward decreasing and then stabilizing

inflation. The Federal Funds effective rate, a measure of short-term lend-
ing rates, was both volatile and surging upwards in the 1960s and 1970s,
peaking at north of 15 percent in the early 1980s. Since then, it has steadily
declined, now resting just north of zero.

Most important for our tale, this moderation facilitated a multi-
decade rally in risk assets, both liquid (stocks and bonds) and illiquid (real
estate, private equity, and real assets). As markets rose, investor capital
flooded in, creating a lengthy virtuous cycle between investor appetite and
market outcomes. The rise of the modern investor class also undergirded
the rise of the modern investment management industry, most notably
the rise of the retail and institutional mutual fund complex. A growing
number of firms launched a growing number of new choices for investors
to participate in the markets. The data in figure 3.2 evidence the sharp
rise in mutual fund offerings from the early 1980s to 2000, at which point
growth flattened. The proliferation of bond and equity products was most
noteworthy.

Many of the investment firms that rose to prominence early in this
phase remain market leaders today. As in many other industries, an early
mover advantage can be critically important for success. Indeed, seven
of the top ten mutual fund firms (in terms of market share) in 1990

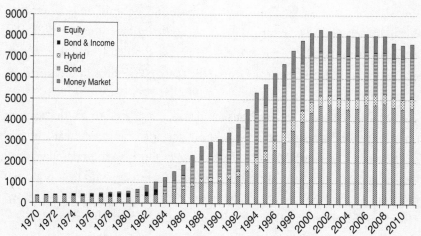

Figure 3.2   Growth of Mutual Funds (Number, by Asset Class), 1970–2011
Source: Investment Company Institute

retained their top ten status by 2010.[8] The "big three" fund complexes—Fidelity, Vanguard, and Capital Group (American Funds)—controlled nearly one-third of market share in 2010 but were also significant players decades ago.

Leaders of the Pack

No two investment firms exemplified this phase of the choice regime more than Vanguard and Fidelity. Together, they became the two dominating forces of the period, driving the evolution of the modern regime more than any of the others, though in different ways.

For Fidelity, it was all about the stars. The goal of the firm was to outperform competitors by tapping the talents of bold stock pickers. The premise was that active management could add value and that Fidelity could attract the best and brightest stock pickers to do so. In a telling quote by Fidelity Chairman Edward C. "Ned" Johnson III, responding at the time to the upstart challenge of passive index funds, "I can't believe that the great mass of investors are [sic] going to be satisfied with just receiving average returns. The name of the game is to be the best."[9]

The firm's modern prominence was based on a popular lineup of articulate fund managers, headlined by its top celebrity, Peter Lynch. A former golf caddy for the president of Fidelity in the mid-1960s and a junior portfolio manager in the early 1970s, Lynch took the helm in 1977 of the then-unknown Magellan Fund, with only around $22 million in assets under management.[10] Over time, Fidelity Magellan grew to be one the largest investment funds in the world, with more than $14 billion in assets when Lynch retired in 1990, affording him superstar status in the world of money managers.

Lynch's outsized bets on household names adhered to his homespun philosophy of "invest in what you know," an idea captured in his books *Beating the Street* and *One Up on Wall Street*. Both were best sellers and helped democratize the notion that everyday investors could beat not only the stock market but also the stock market experts. This point somehow rested comfortably with Fidelity's thrust toward cultivating star stock pickers, who were well publicized as having the ability to beat the market. Lynch helped to put Fidelity on the map, alongside a bevy of other in-house stock and bond pickers who delivered strong returns in the 1980s and 1990s in correspondence to the era's bull run.

Vanguard rejected this superstar approach. While the firm can trace its roots to the actively managed stock-and-bond-picking Wellington Fund, launched in 1929, the Vanguard Group was officially founded in 1974 by John C. (Jack) Bogle and gained prominence by embracing a low-cost index fund model. In direct contradiction to Fidelity's Ned Johnson, Bogle passionately embraced the surging efficient-markets hypothesis and preached that "beating the market" was a fool's errand. Bogle's academic muses included Burton Malkiel, Paul Samuelson, and Charles D. Ellis.[11]

Vanguard's embrace of inexpensive market indexing dovetailed nicely with the rally that began just several years after the firm's founding, as well as the creeping acceptance (more so by investors than fund companies) of the efficient-markets hypothesis. The firm grew spectacularly in the 1980s, from $3 billion in 1980 to more than $50 billion by the fall of 1990. During this decade, Vanguard began to differentiate its lineup, both in equities (e.g., small-cap US, international, emerging markets) and bonds (e.g., long- versus short-term maturities).[12]

While apparently alter egos in terms of both message and swagger, what united Fidelity and Vanguard was their shared skill in selling to an increasingly broad audience. For Fidelity, it was distribution prowess, more than investing genius, that put them at the top of the mountain. By 1990, Fidelity controlled roughly 10 percent of mutual fund assets, with roughly $119 billion in AUM. Vanguard was also aggressive on the marketing front. Its embrace of low-cost indexing, selling funds with no up-front charges, and even cheaper institutional share classes facilitated massive inflows into a variety of products. These two firms spearheaded the transformation of the asset management industry into a consumer products business.[13]

Others rallied to imitate their success. Not surprisingly, the Fidelity model, with its considerably higher profit margins, was much more popular. The Vanguard model wasn't as sexy; few overseeing index funds end up on the cover of *Money* magazine. Thus, while the empirical record supported a move toward passive investing, the surge in product development stemmed from actively managed funds. A number of the investment shops that accelerated their reach during this era remain household names today, including T. Rowe Price, American (formerly Twentieth) Century, Capital Group (which sells American Funds), and Franklin Templeton.

The number of fund offerings more than tripled in the 1980s. While the pace of growth in the 1990s was slightly slower, the decade saw a spike in product specialization. As a result, the choice regime was growing more complex.

The 1990s were the decade of the style box. When research firm Morningstar launched its Style Box Methodology in 1992, it brought together some key undercurrents in both academic theory and product development, thus helping to accelerate further differentiation in the choice regime. First, around that time, pioneering work by economists Eugene Fama and Kenneth French advanced investment theory by arguing that we should define risk more granularly than the dominant model suggested. The Capital Asset Pricing Model (CAPM) employed only one variable, overall market sensitivity (or "beta"), to describe stock market returns. While somewhat accurate, it left a material amount of stock returns unexplained. Fama and French proposed a "three-factor model" that took into account both a stock's market capitalization and its valuation, as measured by book-to-price ratios.[14] With the ability to distinguish large caps from small caps and growth stocks from value stocks, this three-factor model more robustly explained stock returns than did CAPM.Further, these two additional variables became the wellspring of the wildly popular style box now used to categorize all long-only equity funds (figure 3.3).[15]

		Valuation Scale		
		Value	Core	Growth
Market Capitalization Scale	Large-Cap	Large Value	Large Core	Large Growth
	Mid-Cap	Mid-Value	Mid-Core	Mid-Growth
	Small-Cap	Small Value	Small Core	Small Growth

Figure 3.3   The Equity Style Box
Source: Morningstar

The schematic became a gold mine for fund companies. As it grew intellectually defensible to splice equity and bond markets into finer-cut segments in order to both better identify pockets of alpha and build more diversified portfolios (on the assumption of lower correlations among style boxes), it was easy to sell the notion that there should be a wealth of new products to address this need. Investment shops rolled out many new products that aimed to provide exposure to these smaller market segments. It was also no coincidence that the business of indexing took off right around this time, now that there was much more to index. The concept of the index fund was born around the same time—in the mid-1960s—as the efficient-markets hypothesis. Even though the first index fund was launched in 1971, it took years for the index business to gain traction in terms of assets and products.[16] Indeed, it wasn't until 1992 that S&P/BARRA launched their Value and Growth Indexes, opening the door to a slew of other style-based indexes.

Morningstar's Style Box (and other comparable categorization schemes, such as Lipper's) legitimated, institutionalized, and accelerated the enormous growth in the first phase of the modern investment choice regime. Now there was not only a vocabulary but an easily understood graphic to articulate investor demand and fund company supply of products that could be labeled "mid-cap growth," "large-cap value," "small-cap blend," and so forth. Investment consultants, who also grew more influential during this period, embraced the style box, in no small part because it moved the basic choice of allocating between stocks and bonds to a more complex choice across dozens of categories; hence, they had more advice to sell. Furthermore, the advent of Morningstar's "star" rating, a quantitatively derived measure of comparative historical performance, gave further marketing legitimacy to fund companies, consultants, and advisors who preferred to recommend or sell the top-rated funds.

The dominant paradigm during this phase was that of *relative return* investing. The name of the game was outperformance of an assigned benchmark. Actually making money (absolute returns) was not that difficult considering that markets rarely went down. What's clear in retrospect is that, despite there being so many different investment approaches, the choice regime for both institutions and individuals centered on being long the market. Whether it was buy-and-hold value investors or fast-trading growth managers, what united virtually all choices in this era were the principles of being fully long and fully invested. In this context, despite their different histories and offerings, Fidelity and Vanguard sold investors effectively the same product.

Within this context, the principle of "diversification" during this period came to mean spreading one's bets across different style boxes without fully appreciating that the beta of these style boxes to global equity markets was high, especially during shocks and crises. Despite its benefits, the style box ushered in an era of false diversification and hidden risks. PIMCO's Bill Gross recently described a "cult of equity," a shared mindset in which a majority of market participants were socialized to believe that it was always prudent to own "stocks for the long run."[17] This cult, as it were, found its roots in the early modern investment choice regime.

Prehistory

And what of so-called alternative investments during this period of relative return dominance? In the grand scheme of the choice regime, they were largely irrelevant. Even if hedge fund strategies were available to the general public (they weren't) or had strong appeal to large institutions (they didn't), why choose a more complicated path when easy-to-access traditional investments in the most liquid markets were producing satisfying results? At best, alternative investments were a curious sideshow, with some astounding, albeit opaque, results from the likes of Soros, Tudor, Caxton, Moore, Elliot Associates, and others.

Even if we can selectively point to individual hedge funds that delivered good returns, this cottage industry had yet to take on a truly institutional quality, in contrast to most traditional firms with mature business management and client service platforms. To wit, some of the prominent alternative investment firms tanked during the period. Most notable was the well-documented implosion in 1998 of Long-Term Capital Management (LTCM), a highly levered fixed income arbitrage fund helmed in part by Nobel economics laureates. The potential ripple effects of their trades compelled some of the world's largest banks to head off a market meltdown when, as Roger Lowenstein has famously put it, "genius failed."[18]

Not long after LTCM blew up, the industry's largest hedge fund, Tiger Management Company, also failed. Run by the legendary Julian Robertson, Tiger's assets peaked at $22 billion in 1998, a not-insignificant percentage of the entire hedge fund universe at the time. From the fund's 1980 founding forward, Robertson and his team generated spectacular results primarily due to Tiger's "long/short" approach to stock picking, taking large bets on its favorite companies while selling short poorly managed, overvalued firms. As sensible and lucrative as that strategy had been for nearly twenty years, Tiger was ultimately forced out of business by 2000 after the fund declined 19 percent in 1999, compared to a 21 percent gain in the S&P 500.[19] Tiger stubbornly adhered to its sizable short positions on wildly overvalued technology stocks, only to watch those issues skyrocket further. The fund underperformed the market by 40 percent and saw the bulk of its client base demand its money back.

Robertson was ultimately correct, yet the largest, most prestigious hedge fund of the era was shuttered before it could take advantage of its prescience, speaking volumes about the maturity of such firms' risk management protocols, the business stability of the platform, and the overall institutional maturity of the hedge fund industry. While Robertson's lasting legacy was a remarkable string of protégés (affectionately referred to as Tiger Cubs) who became some of the most successful investors of the 2000s, his near-term legacy at that time was someone who could not stay solvent longer than the market could stay irrational.

While numerous hedge fund "market wizards" were afoot during this era, their relevance to the investment choice regime was minimal. That would reverse itself quickly. Most of the investment world was feeling plump in the late 1990s, and only a rarified few heard the bell toll for what was shortly to become a lost decade for many investors. And they were virtually all nontraditional fund managers—quietly signaling the start of the next phase of the investment choice regime.

EXPERIMENTATION

The bursting of the tech stock bubble in 2000 marked the end of the era of economic stability. From an underlying macroeconomic perspective, there are few better examples of capitalism's disposition toward "creative destruction" than the Great Moderation and its aftermath: the dampening of economic volatility, which was broadly interpreted as a heightening of economic certainty, led to an increasing level of appetite for risk.[20] Flows to financial assets both liquid (stocks and bonds) and illiquid (real estate and private equity) increased, and system-wide leverage rose sharply, assisted by innovations in financial engineering and the global growth of the financial industry, itself spurred by the global deregulation of finance, including the growth of non-bank financial-lending mechanisms, sometimes called "shadow banking." Paradoxically, the sources of moderation also planted the seeds of systemic instability.

Granted, the golden era had episodic wobbles: the violent market crash of October 1987; the 1990 US savings-and-loan debacle; the 1994 Mexican peso crisis; the 1997 Asian crisis; and the 1998 Russian default. But in retrospect, in each of these instances, when risk premiums widened sharply, investors were handsomely rewarded for buying "on the dip." Being greedy when others were fearful was the courage-soaked mantra of the time. At minimum, a buy-and-hold strategy always seemed prudent as investors learned time and again that the market always came back.

Bookended by burst bubbles, first in stocks and later in housing, this next phase of the choice regime threw a wrench into traditional measures for selecting investments and constructing portfolios. The losses in traditional equity strategies in 2000–2002 were huge. The NASDAQ Composite has come nowhere close to reclaiming its March 10, 2000, peak of 5,048, even though broad indices such as the S&P 500 eventually clawed back their losses. The original cornerstone of modern portfolio theory—diversification—held firm for disciplined investors with meaningful bond allocations, since higher-quality fixed income strategies held up nicely during the bursting of the Internet bubble. But it was hardly bond investing that captured the public mindshare during this tumultuous period. A different revolution was percolating. Enter "hedge funds."

What Is a Hedge Fund?

Until now, we have been treating the hedge fund category monolithically, but it's critical to deconstruct it in order to see it clearly. Absent that step, we simply cannot understand our current choice regime or make effective investments.

To start, it's easier to define what hedge funds are not than what they are. First and foremost, *hedge funds are not an asset class.* According to Investopedia, an asset class is "a group of securities that exhibit similar characteristics, behave similarly in the marketplace, and are subject to the same laws and regulations."[21] By any stretch of the imagination, hedge funds do not fit this description—just as "mutual funds" are not an asset class. In either case, one is compelled to ask: What exactly does that particular vehicle invest in—and how?

Unfortunately, there is considerable evidence that many investors, including sophisticated institutions, treat hedge funds as a monolithic asset class. As we see more often than not, "hedge funds," "alternatives," or "absolute return" is a distinct category in an asset allocation model, as we can see from any number of plan sponsors, whether it be corporate pensions or public plans, endowments, foundations, insurance companies, or wealth management firms.[22]

At its most sterile but technically accurate level, the term "hedge fund" is a shorthand term for a specific legal structure—specifically a private partnership—that grants a money manager enormous flexibility in trying to reach some investment objective. Likewise, a hedge fund is not a specific investment "strategy." It is not a "type" or "style" of investment that can be coherently mapped into an intelligent asset allocation plan, any more than one can make a meaningful allocation to mutual funds. Because they are completely flexible in their mandate within the structure of a private partnership, what are colloquially referred to as hedge funds can own not only equities and fixed income securities, but also commodities, currencies, and many other esoteric instruments, especially derivatives (e.g., futures, forwards, options, and swaps). They can be long or short any of those securities or instruments.

By mandate, most hedge funds should be indifferent to the broad moves of the market, as they can bet against overvalued securities, as Julian Robertson's Tiger Fund did in 1999 with technology stocks. They can employ leverage, which is available from banks in a variety of different formats. And they can engage in complex trading strategies, often in terms of capturing a "spread" between the perceived values of two or more instruments, as is the case in strategies with nomenclature like arbitrage, relative value, and pairs trading.

Here's the key point: Investors must distinguish between investment risk and the vehicle with which they are gaining access to those risks. Risk and its packaging, though often conflated, are not the same thing.

It is true that flexibility, expressed in any number of ways—the use of derivatives, leverage, complex trading strategies, and so forth—has gained hedge funds a reputation as "speculative." Indeed, this notion does underpin the typical hedge fund's legal structure, which is a limited partnership open only to institutions and wealthy individuals. Risky investments, so the argument goes, should be reserved for those with the wherewithal and the wallet size to endure a sizable loss.

This popular understanding is incorrect. Most hedge fund strategies tend to outperform in down markets, but underperform in up markets. The reason is not complicated: Most hedge funds hedge. Traditional investments do not, which is why they usually lose more money in bear markets. If risk is understood as the chance for permanent capital loss, then it must follow that many mutual funds take more risk than hedge funds do. And if this is true, it puts a premium on understanding how managers take risk, somewhat independent of the legal structure in which they operate. If risk is understood as volatility of returns, which is common in modern finance, there, too, most hedge fund strategies should be seen as less risky. The average standard deviation of returns for most alternative strategies is considerably lower than it is for traditional equity investments.

The easier-to-see distinctions between alternative and traditional investments are the former's ability to own exotic asset classes, short securities, employ leverage, trade derivatives, and engage in complex trading strategies. But there is also a more philosophically profound difference between the two approaches: the objectives of beating a market benchmark versus outperforming the returns of risk-free assets (cash or US Treasury bills). The relative-return orthodoxy, which was nurtured by the efficient markets hypothesis and the advent of indexing, came to full fruition with the advent of the Fama-French three-factor model, Morningstar style boxes, and investment companies' commitment to selling long-only, style-based products.

By aiming to achieve absolute returns—*making money instead of beating a benchmark*—many alternative approaches focus on delivering non-linear, convex payoff profiles. However, that does not mean that alternative strategies cannot underperform or lose money as a result of market conditions, lack of skill, or both. Their focus thus tilts toward risk-adjusted returns, unlike many traditional investment strategies that deliver more linear results. While the old saw states that "you can't eat a Sharpe Ratio," it's also true that investors seeking lower volatility with reasonable returns can garner more consistent nourishment with an alternative approach. The utility of convexity is not supply driven, but demand driven. Needs among investors vary, so a pension plan managing to a specific payout schedule (where undue volatility could disrupt those payments) will likely find strategies offering convexity to be useful. Investors seeking maximum returns over long periods of time might not.

The appeal of this *absolute return* paradigm is grounded in behavioral theory. Investors do not experience the utility of their investments as depicted as a fluid line that flows through a time series of returns. The utility profile of returns is lumpy and episodic, with periods of steep losses especially painful, more so than comparable positive spikes are enjoyable. The principle of loss aversion is always relevant in investing, and it appears that the payoff profile of alternatives, generally speaking, maps most people's loss-averse profiles better than do the more linear payoffs of traditional investments.

This goes a long way toward explaining the periodic popularity of alternative investments. Traditional, benchmark-constrained investments typically capture a large percentage of their markets' upswings and downswings; hence their linear character. Alternatives, on the other hand, address some of our built-in biases. Because of loss aversion, hedge fund returns can often *feel* better because, on average, the lows aren't as low, even though the highs aren't as high. Hedge funds' likelihood of smaller drawdowns means less anguish in holding on to underperforming investments just in order to regain our high-water mark. The flip side is that, precisely because most hedge fund strategies don't keep pace with the market during rallies, we experience feelings of regret. The disappointment that investors in alternative strategies sometimes feel stems from a profound sense of missed opportunity.

Shifting Tides

One of the main objectives of *The Investor's Paradox* is to help clarify the industry-wide consternation over hedge funds. For some observers, it's ultimately a beauty pageant—a comparison of the raw performance numbers. That's necessary, but hardly sufficient. I contend that the ferocity of the ongoing debate is actually indicative of a much deeper undercurrent: that hedge funds broadly defined constitute a pronounced assault on the dominant investment management paradigm. In Thomas Kuhn's rendition of scientific progress, a paradigm is an all-encompassing worldview that allows us to make sense of the world.[23] In the physical sciences an established paradigm relies on specific theories or causal explanations that prove robust in light of the data we observe. More generally, our worldviews—perspectives on how things work, if not precisely calibrated causal mechanisms—filter incoming data points, categorizing and storing them to build a rich mosaic over time. Worldviews are organic; new information can challenge and ultimately change our filters, especially when that information does not fit easily into our established mosaic.

"Normal" science occurs when prevailing theories provide robust explanatory power. Things get interesting when anomalies arise, when what we see doesn't jibe with how we think the world works or should work. When these anomalies persist, full-blown crises can emerge. As a result, people experiment with different worldviews.

One of Kuhn's most important contributions was illustrating that this experimentation and competition were not a tidy academic exercise, but deeply political. It's not only ideas on the line, but livelihoods. The conflict between the orthodox and the heterodox is not exclusively a matter of intellectual accuracy, but also a social process that filters divergent viewpoints, each with vested interests and consequences for individual and group prosperity. For Kuhn, a fully realized paradigm shift is a "scientific revolution." The shift from Ptolemaic to Copernican astronomy (the earth revolves around the sun, not the other way around!) is among the most famous of these revolutions. A true paradigm shift is more than the challenge to the existing paradigm; it is replacing it with a different paradigm.

Through this lens, the investment management industry is in a crisis mode, with no resolution in sight. The "relative return" paradigm that so long dominated the industry has been challenged as a result of certain market events. The reason is clear: When markets consistently appreciate, we want to be long the market; as investors profit, outcomes are judged on a relative basis. When markets are choppy or trend downwards, our first goal is capital preservation, while our second goal is to make money. In other words, we want a linear payoff profile in the first context and we want a nonlinear, asymmetrical payoff in the latter. Who doesn't want full upside capture in a bull market and full downside protection in a bear market? Alas, neither paradigm can make such a promise, because there is, inescapably, a relationship between risk and return.

The past decade was filled with anomalies that could be interpreted as early signs of a potential paradigm shift: high-priced vehicles dramatically outperformed; funds that were bought for "long run" returns returned close to nothing over a decade's span; funds run by the most prominent money managers in the world were inextricably constrained to run structurally bullish, even when they knew their target markets were overvalued; the category of funds that were considered "risky" managed risk much better during market downturns.

Some of the existing beliefs about the upstart paradigm are demonstrably untrue, yet they persist. Alternatives are "riskier" than traditional investments because they feature some combination of derivatives, leverage, shorting, etc. Understandably, some investment failures like LTCM support that impression. But in fact, because most hedge fund managers use hedging techniques, many of them will underperform in up markets and outperform in down markets. This speaks to a lower risk profile, not higher. Meanwhile, there is the belief that because hedge funds are "absolute return" investments, they shouldn't lose money. The most suspect claim in Simon Lack's controversial *The Hedge Fund Mirage* is that hedge fund managers "broke their promise" to investors in 2008 by losing money.[24] Who exactly made this promise? And why would it ever be believed? This notion that investors in hedge funds should always expect positive returns, like they would with a certificate of deposit, is ludicrous. Taking market risk can and will produce losses. In brief, you can believe hedge funds are risky. You can believe hedge funds are safe. You can't legitimately believe both.

The dominant paradigm in investment management is up for grabs. The style box paradigm took decades to dominate product development, asset allocation models, consultant advice, and most important, investor worldview. True, we now find that most major institutional investors make allocations to something called "alternative" investments. Yet they remain a relatively limited percentage of those allocations. Paradigm shifts can take generations to sort themselves out. We've got many years to go with ours.

THE LOST DECADE

Alternative strategies, broadly defined, delivered solid performance during the turn of the century's bear market. In fact, those were glory years for these strategies, launching a variety of challenges to the "normal" methods of fund management, manager selection, and portfolio construction. As the data in figure 3.4 suggest, there were three notable episodes during this phase of the choice regime: the outperformance of 2000 to 2002; the comparable performance from 2003 to 2007; and the crisis of 2008 and its aftermath. We will break apart each of these episodes and explain what

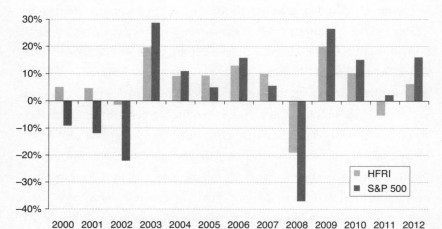

Figure 3.4   U.S. Stock Market vs. Diversified Hedge Fund Index, 2000–2012
Source: Hedge Fund Research

happened and why. In short, these stages were characterized by differentiation, then binge, and finally crash.

Differentiation: 2000–2002

Global stock markets hit a hard landing in the aftermath of the tech stock bubble explosion. From peak to trough in this period, the S&P 500 Index, the MSCI EAFE Index, and the NASDAQ Composite dropped 50.5 percent, 49.0 percent, and 78.4 percent, respectively. Very few traditional funds escaped this carnage. To be sure, the tech-focused shops were slaughtered. Aggressive growth funds offered by the likes of Janus, AIM, and Invesco lost a good percentage of their investors' capital very quickly, thanks to bad investments like WorldCom, Enron, Global Crossing, and JDS Uniphase.

But respected industry bellwethers also performed terribly. Take the Vanguard 500 Index Fund, which dropped 49.1 percent from peak to trough between March 2000 and October 2002. Sold as a low-cost means of gaining "diversified" exposure to US equities, the fund was anything but diversified when the market bottom fell out: at the end of 1999, 28.6 percent of its portfolio was in technology stocks. Wittingly or not, investors in the Vanguard 500 Fund (and other comparable passive indexes) took a speculative bet on overvalued Internet stocks, the kind that Jack Bogle had long railed against. Other major funds tanked as well. Fidelity Magellan, Legg Mason Value Trust, and Growth Fund of America shrank 49.3 percent, 46.8 percent, and 47.6 percent, respectively. Performance revealed many top stock pickers to be as much gamblers as analysts—they bet big and won big until they lost big.

Losses within equity markets during this bear market were not evenly distributed, however, opening an opportunity for funds with more flexible mandates to pounce. While large- and mid-cap growth stocks in technology, media, and telecommunications (TMT) grew overvalued during the TMT bubble of the late 1990s, smaller "old economy" stocks were mostly ignored. This dual dislocation of both capitalization (large versus small) and valuation (growth versus value) factors presented a large investment opportunity.

Figure 3.5 presents data from Morningstar Style Boxes on how the average fund performed during the peak and crash of the TMT bubble.

	1999				2000				2001				2002		
	V	C	G		V	C	G		V	C	G		V	C	G
L	0.6	17.8	42.6	L	5.7	4.2	−33.5	L	−3.4	−14.4	−29.1	L	−15.5	−23.8	−33.2
M	−6.8	1.9	52.5	M	24.6	14.8	−11.1	M	5.1	6.1	−21.6	M	−10.0	−12.4	−32.5
S	−5.2	16.7	46.0	S	18.7	23.2	−12.1	S	18.6	14.6	−12.9	S	−8.2	−14.2	−36.9

Figure 3.5   Mutual Fund Returns (%) by Morningstar Style Box
Source: Morningstar

The value and small-cap factors that were overshadowed in the late 1990s dramatically outperformed in the following years. In 1999, the difference between growth and value funds was remarkable: large-cap growth funds soared 42.6 percent while small-cap value funds actually dropped 5.2 percent. When the TMT bubble burst, however, the reversal in performance was equally remarkable. In 2000 and 2001, small-cap value funds notched 18 percent gains in both years, while large-cap growth funds lost 33 percent and 29 percent, respectively. Figure 3.6 calculates the difference in style returns during the 2000–2002 bear market. While the large-growth/small-value divide was the most extreme, the data reveal a major dislocation among various segments of the US equity market.

This dislocation, while rarely remarked upon in the debate over hedge funds, was the opening moment when alternative strategies pushed into the mainstream. It was also the dawn of the crisis stage of our paradigm shift. Several alternative strategies excelled through this episode, especially hedged equity funds that took advantage of this style dislocation. In effect,

	LG	LC	LV	MG	MC	MV	SG	SC	SV
LG	0								
LC	36.5%	0							
LV	55.2%	18.7%	0						
MG	15.5%	−21.0%	−39.7%	0					
MC	75.1%	38.6%	19.9%	59.6%	0				
MV	86.3%	49.8%	31.1%	70.8%	11.2%	0			
SG	16.8%	−19.7%	−38.4%	1.3%	−58.3%	−69.5%	0		
SC	89.7%	53.2%	34.5%	74.2%	14.6%	72.9%	72.9%	0	
SV	97.6%	61.1%	42.4%	82.1%	22.5%	7.9%	80.8%	7.9%	0

Figure 3.6   A Massive Difference in Style Returns, 2000–2002
Source: Morningstar

this was the revenge period for long/short stock pickers who suffered both poor performance and derision during the late 1990s. Largely vindicating their mentor's approach, Tiger Cubs such as Lee Ainslie of Maverick Capital and Steve Mandel of Lone Pine posted strong results by pressing their shorts on overvalued, poorly managed growth companies and maintaining their long positions in reasonably valued companies that the market had overlooked. Quite the opposite of so-called black-box investing, this was as sound and fundamental as investing could get.

Many hedge fund strategies delivered good performance just when investors needed it most: a period of volatility and market decline. That was true with equity-oriented strategies: long/short equity strategies, which take on more market risk, and market neutral equity funds, which don't. It was also true of more esoteric strategies that relied on arbitrage techniques, taking advantage of wide merger spreads, dislocated convertible bond pricing, and so forth (e.g., HBK, Och-Ziff, Gruss, Paulson, Deephaven, Stark, Carlson). And because of strong momentum trends in global markets across several asset classes, other strategies like global macro and managed futures worked well. In brief, this bear market was a hedge fund manager's paradise. Almost everything worked (figure 3.7).

Ultimately, most hedge fund strategies appealed because they proved more resilient during tough times. It wasn't just outperformance but outperformance and positive gains during down markets that mattered. This is the behavioral explanation for the increased interest and asset inflows. By contrast, if we consider a more widely accepted hypothesis—namely, that investors follow strong performance and alpha—we would likely have seen large inflows to hedge funds in earlier years. Even hedge fund skeptics grant that the 1980s and 1990s were a very fertile time for alternative strategies.

	Long/Short Equity	Market Neutral Equity	Distressed	Convertible Arbitrage	CTA/ Managed Futures	Macro	Merger/Risk Arbitrage	Multi-Strategy
2000	11.92%	11.58%	6.78%	13.84%	16.39%	9.25%	17.26%	14.44%
2001	6.60%	5.98%	13.09%	13.03%	6.45%	9.04%	2.82%	9.33%
2002	−1.30%	6.33%	5.93%	9.95%	17.52%	7.08%	0.53%	5.37%

Figure 3.7   *Hedge Fund Strategy Returns during the 2000–2002 Bear Market*
Source: eVestment

Their performance was quite strong, especially on a risk-adjusted basis. Yet most eligible investors, especially institutions, didn't care much until the 2000–2002 episode.

Thus, relatively few investors actually benefited from this success. Underperformance and industry instability due to the LTCM debacle meant modest industry-wide AUM leading into 2000. Asset growth did not start accelerating until toward the end of the bear market. Figure 3.8 shows the growth in AUM over time: with many trillions invested in long-only vehicles worldwide, hedge funds didn't even top the $500 billion mark until 2001. This was a tiny industry until the TMT bubble popped.

The bear market spurred the first genuine broad-based institutional interest in hedge fund strategies. When pensions, endowments, and insurance companies began to nominally experiment with an alternative *structure* of risk taking, what they were really doing was exploring an alternative *philosophy* of risk taking.

Paradigm shifts do not occur based solely on intellectual merit. Institutional change is always driven by idiosyncratic events and people. This profound, though largely unnoticed, shift in the investment choice regime owed no small credit to the efforts and writings of David Swensen. The midwestern-raised Swensen earned his PhD in economics at Yale and, after several years on Wall Street, returned to New Haven to helm Yale's endowment, which totaled just $1 billion when he joined in the mid-1980s.

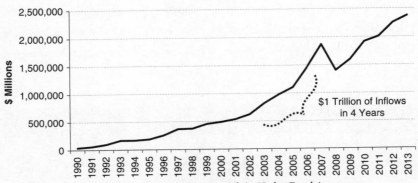

Figure 3.8   Demand Side: Growth in Hedge Fund Assets under Management ($ Trillion), 1990–2013
Source: Hedge Fund Research

As captured in his now-landmark book *Pioneering Portfolio Management*, Swensen and his team at Yale embraced, but then rearticulated, the most foundational concept in portfolio management: diversification.[25] Swensen's tenure mapped nearly perfectly to the onset and trajectory of the Great Moderation. In fact, as Swensen penned the book's foreword in the fall of 1999, the TMT bubble was peaking. In that historical context, Swensen's innovation was not so much the sober discipline of diversification itself, but the means by which he achieved it. In particular, Swensen became a strong advocate of alternative investments, both liquid (hedge funds) and illiquid (private equity and real assets), which would provide endowments and other long-term investors with the tools to find uncorrelated investments, and thus better overall portfolio results.

The Yale model, rebranded more generally as the Endowment Model, generated peer-beating results for Swensen as well as for other institutions that adopted it. And as many institutions and investment consultants in the early 2000s scrambled to deal with the aftermath of the fake diversification embodied in most individual mutual funds, as well as the style box mentality more generally, the Yale endowment and others like it skated through the bear market barely nicked.

With Swensen as the voice of the endowment approach, others quickly moved to mimic it, which helped to drive the genesis of the modern hedge fund industry. On the supply side of the equation, this was clearly reflected in the growth of the number of direct offerings. As shown in Figure 3.9, from the end of the 2002 bear market to the pre-2008 crisis peak, the number of offerings nearly doubled. And because this was a new and complicated area for nearly all institutional investors (with limited exceptions like Yale), intermediaries who specialized in researching and packaging bundles of hedge funds into single portfolios also exploded in number and size during this period. This was the heyday of funds of hedge funds. In the years following the TMT crash, a number of prominent funds of funds were raising more than $100 million in assets *per month*—more than $1 billion per year. Recall that in the early 1990s, the entire hedge fund industry had fewer than $50 billion in *total* assets.

At least for institutional investors and wealthy individuals, who had no legal restrictions on purchasing hedge funds, both the breadth and

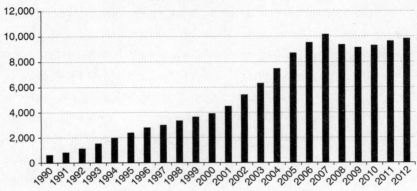

Figure 3.9   Supply Side: Total Number of Hedge Funds, 1990–2012
Source: Hedge Fund Research

complexity of their choice set increased significantly. The investment choice regime was changing rapidly.

The Binge: 2003–2007

The middle of the previous decade was the golden age of hedge funds, a short period of such intense wealth accumulation that it will long be considered a distinct moment in global financial history. With roughly a trillion dollars in new assets raised during this brief span, there was a veritable orgy of buyers and sellers, often coalescing at lavish private investment conferences held in exotic locations. Increasingly, union pensioners, college endowments, and charitable foundations were the beneficiaries of hedge fund prowess, but the front lines of the hedge fund scramble were anything but pure.

This period was a land grab for traders seeking to take advantage of industry tailwinds. The hedge fund "start-up" was all the rage. In 2004 alone, approximately 1,400 new hedge funds launched.[26] Over these few years between 2003 and 2007, the count was in the several thousands, some of which launched with considerable fanfare, such as William Von Mueffling's Cantillon, Jon Wood's SRM, and Jack Meyer's Convexity. Bank proprietary trading operations—known as "prop desks"—were an important source of new talent.

Traders from Goldman Sachs's legendary prop desks garnered extraordinary attention. The same arbitrage and equity desks that had been home to Robert Rubin (secretary of the treasury), Tom Steyer (Farallon Capital), Dan Och (Och-Ziff), Richard Perry (Perry Capital), and Edward Lampert (ESL Investments) in previous decades birthed the multibillion-dollar launches of Eric Mindich's Eton Park and Dinakar Singh's TPG-Axon, as well as other prominent start-ups such as Gandhara, Montrica, and Broad Peak. The other major tribe producing high volumes of new talent during this stretch was the Tiger complex. Though generally less sensational launches than Goldman's, Tiger Cubs such as Hoplite, Impala, JAT, Intrepid, and Tiger Global attracted serious investor attention. Overall, the size of the choice set exploded.

Alongside this flurry of new activity, the hedge fund industry went through its first major wave of institutionalization. As hedge funds increased in size and looked to attract pension fund, insurance company, and sovereign wealth capital, they grew more professional, sophisticated, and to some extent bureaucratized. And much larger: By the start of 2007, there were thirty-three firms managing in excess of $10 billion, a far cry from just a few years prior.[27] These and many other sizable firms grew to accept that more mature business operations would be necessary if they wanted to scale further.

Some of the largest "multi-strategy" complexes such as Highbridge, DE Shaw, and BlueCrest offered multiple products. Far from the old days of "two guys and a Bloomberg," all of the big alternative funds developed sophisticated back-office operations in terms of trading, pricing, accounting, and human resources. These internal developments led to a rapidly expanding ecosystem of brokers, legal advisors, fund administrators, accounting firms, and technology advisors. Some hedge funds found new channels for significant capital infusions, including the public markets. Blue-chip outfits Fortress Investment Group, the Blackstone Group, and Och-Ziff Capital Management made initial public offerings, while others were acquired, most notably Highbridge, by JPMorgan.

At the epicenter of this activity were the banks. As both facilitator and beneficiary of alternative industry growth, the largest global investment banks clamored for a piece of the action. Goldman Sachs, Morgan Stanley, UBS, Credit Suisse, JPMorgan, Merrill Lynch, and Deutsche Bank all aggressively built out their "prime brokerage" units during this period. They were devoted to accelerating the growth of, and then profiting from, their

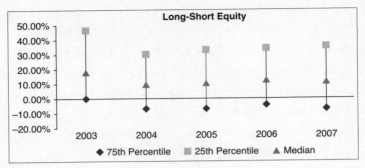

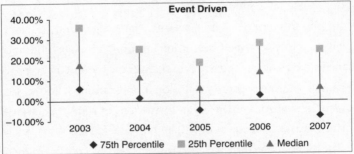

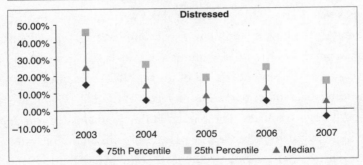

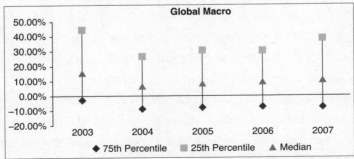

Figure 3.10   Performance Dispersion within Alternative Strategies
Source: eVestment

hedge fund clients primarily by providing leverage as well as stock loan inventory to facilitate shorting. An increasing percentage of the banks' overall revenues began to flow from prime brokerage activities.

In aggregate, the performance of most hedge fund strategies was not noteworthy during this stretch. As earlier data showed, the average hedge fund underperformed in the period between 2003 and 2007. The data in figure 3.10 bring this into sharper detail. Across four prominent alternative strategies, we can see that median performance was solid but not outstanding. In long/short equity, for example, the average fund delivered low double-digit returns from 2004 through 2007. The category's top performers posted impressive gains, although we don't have much insight into what extra risks those managers took to achieve them (a topic we'll explore further in chapter 6). Meanwhile, bottom-quartile hedged equity managers lost money during a period when the stock market marched steadily higher. The same observation about the wide dispersion of returns holds true for other alternative strategies.

During this period of excitement and extraordinary wealth creation, what was happening over in mutual fund land? Nothing interesting. As markets rose, the industry saw healthy inflows and asset growth, as would be expected. The preponderance of assets continued to sit with long-only asset managers. When the hedge fund industry crossed the $2 trillion mark around 2007, the mutual fund industry oversaw at least an order of magnitude more in assets. But in terms of innovative product development, as well as attracting the best talent from business schools and finance departments, the incumbents were back on their heels.[28]

Outside of mutual funds, the long-only world did see one major development last decade: the explosion in size of the exchange-traded fund (ETF) marketplace. Counterposed to traditional, actively managed long-only funds, and aligned with the spirit of cheap indexing, the ETF is an investment vehicle that provides passive exposure to a predefined market segment. Far and away the most popular is the ETF for the S&P 500, whose ticker is SPY and which is typically referred to as a "Spider." In 2013, that ETF sold for a mere nine basis points.

As any good consumer product firms would do in light of a new, profitable market segment, the money business vigorously attacked the

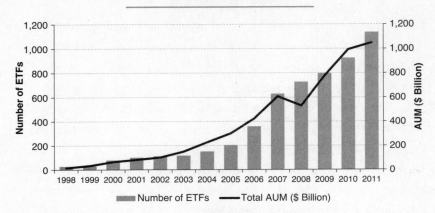

Figure 3.11   ETFs: Total Number and AUM
Source: Investment Company Institute

opportunity to provide cheap, prepackaged, and thinly sliced market exposure. As shown in figure 3.11, both the number of choices and investor
interest climbed sharply in the last decade. With the number of ETFs now
more than 1,100, the choice set has moved beyond basic exposures like
the S&P 500 and other standard market indexes. Investors can now slice
market segments thinner and thinner. For those seeking "diversified" investments in Chinese infrastructure stocks, Indian small-cap stocks, global
wind energy issues, copper mines, or oil equipment makers, there is an
available ETF one click away.[29]

As a result, the investment management industry is increasingly taking
on a "barbell" quality. While most assets still reside in traditional vehicles,
they are being challenged from two directions: thinly sliced beta selling
for a few basis points, and truly active, unconstrained managers selling for
several hundred basis points. Proponents of the former argue that markets
are highly efficient, that stocks pickers add no value, and that investors
should be empowered to pick and choose which low-cost market segments
they want in their portfolios. Proponents of the latter argue that markets
are largely inefficient, that smart money managers unconstrained by arbi-
trary benchmarks or style boxes can add significant value, and that investors should delegate their portfolios to these experts. Both mindsets have
been increasingly welcomed by the investor class. With more choice, more

complexity, and a proliferation of legitimate worldviews, the incumbent paradigm is under assault.

The Crash: 2007–2009

The market crash of 2008 was a cataclysmic event of great historical significance. If the intentions of the Founding Fathers in drafting the US Constitution, the meaning of Abraham Lincoln's presidency in the 1860s, and the causes of the Great Depression in the 1930s are still argued about today, it's fair to say that the book has not yet been closed on what transpired in 2008 and why, despite the fact that many tomes have already been written. Indeed, in the *Journal of Economic Literature,* Andrew Lo of MIT reviewed twenty-one books about the crisis.[30] He concluded that there is no single narrative that emerges from these books and that the interpretations of the crisis are both plentiful and contradictory.

There were numerous perturbations in the global financial system leading up to 2008. We can see with the benefit of hindsight that when the figurative "canary in the coal mine" is actually a flock of birds, not just one, it should not come as a surprise that the mine collapses. For example, in August 2007, the market encountered a sudden crash among fund managers who employed levered quantitative investment strategies. While the "quants" are a small part of the money management industry, including among hedge funds, their prominence exceeds their assets under management due to both the academic soapbox on which many of its portfolio managers stand and the fact that their market impact is increased by using significant amounts of leverage. During the week of August 6, 2007, some important quants endured large losses that, in their own terminology, were many standard deviations away from anything any of their statistical models ever predicted.

The quant meltdown took place in the context of a market that had already begun to destabilize. Generally, there was a peculiar bifurcation in the markets when rapid global growth spurred by emerging markets (EMs) created numerous long opportunities while credit markets grew increasingly unstable. In June 2007, two Bear Stearns funds that invested in mortgage-backed securities (MBS) incurred major losses and were forced to shut down. Another levered credit strategy, Sowood Capital, ran into difficulties, and its portfolio was absorbed by behemoth Citadel that year.

It was in 2007 that "the big short" first paid off. As has been well documented, the last hoorah of the global housing bubble had been driven by the supply of banks manufacturing inexplicably complicated synthetic forms of credit along with the demand from home buyers looking to buy something for effectively nothing. This created an endless menu of complex MBS that could be bought and sold by mutual fund and hedge fund managers alike.

Many hedge fund managers in 2007 were skeptical about what was transpiring in global credit markets—it was more a question of when than if trouble would come. Thus, there were numerous managers who made some sort of short subprime bet in their portfolios, though those bets tended to be small. It was typically one bet within a portfolio of many other bets.

The few who shorted subprime mortgages in size are now legends. John Paulson of Paulson Capital, Steve Eisman of FrontPoint, Michael Burry of Scion Capital, and a few others publicly staked their reputations with large short positions in various MBS tranches and/or indices. They earned fortunes as a result of being right: the subprime mortgage market collapsed over the course of 2007 and certain companies, such as Countrywide Financial, sunk into deeper and deeper problems.

Yet while the mortgage market was tanking, global equity markets were booming. In particular, these were the halcyon days for emerging markets. The fascination with the four major EMs—Brazil, Russia, India, and China—was captured by the "BRICs" acronym. These massively populated yet still relatively poor economies were growing rapidly. By 2007, the combined GDP growth of the four BRIC economies contributed more than 50 percent of all global growth. China was the locus of the excitement and its growth had implications not only for its own equities market (itself not particularly big or liquid), but also for other global segments, especially commodities such as oil and copper.

And then it all came tumbling down. The market tumult that ensued in 2008 was extraordinary. In response, traditional fund managers delivered—predictably—market performance. In the context of the S&P 500 Index declining 37.0 percent that year, the average long-only "large blend" fund declined 37.8 percent. In other words, the average large-cap mutual fund more or less mirrored the market's losses.

Strategy	Rank	Return	Strategy	Rank	Return
Long/Short Equity	25th %	16.41%	Market Neutral Equity	25th %	20.03%
	Median	−14.99%		Median	−0.11%
	75th %	−43.10%		75th %	−19.57%
Distressed	25th %	−2.49%	Multi-Strategy	25th %	16.24%
	Median	−20.69%		Median	−8.29%
	75th %	−39.57%		75th %	−32.44%
Convertible Arbitrage	25th %	−3.63%	Merger/Risk Arbitrage	25th %	9.22%
	Median	−19.50%		Median	−0.84%
	75th %	−40.31%		75th %	−12.45%
Macro	25th %	28.07%	CTA/Managed Futures	25th %	61.15%
	Median	0.62%		Median	11.45%
	75th %	−26.36%		75th %	−24.90%

Figure 3.12   *Alternative Strategy Performance in 2008*
Source: eVestment

The data in figure 3.12 survey how a variety of prominent alternative strategies performed. There are two key points. First, all of these strategies on average performed much better than the overall market. The most direct comparison is the long/short equity strategy compared to a long-only equity strategy. While the average large-cap mutual fund was down 37 percent, the average hedged equity fund was down only 15 percent. Other strategies, such as distressed debt or convertible arbitrage, performed worse but still beat the market. Some strategies that bet on moves in interest rates and sovereign debt, such as Global Macro, delivered positive returns.

However, the return pattern looks very different from what we saw in 2000–2002. In 2008, the entire market gapped down—there was a violent global liquidity squeeze that devalued nearly all risk assets. Some declined more than others, but the trend was sharply negative across the board. There were also certain regulatory interventions by some national authorities, specifically a ban on short selling certain securities, that hamstrung fund managers who were otherwise well positioned to profit from their bearish worldview. Contrast this to the opportunity in 2000–2002, when major dislocations were available for fundamental investors to trade. In other words, these two bear markets were very different in character. Thus, the *environment to be skillful* (an idea we will revisit in chapter 7) was markedly different.

The second observation is the wide divergence of returns within and across strategies. Look at long/short equity again. While the median fund lost 15 percent, funds in the category's top quartile gained at least 16.4 percent while those in the bottom quartile lost at least 43 percent. Even excluding outliers, there was an approximately 6,000 basis point performance gap between the twenty-fifth and seventy-fifth percentiles, which is massive. Meanwhile, these hedge fund strategies performed very differently from each other. Investors in global macro funds were able to eke out gains in calamitous market conditions, while distressed-debt investors lost significant capital. These data further substantiate that references to something broadly called "hedge funds" obscures more than it illuminates.

As with any data, there is no objective analysis of these numbers. For some, alternative investments are understood as "absolute return" vehicles that should not lose money. From that vantage point, any losses are condemnable. In my view, that's unfair. The reality is that many alternative investors took steps to protect capital during this bear market, whether it was being short equity, short credit, or long volatility. And some actually did a fine job, which the range of outcomes in Figure 3.12 clearly demonstrates.

The more important point is the methodological one, which sets up chapter 4 in a few pages. The reason for unsatisfactory outcomes in investing is that outcomes do not meet expectations. If your expectation is that a fund manager should never lose you money, then it's fair to be disappointed when they do. But is it fair to hold that expectation in the first place? The tough thing about alternative managers is that the process of setting expectations of what they will do and how they will perform is much harder than it is for traditional managers.

THE NEW NORMAL

The crisis of 2008 and its aftermath marked the end of the Great Moderation. The factors that first coalesced in the early 1980s had fully run their course, with the explosion of the housing and leverage bubbles marking the onset of more uncertain times—what asset management giant PIMCO has now famously called the "New Normal."

In turn, the modern investment choice regime has entered its third phase, one that is just beginning. I make two arguments in this final section. The first is that we will not see lengthy, multiyear rallies in the prices of risk assets—the kinds that were common during the Great Moderation—for the indefinite future. Fundamentals don't support that outcome. The second argument is that, as a result of the first claim, manager selection will matter more than ever going forward—more so than during the pre-modern choice regime of the 1950s to 1970s, and more so than during the Great Moderation.

Let's tackle both arguments in turn.

The Great Contraction

The conditions for a sustained bull market in risk assets are absent because we have entered a period of broad-based financial deleveraging. These periods, of which there have been many over the centuries, have almost categorically proved to be difficult periods in terms of economic growth and, in turn, consistent financial market performance.[31] Recall the virtuous cycle of the early 1980s with declining interest rates, declining inflation, accommodative policy innovations, and a sustained rally in risk assets. Whether it was changes in the microstructure of developed economies (e.g., inventory management), geopolitical quiescence, new thinking about monetary policy, or just plain luck, the only point that matters to us is that these factors' collective impact on the dampening of economic volatility have run their course.

The impact of that dampening wasn't all positive, however. The darkest undercurrent of the Great Moderation was the massive accumulation of debt. As interest rates over the era gradually declined from double-digit to low single-digit rates, consumers, corporations, banks, and governments amassed large debt burdens. There is a long history of societies that have taken on massive debt loads that drove financial crises and ultimately the imperative to delever. In their magisterial 2009 study *This Time Is Different*, Carmen Reinhart and Kenneth Rogoff systematically collected data on more than 200 financial crises over the past millennium. The events of 2008 may have felt distinctly calamitous. But the authors ominously proclaim: "We have been here before." Where is that exactly? Reinhart and Rogoff observe:

> If there is one common theme to the vast range of [financial] crises . . . it is
> that excessive debt accumulation, whether it be by the government, banks,

corporations, or consumers, often poses greater systemic risks than it seems during a boom. . . . Private sector borrowing binges can inflate housing and stock prices far beyond their long-run sustainable levels, and make banks seem more profitable and stable than they really are. . . . Debt-filled booms all too often provide false affirmation of a government's policies, a financial institution's ability to make outsized profits, or a country's standard of living. Most of these booms end badly.[32]

Thus, our deleveraging cycle will undercut our growth prospects in coming years. There is no fine-grained algorithm to predict how long it takes for a deleveraging cycle to run its course, nor its precise impact on growth. However, credible analysts suggest that it can take upwards of two decades. The unwinding of excessive debt burdens can lead to extended periods of low interest rates such as we're experiencing now. Yet the availability of cheap financing does not necessarily translate into growth prospects by way of balance sheet expansion. For instance, right now, despite low rates globally, large corporations continue to hold record levels of cash, meaning that the demand for free money is less than one might expect.

There are significant negative growth consequences to a debt burden and its unwinding. Deleveraging has a variety of other pernicious economic and social consequences as well. We can expect higher unemployment that feels more structural than cyclical, and an aggravation of real economic inequality, which could further decelerate growth; the transfer of private risk into sovereign risk, which, among other outcomes, portends the sharp rise of government direction in economic affairs, with potentially serious consequences for incentives and efficiency; depressed international trade, higher geopolitical tensions, and a continued assault on the "free markets" orthodoxy from the corners of the world that don't espouse it; and the looming specter of stagflation—muted growth alongside necessarily higher future inflation driven by the massive expansion of the monetary base.[33]

Nor is it just deleveraging that portends lower growth prospects. While many economists believe that growth will return to its natural long-term equilibrium rate, prominent growth theorist Robert Gordon suggests, in a controversial counterargument, that economic development is not a smooth linear process but instead lurches forward episodically based on historically specific moments of innovation.[34] Growth is not a given: "There was virtually no growth before 1750, and thus there is no guarantee that growth will continue indefinitely. . . . The rapid progress made over the past 250 years could well turn out to be a unique episode in human history."[35]

Gordon suggests that the first and second industrial revolutions in the United States (steam and railroads in the first; electricity, the internal combustion engine, running water, indoor toilets, communications, entertainment, chemicals, petroleum in the second) drove periods of rapid growth that have run their course. The second industrial revolution was more robust, as it featured many positive inventions (airplanes, air conditioning, interstate highways) and other occurrences (women entering the work force, urbanization, transportation speed). The third industrial revolution (computers, the Internet, mobile phones) has had much less of an impact in terms of real per capita GDP growth. But even if it had had a greater impact, there are now a series of relatively unprecedented historically specific challenges with which we need to contend, namely, demography, education, inequality, globalization, energy constraints, environment challenges, and the post-crash overhang of consumer and government debt.

What, then, are the implications for financial markets? After spilling much ink in chapter 2 on the futility of predictions, it would be foolish for me to offer my own here. But I do want to make the case that the roughly twenty-year run in stocks and thirty-year run in bonds were driven by a mix of historically specific variables that are no longer present. Absent those forces, it is highly unlikely that we will enjoy the market tailwind of the previous generation. Thus, we can be very confident about what is *unlikely* to happen: a steady multi-decade rise in the price of risk assets. This is a modest claim.

The case with fixed income instruments is relatively easy to make. Broadly speaking, the price of high-quality bonds is inversely related to interest rates. As rates go up, the price of bonds goes down. This is mathematically inescapable. Currently, interest rates are close to zero, meaning that they can go in only one direction: up. Thus, bonds will continue to generate very low yields until, at some point in the coming decade, rates rise and the total return on bonds declines.

The case with equities is trickier. There are arguments pro and con for why equities will do well in coming years, very much driven by the manners in which interest rates and inflation rates proceed. Conventional wisdom would state that rapidly rising interest rates and inflation should be bad for stocks, but we'll just have to see. Instead, let's look at only one very credible historical statistic that's probably about as good as it gets. One of the more reasonable notions in equity research is that when stocks are at extremely high valuation, they are likely to do worse in coming years. When stocks are very cheap, they are more likely to do well. Economist Robert Shiller captured this idea in rolling ten-year windows on price-to-earnings (P/E) ratios. This measure has come to be known as "Shiller's P/E" (figure 3.13).

The relationships in the data are pretty clear. At the start of any rolling ten-year window, the market will have a valuation as measured by a P/E ratio. These P/Es can be broken out into deciles. At points where the market would be considered extremely cheap, such as P/Es between 5 and 9, the average annualized forward real return of the market has been 10.3 percent. During those windows, the best real return ever experienced was 17.5 percent, while the worst was 4.8 percent. On the other hand, when P/Es

Starting P/E		Avg. Real 10 Yr. Return	Worst Real 10 Yr. Return	Best Real 10 Yr. Return	Standard Deviation
Low	High				
5.2	9.6	10.3%	4.8%	17.5%	2.5%
9.6	10.8	10.4%	3.8%	17.0%	3.5%
10.8	11.9	10.4%	2.8%	15.1%	3.3%
11.9	13.8	9.1%	1.2%	14.3%	3.8%
13.8	15.7	8.0%	−0.9%	15.1%	4.6%
15.7	17.3	5.6%	−2.3%	15.1%	5.0%
17.3	18.9	5.3%	−3.9%	13.8%	5.1%
18.9	21.1	3.9%	−3.2%	9.9%	3.9%
21.1	25.1	0.9%	−4.4%	8.3%	3.8%
25.1	46.1	0.5%	−6.1%	6.3%	3.6%

Figure 3.13   Shiller's P/E
Source: Cliff Asness (2012), "An Old Friend: The Stock Market's Shiller P/E," AQR
Capital Management, *November, www.aqr.com; cf. www.multpl.com/shiller-pe*

are greater than 25, markets have rarely done well: the average return was just above zero; the best return ever at that valuation level was 6.3 percent.

By this form of measurement the market was valued at a P/E of 21.4 toward the end of 2012. At that level, the average return on the market has been about 1 percent. While anything is possible, the tendencies are pretty clear. Rich markets generate modest returns. There are anomalies, but you've got to be lucky to achieve results outside the historical bounds. Even if the market began to trade at a significant discount to the end-of-2012 multiple, the chance of achieving double-digit annualized returns from equities would be historically unprecedented.

These data form a reasonable basis for long-term expectations. In short, bonds are priced very rich and stocks aren't cheap. It's not going to be an easy road forward, with the likelihood of mid-single-digit returns being the norm. James Montier has recently referred to this as "the purgatory of low returns." He strains to imagine a scenario wherein the returns of a standard stock-and-bond portfolio will exceed low-to-mid single digits in coming years.[36] Likewise, Bill Gross wrote in late 2011, "The investor class [will be] continually disenchanted with returns that fail to match expectations. If you can get long-term returns of 5% from either stocks or bonds, you should consider yourself or your portfolio manager in the upper echelon of competitors."[37]

Picking Winners in the New Normal

Investment choice matters more when the market lacks a brisk tailwind. In the pre-modern era, between the mid-1960s and the early 1980s, the US equity market was flat, albeit with large up-and-down swings along the way. During that time there were relatively few choosers and few choices. Don't forget that index funds weren't even invented until the 1970s, so the notion of beating something called "the market" is a recent historical phenomenon.

In retrospect, manager selection was relatively easy during the 1980s and 1990s. That is less a comment on the stock and bond pickers themselves, who enjoyed a steady tailwind, albeit with the occasional moment of intense volatility. Rather, it reflects the fact that a diversified menu of asset managers, in aggregate, delivered attractive returns in those years. It's not an accident that the classic "60/40" portfolio allocation model (60 percent equities, 40 percent bonds) dominated during this period. With both types of risk assets generating positive returns the investor's main task was to dial the level of equity and bond risks to an appropriate level. While skill could vary, most standard outcomes were reasonably attractive. The current choice regime, by contrast, maps a massive and complicated choice set onto befuddling market conditions. There are many ways to think about building portfolios, and the "60/40" method is challenged and increasingly supplanted by other frameworks.[38]

In this great contraction, manager selection arguably matters more. The barbelling of choices between cheap ETFs and expensive alternatives reflects two different approaches to choosing the right investments. First is the do-it-yourself mindset. The challenge here actually is choosing the right asset classes. Should I be in stocks or bonds? How much exposure to commodities is prudent? Will emerging markets continue to grow rapidly, and should I have an allocation to those markets? These are all reasonable questions, none of which has anything to do with choosing the right fund manager. In fact, for those who see the primacy of asset allocation over security selection in driving investment performance, the critical task is making sure you're in the right race, rather than riding the right horse. What's novel about the current investment choice regime—and the advent of ETFs in particular—is that you have cheap access to any race you'd like. Another way of putting it is that do-it-yourself investors want to work exclusively with hedgehogs, who deliver one big thing.

Other investors or advisors won't or can't pick the right race, but they will try to pick the right horse. They effectively take an outsourcing approach to their investment portfolio. With a prominent subset of hedge funds, the idea is to achieve a targeted risk-adjusted return by any means necessary, meaning that shifting among asset classes and investment styles is not only legitimate; it's sought after. These investors want to work with foxes, who know many different things and will adapt their strategy to an evolving set of opportunities and risks. The truth is that there are very few investors or advisors who operate exclusively in one camp or the other.

We have entered an era of "convergence." Investors, from individuals to the largest institutions, now have a choice ranging across the entire spectrum, from hedgehogs to foxes. What underlies this transition is, thankfully, a disconnection of the investment risks that we want to take from the legal structures through which we access those risks. Returning to an earlier, critical point, hedge funds are not an asset class—"hedge fund" is a colloquial term that refers to a very specific form of private partnership. What specific market risks the hedge fund takes are largely irrelevant to the structure of the vehicle in which those risks are delivered.

The increasing disconnection of risk from packaging is a hallmark of the modern investment choice regime. Everyday investors have growing access to a broadening spectrum of so-called liquid alternatives—hedge fund strategies available in liquid vehicles like mutual funds. There has been a steady, steep rise in the level of assets in this category. Between 2003 and 2012, there was a tenfold increase in assets to approximately $300 billion. The choice set of US mutual funds, ETFs, and vehicles structured for European investors numbers in the hundreds and is climbing.

While there are certain regulations that restrict (but do not eliminate) these liquid vehicles' exposure to leverage and derivatives, the available strategy menu increasingly mimics that which has been available to hedge fund buyers, including long/short equity, market neutral, short-only, long/short credit, and global macro (e.g., currency trading). On top of these direct offerings, a number of funds of funds have already offered, or plan to offer shortly, pools of underlying alternative manager allocations. For example, Fidelity recently teamed with Arden Asset Management to offer hedge funds to retail clients.[39] It appears that we are at the beginning of the next big thing in global asset management. Indeed, Citi estimates that by 2017, there will be roughly $900 billion invested in liquid alternatives, triple the current level.[40]

THOMAS KUHN ARGUES in *The Structure of Scientific Revolutions* that advances in thinking about the world do not happen smoothly, but rather stem from "a series of peaceful interludes punctuated by intellectually violent revolutions." And in those revolutions, "one conceptual world view is replaced by another."[41] In the investment choice regime, there remains one dominant paradigm that is under heavy assault by another. But the castle has not been breached. What we now have is a mess of tribal loyalties toward one way or another of doing things.

Investors confront the timeless difficulty of making effective decisions alongside the specific difficulties of their times. In chapter 2, we revealed the near impossibility of picking winners versus losers due to statistical, epistemological, and behavioral constraints. In this chapter, we explored the interplay of the evolution of the global economy and its consequences for the investment management landscape—the players, the products, and the buyers. Together they combine to form our challenge.

It is now time to turn the tables, to extract simplicity from the clutter. What follows in the balance of *The Investor's Paradox* is a guidebook for navigating the current investment choice regime.

PART II

SOLUTION

4

ADAPTATION

*Managing our expectations is perhaps the most difficult challenge of
choice, but one way to do so is to look to those who have shown how
constraints create their own beauty and freedom.*

—Sheena Iyengar[1]

THE HERO WITH A BILLION DOLLARS

Stories are the lifeblood of the human experience. We not only love stories,
we need them to add meaning to our existence. As Joseph Campbell suggests in his classic *The Hero with a Thousand Faces*, we rely on myths to
make sense of our ordeals and achievements, both little and big. That these
stories tend to have similar narrative structures across cultures, as Campbell wonderfully illustrates, only speaks further to how core storytelling is
to both the individual and the collective experience. Stories define us.

We use stories to make sense of the world because our brains are not
wired to think well statistically. We have multiple, often conflicting thought
processes: "slow" thinking that is analytically prodigious but often inactive
or even "lazy," as Daniel Kahneman describes it; and "fast" thinking that
is almost always humming away in the background, like the faint whir of
our desktop computers, eager to process new information but profoundly
vulnerable to a multitude of biases.[2]

Goodness knows the markets produce great stories. In *Devil Take the
Hindmost*, Edward Chancellor refreshes Charles Mackay's *Extraordinary
Popular Delusions and the Madness of Crowds*, guiding the reader through

some of the spectacular crises of recent centuries, including the Dutch tulip craze of the 1630s, the South Seas Bubble of 1720, and the stock market crash of 1929. Chancellor finished his book in 1998, just months too early to delve deeply into the dramatic demise of Long-Term Capital Management, a story wonderfully captured by Roger Lowenstein's *When Genius Failed*. Michael Lewis, the closest modern finance has to its own Charles Dickens, has treated us to many wonderful tales, including bookend works, *Liar's Poker* and *The Big Short,* which detail the mortgage-backed security market's fascinating genesis and its cacophonous explosion.[3]

In the world of money, it is people as much as events themselves that capture our fancy. There's no shortage of larger-than-life individuals— heroes and villains alike. Hero narratives are especially abundant driving the mystique of the hedge fund manager. In *The Greatest Trade Ever,* Gregory Zuckerman detailed the most lucrative investment of all time: John Paulson's massive short position in subprime mortgages in 2007, which personally earned him billions.[4] The *New York Times* review of the book said it "reads like a thriller." Scott Patterson's *The Quants* is an expertly constructed narrative about traders such as Cliff Asness of AQR and Boaz Weinstein of Saba Capital, who employ highly sophisticated techniques to beat others and earn inexhaustible fortunes.[5] Of course, villain narratives also abound—witness the number of recent books on Bernie Madoff.

Alas, these stories—even the well-written ones—are largely irrelevant for navigating the investment choice regime. Yet we continue to use them as touchstones for identifying "moneymakers." The mindset is: let me understand the characteristics of these successful traders and then I will either trade like that myself or go find others who do.

In the real world, choosing money managers just doesn't work this way. For those needing to separate signal from noise, there are two basic methodological problems with the popular approaches. One is the obvious case of sample bias. Seeking out the most successful in a particular industry and writing at length about their accomplishments does not take into account others who were similarly well pedigreed and resourced but didn't land in the winner's circle. What really separates the winners from the losers remains a mystery. In scientific terms, we are "selecting on the dependent variable," thus skewing our insights.

Second, we instinctually generalize from a small number of other situations (sometimes just one) to what we perceive to be broader tendencies. How we see the world tends to be episodic, not statistical, so we naturally gravitate toward compelling stories to make sense of it all. We then take the next leap to implicitly or explicitly identify patterns or rules based on them. Those perceived patterns, as pointed out in chapter 2, rarely exist in reality.

Claiming tendencies or rules based on sample universes in which the nature of the underlying constituents varies widely is a statistically shabby exercise. That's why some investment databases, especially for hedge funds, aren't helpful. Even in the few instances where the data's systematic biases are addressed, we still know very little about any single fund's important risk attributes. With standard long-only categories, such as large-value equity or intermediate high-grade bond, there is mostly homogeneity among the constituents' portfolio attributes and benchmark target, thus you can make "apples for apples" comparisons. On the contrary, in categories such as long/short equity, distressed debt, or global macro, we do not know how any individual constituent's portfolio is positioned (e.g., leverage level, exposure to multiple asset classes, use of derivatives, etc.), so meaningful comparison is often impossible.

RESEARCH IS RESEARCH:
THE IMPORTANCE OF METHOD OVER CONTENT

How then do we jump from stories to structured insight, from retellings to rigor? Across campus from the business and economics departments, in the slightly less lucrative field of epistemology, there are some pretty basic solutions at hand. Indeed, moving from unstructured data to structured insight is hardly a new issue for philosophers of science. In 1892, Karl Pearson put it bluntly: "The field of science is unlimited; its material is endless; every group of natural phenomena, every phase of social life, every stage of past or present development is material for science. The unity of all science consists alone in its method, not in its material."[6]

Consider two key points. First, as Pearson notes, experience presents "endless" detail. Whether our favorite topic is the Ottoman Empire, the

US Civil War, or money management, we can spend lifetimes learning. Yet like the fictional Harvard law student in *The Paper Chase,* who has a photographic memory but lacks the ability to synthesize his mental encyclopedia, prodigious detail is ultimately insufficient. It is learning without understanding, cataloging without analyzing.

Second, method supersedes content. That means that *how* to think is more important than *what* to think when it comes to solving puzzles. Sourcing and processing incomplete information is a higher-order affair than just collecting it. Method to what end? It is to explain, to understand something bigger than the immediate facts at hand. Unawareness of these rules of the road leads to bad storytelling. It is also one root of bad investing.

Our methodological goal is *inference.* How do we form reliable expectations when the future is inherently unknowable? This query dovetails with behavioral issues already touched on in chapter 2. We want to make good decisions that produce future satisfaction, but we are wired in a way that compels us to act in a manner that doesn't fit the traditional narrow definition of what is "rational." The bar is raised even higher when we try to anticipate how other people will behave or decide, which leaves us guessing at their biases.

Let's stick for a bit longer with dead philosophers. Thinking on how to form reliable inferences dates back to eighteenth-century Scotland, when David Hume—whose prodigious contributions have been overshadowed by those of his friend and countryman Adam Smith—penned the foundational modern treatment of the problem of induction. In his 1748 *Enquiry Concerning Human Understanding,* Hume explored how to understand the relationship between cause and effect. How do we reliably form expectations for what comes next? Hume raises the debate on the rules for inquiry that we're still vetting 350 years later.

His depressing philosophical conclusion was that neither deductive nor inductive reasoning provides theoretically reliable grounds for knowing what we think we know. The search for certainty is a bottomless pit. But Hume's pragmatic perspective, which has become a foundation of modern philosophy, was more uplifting in acknowledging that *practical skepticism is good enough most of the time.* We only draw conclusions from our experiences, which are necessarily limited and messy. Experience trumps logic in the effort to establish expectations for what comes next.

For us as investors—especially when hiring people, rather than buying securities ourselves—this is important. Like Hume's, our solution is ultimately pragmatic, relying on the only things we know we can observe: past behavior, habit, or what Hume calls "custom." He defines custom as "the great guide of human life. It is that principle alone which renders our experience useful to us, and makes us expect, for the future, a similar train of events with those which have appeared in the past."[7] In other words, it's reasonable to expect that what happens tomorrow will look more or less like what happened today. In the parlance of modern institutional economics, there is "path dependence," a notion Hume theorized three centuries ago: "All our experimental conclusions proceed upon the supposition that the future will be conformable to the past."[8] This is hardly an airtight assumption, but it's about as good a starting point as any in attempting to form reliable expectations for future outcomes.

As a practical matter, we start with a working hypothesis, a formalized expectation for certain outcomes given a set of preexisting conditions. It is basically a statement of expectations against which we judge as many observations of the relevant phenomenon as we can find. The working hypothesis tees up the research process. How to first form working hypotheses? Legendary physicist Richard Feynman famously sums it up: "We guess."[9] A hypothesis can be as simple as descriptive conjectures—Who will win the election? How old is the universe? What will my fund return? How many games will our new left-hander win?—or it can postulate relationships among numerous complex variables, answering questions ranging from why nations sometimes go to war or why some investment firms succeed while others do not to why hundreds of millions of stars appear to be gravitating toward one "cosmic hotspot" in the distant reaches of the universe.[10]

Once we have made our guess, we figure out if the evidence is on our side. We test our hypothesis with observable data, which will either support or contradict our supposition (or present some shade of gray). In either case, but especially when what we see doesn't square with what we expected, we collect more data in order to establish as robust a set of inferences as possible. What results over time is an iterative process in which we tweak our working hypothesis and data collection efforts to ultimately arrive at stable, reliable expectations. We engage in this exercise with one of two goals in mind: to understand how a *specific* person or group will act through time, or to understand how a certain *class* of people or groups will react under comparable circumstances.

From a neurocognitive view, our brains are always rapidly and subconsciously setting these expectations. On my next step the ground meets my foot, it gets dark at night, cars stop at red lights, and that cup of Starbucks coffee tastes exactly the same whether I'm on the north side of Chicago or in the south of France. The world makes almost complete sense to us at almost every moment. The power of Hume's "custom," when you stop to consider it, is great.

The line between the physical and emotional is quite blurry when it comes to the exercise of inference building. Expectations aren't just mind games; they are rooted in powerful biological forces. This sense of predictability and control is existentially satisfying. Take the simple example of how we drink and enjoy wine. A team of oenological researchers conducted 6,175 double-blind wine tastings (meaning neither the drinkers nor the servers knew the details of what was being served or drunk) to better understand how expectations of price impacted the perception of quality.[11] They arrived at their conclusions not only through surveys, but also through fMRI readings—scans that measure brain activity by tracking the levels of oxygen in the blood flow. What they found was that in a controlled experiment, the correlation of price to enjoyment was slightly *negative.* "On average, individuals who are unaware of the price do not derive more enjoyment from more expensive wine. In fact, they enjoy more expensive wines slightly less."

The critical twist occurs when consumers' expectations are manipulated. If we take wine from the same bottle and pour it into two distinct bottles with two fake price tags, one rich and the other cheap, customers will enjoy the exact same wine differently depending on whether they think they're drinking an expensive wine. Consumers prefer more expensive wines when they are *told ahead of time* what each bottle costs.[12] The physical enjoyment, as measured by the fMRI results, is higher when we believe we are drinking a fancier wine. Other studies corroborate this find-ing.[13] Our physical and mental faculties are inextricably connected.

PLAYING BY THE SAME RULES

Choosing investments is a form of research, no different from any other form of empirical inquiry. Dynamic inference building is as applicable to figuring out how fund managers work as it is to anything else. Manager due diligence, like any form of research, should prioritize method over content. Method should trump storytelling.

Good research is a dynamic process of hypothesis building, testing, and reformulation. It is flexible and adaptable. To the contrary, conven-tional fund research is fulfilling a predetermined checklist of attributes. I think it's fair to say that checklists dominate the field of manager re-search. In the traditional world, those like Morningstar and Jack Bogle direct us to review the "five P's": portfolio, people, process, performance, and price.[14] By whatever measure the researcher chooses, a "good" invest-ment is one that ticks the right boxes. Stable management team? Check. Competitive historical performance? Check. Well-articulated, sensible investment process? Check. Reasonably priced? Check. There is little written about hedge fund due diligence, but the mindset is similar—just with a much longer list.

There is nothing inherently wrong with checklists insofar as they for-malize a repeatable, coherent process.[15] It's good to identify the issues of most importance to the task at hand. Thus, a portfolio manager's pedigree, how many stocks are in the portfolio, and the level of fees are all relevant for our inquiry. But if that were all it took, none of this would be all that challenging. We could just download the list and send it off to the manager to fill in the form. There would be, at its logical conclusion, a tidy, robotic due diligence process.[16]

But this isn't the way manager due diligence actually takes place, or should. This is because we are dealing with people, not objects. The meth-odological goal is still inference, but forming reliable expectations in a dy-namic environment about biased, sentient beings is a unique challenge. People, even when they work within a fully specified set of rules and pro-cedures, are unpredictable.[17]

So, in short, we make it up as we go along. And in many instances, that's the key to success. Setting expectations about complex social phenomena is a painstaking task. We must deal with constant change and update our expectations intelligently. In other words, we must adapt. When we don't adapt, and when expectations are mismanaged, physical and emotional disappointment results. Investment research centers on a social, interactive process of inference building. That's especially true when we navigate the modern investment choice regime by hiring experts rather than analyzing securities ourselves.

The specific method for choosing investments is an expression of the general method of empirical inquiry. We form hypotheses, whether they are descriptive conjectures or causal relationships; collect evidence to either verify or disconfirm the hypotheses; and evaluate the gap between what we expected and what we observed. The size and nature of that gap will suggest how, if at all, we revise our expectations. The crux of the issue remains the method: forming and updating reliable inferences about future behavior.

The magnitude of the challenge in any phase of the investment choice regime is determined by how difficult it is to update our expectations in response to changing circumstances. And here's where the general method meshes inextricably with our historically unique circumstances: at this time of convergence between traditional and alternative paradigms of investment management, any increase in the flexibility of managers to navigate uncertain times, however tiny, puts a further premium on our ability as choosers to adapt our own expectations for how others will conduct themselves in different environments. Thus, it allows us to adapt.

ADAPTIVE INVESTING

Let's describe each step in the process of adaptive research, starting with expectations formation, moving to information gathering and analysis, and concluding with the thorny issue of updating.

Expectations

Inference building in the social sciences is messy, but at least we start with one advantage over the physicists. Richard Feynman and his sort must start with an educated guess about the particles and other subject matter with which they cannot directly engage. We have available and sentient subjects. Thus our starting point is not "We guess," but instead "We ask."

The first step in investment research is establishing expectations for how the manager will run his program—both his portfolio and his business. What are the rules of the road? We should strive to state our expectations as testable hypotheses. By "testable," we mean that there are observable, measurable data to collect; and by "hypotheses" we mean that we are looking for conditional outcomes. Under what conditions do we expect the manager to do certain things? For a global macro fund, for example, we want to know not only how much of its portfolio will be exposed to commodities but under what market circumstances it will vary its exposure within its stated limits, or perhaps go beyond those limits. For a long-only bond manager, what would cause him to increase the duration of the portfolio? And so on. Generally, we're asking under what circumstances a manager will make certain choices. Conditionality facilitates the process of adaptation.

The "first law of manager due diligence" is that the less constrained a manager's mandate, the more difficult it is to set expectations. The upward sloping line in figure 4.1 captures simply why investors find hedge funds more confusing than mutual funds, why multi-strategy funds tend to defy definition more than single-strategy funds, and why ETFs appear to be an easy alternative to actively managed funds. By degrees of freedom, I mean the number of active investment decisions a portfolio manager can legitimately make.

Variability in the degrees of freedom doesn't linearly map onto the labels of "traditional" versus "alternative." It's a spectrum. An equity market neutral hedge fund manager with limited discretion over its neutral positioning and a stable amount of leverage has few degrees of freedom, not unlike a benchmark-driven long-only fund. By contrast, some "go-anywhere" mutual funds can shift around exposures between stocks and bonds, shift in and out of emerging markets, vary leverage, and even short stocks.

At the far end of the spectrum are vehicles with breathtaking degrees of freedom. Multi-strategy hedge funds, which have attracted many

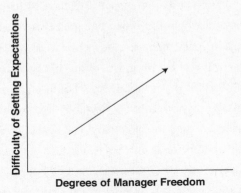

Figure 4.1   *The First Law of Manager Due Diligence*

billions of investor capital, can do with it more or less whatever its executives please. In its heyday, Milwaukee-based Stark Investments managed as much as $14 billion in equity capital (and more than that on a levered basis), focusing not only on its legacy expertise in convertible bonds and related skills in credit and equity research but also on areas as far afield as financing motion pictures and structuring private loans to Asian tycoons. Other firms, such as Brevan Howard or Bridgewater, manage massive sums invested across a very broad array of asset classes. Paulson has jumped from merger arbitrage to subprime mortgages to gold. This is not to suggest that in each of these cases, and in hundreds of others like them, there is not a sound investment philosophy and process underlying these decisions. That said, the fact that Stark is no longer in business, while Brevan Howard has thrived, demonstrates that some organizations are much better at adapting to change than others.

The less constrained an investment, the harder it is to set expectations. A hallmark of the absolute return paradigm is its freedom from rigid benchmark constraints. In reality, there is no such thing as a wholly unconstrained mandate. There are always rules that proscribe, some externally imposed by clients or regulators, others internally imagined and implemented. Investors will necessarily struggle with the balance between focus and opportunism among semi-constrained choices. For example, what does "style drift" mean for unconstrained funds that can more or less do what they want? By the same token, what does "opportunistic" mean for portfolio managers who have only a narrow list of securities from which to choose? As portfolio managers make decisions that don't square with our wants and needs, we are confronted with tough choices irreconcilable by algorithm or anecdote.

We have a Goldilocks problem on our hands. If we set expectations for something important—how a fund picks stocks, takes on leverage, works with counterparties, etc.—too narrowly, we will observe violations too frequently. Set expectations too broadly and we enable an "anything goes" attitude or an undisciplined process, leading us to under-observe violations of the manager's true program, whatever that might be. An unintended consequence of this "too cold" mindset is that it leads to performance chasing. Without reasonably firm expectations for what a manager is going to do, we end up focused on the very thing no one can control, which is performance.

Figure 4.2 captures the spectrum along which investors must now choose. In one direction, there are many choices an investor legitimately maintains, while in the other direction there are few. Here we can see that our choices range from tightly constrained investment opportunities—ones that are tied to either a specific style box or benchmark—to those that have complete freedom to approach any opportunity they like.

This is where chapter 2's ahistorical concepts and chapter 3's historical narrative dovetail. One of the key features of the modern investment choice regime is that the investor class has an abundance of choice across this entire spectrum, compared to an earlier era, when traditional and alternative channels were separate.

The graphic also sheds further light on the fox/hedgehog distinction. Fund managers who know "one big thing"—which, in the traditional space,

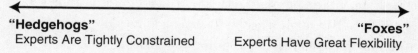

"Hedgehogs"
Experts Are Tightly Constrained

"Foxes"
Experts Have Great Flexibility

Figure 4.2: The Spectrum of Investment Flexibility

means that markets will go up over the "long run"—are probably, all else being equal, less likely to succeed in challenging markets. Managers with more flexibility who know "many little things" are more likely to get things right in uncertain times. Appreciating that the market may move downwards or sideways for long periods of time, or that their area of expertise may be out of favor compared to other opportunities, foxlike experts have a better chance of figuring out how to win. Adaptive manager research is useful in proportion to the discretion that we allow our experts (i.e., fund managers) to have. And thus the deeper layer of our investor's paradox: we would like to rely on foxes as our experts, yet their very natures make them difficult to pin down. Setting expectations for a fox is far more difficult than setting expectations for a hedgehog.

Outcomes

There's a funny scene in Rodney Dangerfield's *Back to School* when his character, Thornton Melon, a retired millionaire who returns to college, instructs one of his lackeys to expand an assigned report in order to get a better grade. "Where's the lab report on psychology? It's too light. It feels like a 'C.' Bulk it up and add a few multi-colored graphs." Melon believes what most naïve researchers do, which is that more information gives us a better chance to get the right answer. Or at least to give the impression that we know what we're talking about.

Those who engage in data mining—collecting as much information as possible—expect that the truth will reveal itself at some point. They believe that their gut intuition or mental models will guide them through the morass of data to the right answer. The "old-school" baseball scouts in Michael Lewis's *Moneyball* relied on various rules of thumb for distinguishing good prospects from bad: a young athlete "looked like" a major leaguer, for example. Likewise, in manager research, old-school talent scouts rely, wittingly or not, or various forms of pattern recognition to identify great managers, colloquially known as "moneymakers." Mature research, on the other hand, is theory driven. It starts with a set of priors that guide our explorations. Absent the hypothesis testing framework, we are on a rudderless voyage, a pointless campaign to know "more."

The sources and nature of information themselves are complex and open to interpretation. Information is not a pebble—hard, discrete, immutable. It is malleable in the eyes and hands of its collector. What information do we need to test our hypotheses? A common belief is that in research, the "real" data are numerical. But there's nothing magical about quantitative data. Hypotheses drive the type of information we need, which may be numerical, verbal, or both. Moreover, how do we source our data? They could come directly from our subject, from others, or through truly independent research. The independence and veracity of data vary considerably. Much of the information sourced in clinical settings comes directly through interaction with our subjects, meaning that the actual exercise of research can alter the outcome itself, what scientists call the Heisenberg Uncertainty Principle.

Our counterparties usually don't make the findings stage easy. This is true in any clinical scenario. Most therapists don't have open, honest, and self-aware clients; they face a matrix of reticence, dysfunction, stubbornness, and ignorance. When we are conducting manager research, our subjects sometimes cannot comply: the information we seek is legally confidential; they truly don't know the answer; or multiple subjects will deliver disparate answers that are hard to untangle. Other times, they *can* comply but won't. Experts for hire don't necessarily want to tell you how they arrive at the results you desire, whether to protect their trade secrets or simply to create the impression of mystery. Telling someone they can't have something is a sure way of making them want it.

With investments, transparency is critical. This is less of an issue than most make it out to be. There is much hand-wringing over hedge fund opacity (they are "secretive"!), but at this stage, it's largely a red herring. There was certainly a period when some funds would not tell you what they owned, how they made their investment decisions, or the details of their business model. Now nearly everyone is an open book, within reason, based in no small part on investor demands. All major US hedge funds are now registered with the Securities and Exchange Commission (SEC), so some important details such as the stocks they own are now easily available. The snapshot in figure 4.3 took a few minutes on the SEC website to

Hedge Funds					Mutual Funds		
Viking	**Lone Pine**	**Tiger Global**	**Maverick**	**Third Point**	**Contrafund**	**Growth Fund of America**	**Vanguard 500**
Time Warner	Priceline	Apple	Macy's	Yahoo	Apple	Amazon.com	Apple
News Corp.	Google	Liberty Media	Apple	AIG	Google	Gilead Sciences	Exxon Mobil
Danaher	Cognizant Technology Solutions	Yandex	Qualcomm	Delphi Automotive	Berkshire Hathaway	Google	General Electric
Capital One Financial	Dollar General	Mastercard	Express Scripts	Murphy Oil	Wells Fargo	Home Depot	Chevron
Qualcomm	Equinix	Groupon	Family Dollar	News Corp.	Coca-Cola	Oracle	IBM

Figure 4.3: Top Five Holdings of Prominent Hedge Funds and Mutual Funds
Source for the mutual funds is www.morningstar.com. Source for the hedge
funds is www.sec.gov. All portfolio holdings are as of 12/31/12.

compile.[18] Any fund that wants to raise real money needs to be an open book. Most are.

More importantly, all firms with serious growth plans have taken great strides to "institutionalize" their business. Among other things, this means that all top hedge funds, let alone all major traditional asset managers, now have sophisticated sales efforts dedicated to providing specific information on the risks they take and how they take them. Nowadays, there is no investment consultant or institutional investor who would proceed in their due diligence without nearly full transparency into a fund's operations.

With limited information, there is little to evaluate. The fewer the data points, the harder it is to establish expectations, and the more we are forced to rely on stories to frame our decision making. At the same time, we should be careful in wishing for "more" information—the Thornton Melon syndrome. As individuals or in groups, we can handle only so much of it.[19] There comes a tipping point when the overabundance of information is self-defeating and undermines effective decision making. No single pebble of information is unmanageable, but a tall bucket of pebbles is practically unmovable.

As hard as it is to resist, this observational stage is not the place for analysis. I realize it's sometimes impractical to distinguish one step from the next, but we must acknowledge that we risk adding various biases into our data collection efforts if we engage in fact gathering and judgment contemporaneously. True, our brains are wired to continuously seek patterns that collapse observation and analysis into the firing of a synapse.

But we can, and should, still distinguish fact from opinion. In testifying to Congress about the colossal failure of US intelligence on Iraqi weapons of mass destruction, Secretary of State Colin Powell observed:

> An old rule that I've used with my intelligence officers over the years, whether in the military, or now, in the State Department, goes like this: Tell me what you know. Tell me what you don't know. And then, based on what you really know and what you really don't know, tell me what you think is most likely to happen. And there's an extension of that rule with my intelligence officers: I will hold you accountable for what you tell me is a fact; and I will hold you accountable for what you tell me is not going to happen because you have the facts on that, or you don't know what's going to happen, or you know what your body of ignorance is and you told me what that is.[20]

Separate what you know from what you think. At the observational stage, what you observe will not exactly match your expectations. But be patient, and avoid amending the information collection process in midstream.

Mind the Gap

We want to understand the gap between our expectations for what we anticipate happening and the actual outcomes. Did our experts conduct themselves in the way we anticipated? Were we satisfied with the results? Even when others appear to meet certain expectations, there's still the question of whether they did so for the reasons we thought they would. For example, a fund manager delivers great numbers by investing in markets that aren't part of his mandate. Are we pleased that our US equity manager put up great numbers by piling into Chinese stocks? It's the right outcome for the wrong reason.

In analyzing the gap between prediction and results, we must first consider whether they've actually violated our expectations, or if we've somehow misunderstood or mischaracterized their intentions. This is a tricky issue. We engage it head-on in chapter 7's treatment of skill. Suffice it to say that defining skill as the ability of fund managers to meet their clients' expectations is a heterodox, nonstatistical, and ultimately *social* definition. In this view, skill is as much a subjective, discursive phenomenon as it is an objective, financial measurement. Ultimately, skill is the ability to fulfill one's promises.

For now, let's focus on situations where the manager appears to be clearly out of bounds. There is a simple, easy-to-follow rule for anyone who violates our expectations: Fire them, right? We thought they were going to invest in the United States but then they allocated to European securities. They claimed they were going to make 12 percent per year; they didn't. We heard them say they had nearly all of their net worth in the fund so as to "eat their own cooking"; they don't. If the point of going through so much painstaking work is to understand what a potential investment partner will provide for us, and then they don't deliver, it's probably time to move on.

If only it were so easy. Choosing to exit is hard. Selling something is often a more difficult choice than buying something. It's usually at the point of sale for any new purchase—a smartphone, car, board game, clothing, hedge fund, power saw, etc.—that we are most excited about the process of choice. At that moment, it's all possibility and promise. We've been convinced by others or ourselves (usually both) that the features and benefits overwhelm whatever potential drawbacks might exist. Then that moment is gone. And we have to live with our decision.

Changing your mind is hard. It's even more so when it involves admitting a mistake. There are a remarkable number of biases that make this process painful. A powerful bias is the so-called endowment effect, which states that once you possess something, by definition, it becomes more valuable to you. In one of the final scenes of *The Jerk*, Steve Martin's rags-to-riches-to-rags character Navin Johnson is suddenly destitute and insists on keeping possession of an ashtray, thermos, lamp, matches, and some other objectively worthless items. But he valued them dearly because they were *his*. The fact that none of us is an imbecile like Navin shouldn't lead us to think that we don't act on the same impulses.

We grow emotionally attached to our possessions, including our investments. The principle of loss aversion aggravates matters, because once we're in a losing situation, we feel even more compelled to hold our losers until we get back up to scratch. We don't want to change our minds and, in trading terms, "mark to market" our error. Not selling means not changing your mind. There is also the matter of so-called switching costs, a concept tied to satisficing, from chapter 2. We might not like what has transpired, but there are measurable costs involved in selling one investment and choosing another. We can justify not selling by choosing to believe that what we have, though somewhat disappointing, is good enough. Finally, returning to a central premise of the book: we're buying and selling people, not tickers. Being patient—nice, even—might just feel like the right thing to do.

We actually don't fire our experts very often. In addition to the multiple biases that suggest we shouldn't, the fact is that the experts we hire meet most of our expectations most of the time. Even when there appear to be triggers, the decision to exit is still highly subjective. Did they violate our expectations *enough*? To couch the concept of satisficing in statistical terms, the expectations we set tend to be confidence intervals, not point estimates. There's a range of acceptable behaviors and outcomes. This is why investing is rarely dramatic. The stories that stick in our minds are the blow-ups and home runs, but in the aggregate, they're the exception. Reality is less exciting.

THE ART OF IMPROVISATION

When evaluating fund managers, the more challenging and fascinating task centers on our ability to reset our expectations in synchronicity with adaptable, foxlike experts. The more flexibility we afford them, the more we must engage in an iterative process of setting, managing, and resetting expectations.

All experts have rules that guide them, but the truly innovative ones must depart at times from standard protocol; they must improvise. What are the rules for changing the rules? At first blush, the notion itself seems oxymoronic. Casually put, to improvise means to make it up as you go along. Across many domains, however, there are rules for changing the rules, explicitly or tacitly. An obvious example comes from the sphere of politics, where meta-rules are known as constitutions. They formalize the means by which the rules for governance can be legitimately changed. How national constitutions are written is fraught with conflict, precisely because the stakes are so high. In other fields of human endeavor, the lack of formal constitutions shouldn't suggest an absence of process behind adaptation, even though it might not be codified. This is clear, for example, through various forms of art, especially music.

The greatest accomplishment in the history of jazz was improvised. In early 1959, Miles Davis, already a major celebrity, brought together several other luminaries such as Cannonball Adderly, John Coltrane, and Bill Evans, to record an album that aimed to depart from established tradition. Up to this point, Davis had been an aficionado of the bebop tradition that had been prominent during most of the 1940s and 1950s. A natural innovator, Davis regularly advanced his craft, as can be seen in his helping jazz progress from bebop of various stripes to cool jazz to modal jazz and beyond. By the late 1950s, "Davis was looking for ways to break out of the straitjacket of bebop. Even on *Milestones* it was evident that he was looking for something new, and that simplicity might be one way out of the current corner he'd worked himself into."[21]

An instant classic, *Kind of Blue* is, according to the Recording Industry Association of America, the best-selling jazz album of all time. To say it represented a seminal breakthrough in the history of music is incontrovertible. Yet its creation also speaks to the creative process in the arts and beyond. The album was recorded in two sessions, over a sum total of about eight hours, on March 2 and April 22, 1959, at Columbia Record's 30th Street Studio in New York City. The musicians barely rehearsed. They did not have the music ahead of time, as there really wasn't any to distribute. According to the album's liner notes, pianist Bill Evans said that "Miles conceived these settings only hours before the recording dates."[22] To observe that *Kind of Blue* was improvised is hardly to claim that it was an undisciplined, haphazard effort. According to Wynton Marsalis, "In Jazz, improvisation isn't just making any ol' thing up. Jazz, like any language, has its own grammar and vocabulary. There's no right or wrong, just some choices that are better than others."[23] By assembling a group of true experts with a shared sense of the foundational processes that undergirded their craft, Davis was able to find something of beauty without the benefit of a map.

Structured spontaneity is all around us, once we start looking. In his wonderful book *Streetlights and Shadows,* Gary Klein brings together decades of his research on adaptive decision making, showing that experts figure out how to succeed by hook or by crook.[24] Some of his more notable work regards firefighters, whom he has been studying since the 1980s.[25] In evaluating how experts make critical decisions under pressure, Klein learned from firefighters that nonroutine events are common and that they must adapt to whatever is in front of them. Of course, there is the textbook process—codified, ordered, and sensible. But it often falls short: "procedures can erode expertise" is one of Klein's more fascinating insights. He tells the story of a veteran fire commander who recounted a "simple" house fire. While the fireman considered the incident "trivial," Klein discovered a complex series of decisions that were in no way obvious to either a layman or even conventional practice, including the decision to extinguish the fire from outside the house rather than from inside.[26] The matrix of decisions, made quickly and "without thinking," stemmed from extensive experience and a core set of principles that should not be violated. As in other tales, of airplane pilots, meteorologists, and soldiers, the firefighters of Klein's studies leveraged their expertise to make sense of ambiguous situations.

And yes, even high finance—puffed up with its complex algorithms and rigorous processes—is a world filled with artful creation. The "greatest trade ever"—Paulson's massive short on the subprime market—was improvised. That's not to say it was a fluke or an accident; not at all. On the contrary, the clarity of thought and expedience of decision making that John Paulson, Paolo Pellegrini, and the rest of the team demonstrated quickly elevated them into the pantheon of great investment stories. Of course, among serious investment professionals with strong pedigrees and long track records, one rarely hears any investment ideas that seem patently foolish—these are typically thoughtful, meticulous, and articulate individuals. When the Paulson team was initially pitching its idea to institutional investors in the middle of the last decade, the thesis had merit—just as did those who believed the bull market would continue indefinitely. In the end, only a small number of investors allocated to either Paulson's fund or others like it that were shorting subprime mortgages.

There is virtually no way to have known Paulson would pull it off. There was little in his long career as an expert in trading around corporate events to suggest acumen in structured credit. To be sure, Paulson is a smart, nimble professional, just as Miles Davis was a talented, nimble musician. Each of their landmark achievements is, after the fact, no surprise. In the frame of his own vocation, each responded to many years of pent-up environmental tensions and a largely untapped opportunity to resolve them. Yet that doesn't mean anyone could have anticipated the impact of the Big Short or could have guessed that the greatest jazz album of all time would have been recorded, without rehearsal, in only a few hours.

Like jazz musicians and firefighters, less constrained finance experts improvise within a set of rules. The central task of investment research is to articulate those rules and understand how they could change over time. As one very successful fund manager put it, "Traders who are successful over the long run adapt. If they do use rules, and you meet them 10 years later, they will have broken those rules. Why? Because the world changed."[27] Resolving the tension between consistency and adaptation, between discipline and innovation, is difficult. Paradoxically, in the New Normal, flexible experts are more likely to help us succeed, but precisely because setting expectations for flexible experts is so challenging, the more we rely on those most able to help us, the more likely it is that we will be disappointed by the mismatch of expectations and outcomes. Indeed, the obvious difference between Davis and Paulson is that we can simply enjoy jazz (or not), but we have to intentionally choose a wily financial expert when the consequences of being wrong can be substantial.

The source of success (failure) for many managers has been the ability (inability) to adapt over time. These changes are responses to a changing market environment—both opportunities and threats—or new business imperatives. Innovation is a central component of adaptation. Look at some of the more successful alternative managers still in business today: Citadel, Canyon, HBK, Carlson, Baupost, Elliot, Moore, Och-Ziff, Tudor, Millennium. What they do today, both as investors and as businesses, resembles but is not identical to what they've done in decades past. There is likely a distinct investment philosophy and organizational culture at work, but certain things change along the way to help them survive and thrive. What those "things" are and how they work is a central question in investment research. While those are not easy questions, the even more difficult question is why some firms succeed at adaptation and others do not. There were undoubtedly highly capable individuals at Tiger, Stark, Marin, DB Zwirn, Amaranth, and Peloton as well. It just happens that none of these organizations has survived.

ARBITRAGED

The theme of adaptation runs through the history of alternative investing, not only at the individual fund level but across strategies. It's not enough to know any particular manager's strengths and challenges; we must also consider the broader context in which they are operating, fully appreciating that few, if any, can reliably predict what the future holds.

Arbitrage is one of the classic notions in finance: that there are profits to be made by trading two or more securities simultaneously where there is an anomalous price relationship among them. In its purest form, arbitrage should yield riskless profits, but that seldom happens. The more commonplace usage of the term refers to the art of trading multiple securities whose value should either converge with or diverge from each other.

Merger arbitrage is a classic hedge fund strategy. The tale of its prominence, decline, and reformulation is a good example of how adaptation works in the real world of investing. Merger arbitrage aims to profit from the completion of a corporate acquisition. Generally, on the announcement of an intended merger, the price of the stock of the company being acquired does not trade up fully to the proposed purchase price. Acme Corp. wants to buy Coyote Corp. for $90 per share. On the announcement, shares of Coyote jumped from its current price of $75 per share to $89 per share. So in any merger of two publicly listed companies—Exxon and Mobil, Time Warner and AOL, Citicorp and Travelers Group, etc.—the target's stock price spikes upwards on the news but stops short of the announced price.

This creates an opportunity for the arbitrageur to profit from the "spread" between the current price of the stock and the price of the proposed acquisition—in the case of Coyote Corp., the $1 between $89 and $90. For reasons ranging from antitrust laws to the fundamental health of the companies in question, the bigger the spread, the more concerned investors are about the deal getting scuttled. (This strategy is sometimes called "risk arbitrage" because investors are assessing the riskiness of the deal.) If the deal closes, the manager earns the spread. If it falls apart or is renegotiated at less attractive terms, the stock of the target company tends to fall sharply, causing significant losses.

Merger arbitrage had been a profitable strategy for decades. As shown in figure 4.4, the strategy yielded strong results in the 1990s. Rolling one-year returns tended to run between 10 and 20 percent, with relatively little volatility. Further, because the consummation of any particular deal is idiosyncratic—it depends mostly on the details of the deal, not broader stock market or macroeconomic concerns—the strategy has had a very low correlation to stocks and bonds, making it an attractive alternative investment.

A large number of hedge funds emerged to focus on this strategy in light of growing investor demand. Figure 4.5 shows a roughly sixfold increase in the growth of pure merger arbitrage offerings. This growth understates the trend because it doesn't fully capture more diversified shops that had large allocations to the strategy. Luminaries in this field included Kellner DiLeo, Och-Ziff, ORN, Harvest, PSAM, Gruss, Angelo Gordon, Sandell, Paulson, Halcyon, and York.

Then things changed. In 2001, the returns for the strategy fell precipitously. Returns barely cracked 10 percent; the previous decade's floor now became the ceiling. A study by Gaurav Jetley and Xinyu Ji evidences the major decline in arbitrage spreads over the past two decades.[28] They found that for mergers announced since 2001, on the first day's news of the announcement, the deal spread was 520 basis points lower than the

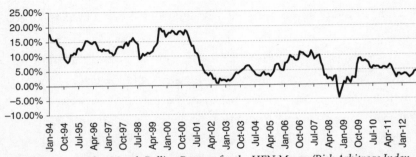

Figure 4.4   Twelve-Month Rolling Returns for the HFN Merger/Risk Arbitrage Index
Source: eVestment

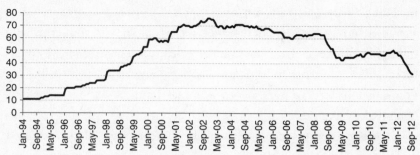

Figure 4.5   *Number of Constituents in the HFN Merger/Risk Arbitrage Index*
Source: eVestment

spread for deals announced between 1990 and 1995, and 290 basis points lower for deals announced between 1996 and 2001. Several factors driving this spread compression, including lower interest rates, changes in typical deal structures, and the sharp influx of capital from investors pursuing this strategy (from less than $100 million in 1990 to more than $22 billion in 2007), reduced the potential opportunity.[29] In a sense, the arbs had been arbed.

A decline in merger spreads is hardly the sexy or controversial item that many associate with the global hedge fund industry. But it is exactly this sort of regular event that subtly but powerfully drives industrial change. In this case, spread compression and other structural factors related to the merger market actually contributed to a material restructuring of the industry, providing a primary example of how foxlike experts adapt to changing circumstances. While a sole focus on merger arbitrage was sufficient for many managers (and their investors) for decades, by the turn of the century, it was almost impossible to build a stable franchise around just half of the business cycle. As mergers came and went, and abundant capital compressed spreads, there were both cyclical and structural drivers for managers to broaden their mandates.

Enter the "multi-strategy event" fund. While there had long been funds that rotated across different strategies, the decline in the bellwether merger arbitrage strategy compelled a number of managers to change their path. Some managers closed their dedicated merger funds, while others shifted away from merger arbitrage toward a broader range of corporate events—including distressed debt and other special corporate reorganizations. Merger arbitrage became but one tool in the tool kit, and an increasingly unimportant one at that. The number of constituents in the eVestment Merger/Risk Arbitrage Index fell by half over the last decade. There are now only a handful of pure merger arbitrage funds, and they garner limited investor attention.

Event-focused managers adapted to new challenges. Some achieved much more success than others. The challenge from the investor's point of view is trying to understand these changes as they take place in real time. In investments, much is made of "style drift"—moving away from one's core competence. But in this case study, there is not much difference between drift and opportunism. The manager is improvising in order to save his business. When merger spreads declined in the early 2000s, it wasn't yet obvious that the whole strategy was in decline—which in hindsight it was. There was nothing predestined about it, nor was it a given that building capabilities in distressed securities, equities, and other areas was the proper recipe for success.

Just because a fox is cunning does not mean that it will always be right. In hiring foxes to do our bidding in the market, we must appreciate that the ability to adapt brings a higher chance of survival, but also a much greater degree of unpredictability and uncertainty.

THE FOUR QUESTIONS

This chapter has delivered an adaptive approach to making good investment decisions. Drawing on the basics of inference building from the philosophy of science, I have walked through the cycle of establishing and managing expectations. It's not as easy as building a fulsome checklist of desirable attributes, but it is a sturdier tool applicable across any effort at choosing the right financial experts.

What's left to accomplish is applying this method in the areas that matter. To be sure, one can become overwhelmed by the endless information available to us about investments. Look at the supposedly "simple" end of the spectrum by taking a quick glance at any mutual fund profile on Morningstar.com. What you'll see is pages and pages of information on topics ranging across portfolio positions, returns, volatility, expenses, exposures to certain asset classes, sectors, and countries, and so on. What's signal and what's noise is tough to sort out. With less constrained vehicles that don't fit tightly into a style box, the exercise is even harder.

I believe there are four basic questions that structure investment due diligence. These are the topics on which we form expectations about the experts we hire and then adapt over time to changes in them, the world around us, and ourselves:

- ✓ Trust
- ✓ Risk
- ✓ Skill
- ✓ Fit

The overriding goal of *The Investor's Paradox* is to simplify complex investment choices. By focusing our inquiry on these areas, we can find simplicity in a world of overwhelming choice.

Can I Trust You?

No single investment can make your portfolio, but any single investment can break your portfolio. One bomb can ruin your entire firm. Just ask the professional investors who invested with Bernie Madoff. Many of them are either out of business or a shell of what they were previously. Yet the evaluation of trust is more than a forensic analysis reserved for accountants, lawyers, regulators, and other specialists in what has become known as "operational due diligence." At a deeper level, it is a tricky psychological engagement to size up others as potential long-term partners with whom we have a true alignment of incentives. This is the topic of chapter 5.

What Do You Do?

If you had only one question to ask a fund manager, this would be it. If you walked into his office knowing literally nothing about him, simply started the conversation with "What do you do?," and actively engaged him with the appropriate follow-up questions, you could more or less establish all of the core investment expectations for the fund at hand. Not that this is an easy task. Sometimes the risks a manager is taking are obvious, but often they're not. In my experience, there are five broad types of risks fund managers choose to take. Understanding how to think about those five risks is the topic of chapter 6.

Are You Good at Your Job?

Is the expert you hire skillful? In finance, there is a conventional notion of "alpha" that captures outperformance relative to well-defined benchmarks. This is a useful but narrow concept. In the real world of selecting managers, the dynamic of what counts as a satisfying arrangement moves well beyond sterile, statistical analysis and enters a realm of social engagement of managing expectations. Skill is about keeping one's promises. This is the topic of chapter 7.

Are You the Right Fit for Me?

The question of fit is an orange compared to the three previous apples. We had been asking questions directly to or about the manager, but now we are asking more personal questions: What is *my* objective? Some investors want a hedgehog—a specific piece in a well-designed puzzle, a fund that does one thing and doesn't veer from its mission. They want a round peg for a round hole. Others want a more flexible offering with more degrees of freedom. They want a fox. Fitting a cunning fox into a dynamic portfolio is a hard task. Both the type of peg and the shape of the hole shift over time. A long-term stable fit is nearly impossible. While fully addressing the question of fit is beyond the scope of *The Investor's Paradox,* I conclude the book in Chapter 8 with some thoughts about how we manage our own expectations, independent of the managers we choose.

Readers may note one surprising omission from these four questions: performance. If there's one topic that everyone thinks about and talks about, it's returns. This makes sense: returns are the "product" for sale. So why the omission? Most pragmatically, it's because performance chasing doesn't work. Like a sugar rush, great returns feel good for a while and then dissipate, as a manager can rarely consistently meet or exceed our performance expectations. Still, we want to be with a winner, so we gravitate toward those who have generated strong recent performance. Yet buying high and selling low is a losing strategy. Performance chasing triggers some of our more influential biases, typically not for the better.

A UNIFIED APPROACH

Because I was fortunate to start my investment career covering mutual funds at Morningstar and then moved into the hedge fund industry, I had the opportunity to train as a practitioner in both worlds. One thing became clear in the transition from one to the other, as well as in retrospect: the questions of interest and the means to answer them are very much the same. In discussing this observation over recent years with friends and peers in the money management business, I have been struck by how stridently some object to this point of view. The common refrain is along the lines of: hedge funds are a different "asset class" than mutual funds!

As I've argued, they are not. I've dismissed as incoherent the thought that hedge funds are an asset class worthy of a distinct set of perspectives and tools. Instead, the important distinction is that between the risks you choose to take and the structure through which you own them. To conflate risk and packaging is to confuse the conversation.

As convergence continues apace, in directions that we cannot predict, what I hope to accomplish is a vocabulary and set of tools for choosing the right funds for any particular purpose regardless of which form it takes. We have one set of choices that vary by matter of degree, not type. The peculiar vocation of fund research has always been split into two camps, one for traditional vehicles, another for alternatives—what few books have been written on due diligence have hewed to one camp or the other. These worlds did not overlap.

Now they must. To understand them, we'll now see how our dimensions of trust, focus, skill, and fit can serve as a north star for fund research of any stripe.

5

MADOFF'S HOBGOBLINS

I looked the man in the eye. I found him to be very straightforward and trustworthy. We had a very good dialogue. I was able to get a sense of his soul.

—President George W. Bush, on his first meeting with
Russian President Vladimir Putin (June 16, 2001)

THE BIG STORE

The term "con man" is now so common that we mostly forget it is an abbreviation of "confidence man." While we all know that con men cleverly scheme to rip us off, most people think they do so by concocting a way for us to trust *them*. That's true, but it's only the second stage of the scheme. The first, more insidious angle is when the con man feigns confidence in *you*. This is the hard edge of the con: before receiving confidence, the rogue offers it.

Limehouse Chappie, Devil's Island Eddie, Barney the Patch, Jimmy the Rooter, and a slew of "Kids"—the Hashouse Kid, Umbrella Kid, Narrow Gage Kid, the Keystone Kid, and Yellow Kid Weil—are some of the colorful characters in David Maurer's little-known gem *The Big Con*, originally published in 1940. A professor of linguistics at the University of Louisville, Maurer spent much of the 1930s earning the trust of these men who made their living malevolently earning the trust of others. Maurer meticulously documented the coming-of-age of the sophisticated scam artist during the interwar years. As an expert in linguistics, he was well equipped to appreciate how the nuance of language and communication influenced interpersonal relationships.

It's a colorful history, and it's hard not to find these men and their deeds engaging, even fascinating. Naturally, their elaborate schemes are the stuff of countless books and movies, including *Ocean's 11, House of Games,* and *The Grifters.* In fact, while you may not have heard of *The Big Con* (I hadn't until I started poking around the history of fraud), you've probably seen and enjoyed *The Sting,* starring Paul Newman and Robert Redford, which was inspired by Maurer's true-life stories.

Well before Bernie Madoff and other modern financial crooks, Maurer explained who perpetrates these sophisticated scams:

> Although the confidence man is sometimes classed with professional thieves, pickpockets, and gamblers, he is really not a thief at all because he does no actual stealing. The trusting victim literally thrusts a fat bank roll into his hands. It is a point of pride with him that he does not have to steal. Confidence men are not "crooks" in the ordinary sense of the word. They are suave, slick, and capable. Their depredations are very much on the genteel side.[1]

That the con men are dastardly is no surprise; after all, bad men aim to do bad things. What's more interesting is that the best of them are also bright, articulate, and charming. They just happen to lack any sense of compassion for their victims. The qualities of the "mark," or victim, are the key to any successful con. In all of Maurer's tales, scams work because the mark is vulnerable. Not from a lack of intelligence or sophistication; most marks are not, in Maurer's words, "blockheads" or "numbskulls." Quite the contrary: a "roper" (the con man charged with finding the marks) *prefers* to find smarter targets. "The higher a mark's intelligence, the quicker he sees through the deal directly to his own advantage."[2]

The environment in which con men work also makes a big difference. As Maurer points out, we're not talking about petty thieves or pickpockets. These men are willing and able to engage in predatory psychology and take advantage of inescapable human biases. Thus, context matters. Indeed, beyond the colorful characters, what Maurer successfully documented was how sophisticated scams, even in those early days, were institutionalized.

Hence the introduction of the "Big Store," a fabricated establishment such as a poolroom, broker's office, or casino that gave marks confidence that they were dealing with legitimate individuals. "Stores are set up with a careful attention to detail which makes them seem bona fide."[3] Recall the fake off-track betting parlor in *The Sting*.

This institutionalization isn't trivial. The appearance of legitimacy is what facilitates the "long con," an extended scam in which deep relationships form over many weeks or months, or longer. The payoff can be huge. The "short con" is lower risk, for lower reward. It takes place quickly and doesn't require deeper feelings of trust. The long con always involves the Big Store because that's what encourages *you to go to them*, not the other way around. The con men have something you want, at least at first. As you grow to accept the legitimacy of the firm, store, or casino you're engaged with, the likelihood of trusting its proprietors increases. At a certain point, they have you—perhaps because you want to be had.

I WANT TO BELIEVE

If only psychology were as simple as dividing the world into good guys and bad guys. Of course, it's not. To get at an adaptive notion of trust in modern society, we have to engage in an intellectually honest (and sometimes uncomfortable) exploration of our motives, aspirations, and fears.

Fortunately, we have television to help us. *The X-Files* was a popular science fiction program that aired from 1993 to 2002. It juxtaposed two protagonists, Fox Mulder and Dana Scully, who served as the modern archetypes for the believer and the skeptic, respectively. This existential tension grounded the show's exploration of the supernatural. According to the show's creator, Chris Carter, "Mulder and Scully came right out of my head. A dichotomy. They are the equal parts of my desire to believe in something and my inability to believe in something. My skepticism and my faith."[4] This tension between skeptic and believer—among us as well as within us—is more present than we might acknowledge.

The show's meta-quest was to discover the "truth" about the existence of the supernatural. In fact, the dueling mottos of its protagonists were "I want to believe" and "The truth is out there." Agent Scully was a scientist by training, driven by the belief that the truth is discoverable by reasoned scientific inquiry, that objective reality will be revealed through careful investigation. That which does not square with our conventional expectations of how the world works, she felt, can be explained, eventually, through measured consideration. Agent Mulder was a believer, though not a Pollyanna. He was as diligent an investigator as his partner, but he believed there are certain things in the world that don't square with conventional wisdom; that sometimes there is an unbridgeable gap between what you know to be true and what you can scientifically prove. Mulder was comfortable jumping that gap; Scully was not.

There is a little Scully and Mulder in each of us, and it comes out in the day-to-day dealings with others. In a complex division of labor, we rely extensively on others to achieve the outcomes we desire. That exercise includes hiring experts, which in the domain of finance includes fund managers. Especially for professional fund pickers, there is the dedication to diligent inquiry, to discovering the true nature of the managers—their focus, skill, and reliability. In the modern money industry, this is typically a group effort with teams of analysts, investment committees, and reams of data subject to analysis and discussion. The purpose of that investment process is to get to the right answer. But there is also an element to the process, rarely acknowledged, that requires some measure of faith in our experts to have the right answers, to figure things out on our behalf. For those who can't avail themselves of a large research staff who can dig into the "truth," the willingness to operate on faith is even more germane.

An important underlying theme in *The Investor's Paradox* is the notion of confidence. We hire experts to whom we afford varying degrees of discretion to act on our behalf. Satisfaction comes when outcomes match our expectations. Confidence is the connective webbing between expectations and outcomes. It would be maddening if we had to wait for every measurable outcome, in every instance, to reevaluate our experts. Instead we take mental shortcuts, effectively assuming across multiple instances that expectations and outcomes will match up reasonably well, if not perfectly. We grow confident in that rhythm of events. This is why, at some deeper level, the real commodity being traded in financial services is confidence itself. The foundation of trust is based on doing what you say you're going to do. It is fulfilling one's promises.

Yet it's not that simple. The long con demonstrates how the source of trust—confidence—can also be a source of skullduggery. It's the establishment of that trust—living up to your word, behaving in line with expectations, acting consistently—that allows for betrayal. To resolve this, let's use the adaptive mindset spelled out in the previous chapter to explore the idea of trust. First, we'll dig into the Madoff affair. Then we'll examine more broadly the social institution of trust in the world of money.

THE LIPSTICK BUILDING

Bernard Madoff built his own version of the Big Store in 1960, when he established Bernard L. Madoff Investment Securities LLC (BLMIS), a legitimate broker/dealer. A pioneer in the field of electronic trading, the firm eventually became one of the largest "market makers" on Wall Street. When BLMIS first started, the stock exchanges were still clunky, paper-based operations. Madoff was a visionary in seeing how the major exchanges could either be transformed or worked around by new technologies. Profiting from this trend, BLMIS became one of the more prolific dealers on the New York Stock Exchange and was, at peak, the largest market maker on the upstart NASDAQ exchange. Although BLMIS was not a household name outside of New York, insiders knew the Madoff broker/dealer was a serious business. Bernie (as he was commonly known) was a prominent member of the New York financial community, including serving as chairman of the National Association of Securities Dealers.

The basic history of the Madoff affair is well documented.[5] On the back of his emerging brokerage business, Madoff began to lure clients in order to manage their assets. Brokerage and asset management, though both "financial services," are very different businesses. The former is a transaction-based service, facilitating the real-time buying and selling of securities; dealers aim to extract the small price difference between what a buyer bids and what a seller asks for. Asset managers serve as fiduciaries for their clients, who allocate their capital to experts who then attempt to earn a certain rate of return on those assets. Both are completely legitimate businesses. It's just that combining them under one roof is fraught with potential conflicts of interest, insofar as what might be good for the broker at any one time is not necessarily good for the client.

Whether Madoff was a fraudster from the earliest days of his career is not known and largely beside the point. What is clear is that he ultimately used the legitimacy of the brokerage business to raise assets for his questionable money management business. The earliest relationships were personal. Madoff leveraged the network of his father-in-law, Sol Alpern, a successful accountant. Alpern actively solicited capital from associates, sometimes promising that his son-in-law could deliver 20 percent year-in and year-out.[6] Erin Arvedlund describes individuals such as Michael Engler, a Minnesota businessman and World War II veteran, who in turn steered others to invest in Madoff: "It was this high level of trust that led smart and savvy people—especially in the Jewish community—to invest with Madoff over the ensuing years without asking serious questions. And they were not driven by greed . . . but rather by the desire to invest in their futures with someone they felt they could trust."[7] In these early years, the types of clients brought into the scheme tended not to be financially sophisticated, so it is unlikely that they asked penetrating questions as to how the money was managed.

Over time, Madoff employed other solicitors—what David Maurer would call "ropers" or "outsidemen." Early on, the most prominent of them were Frank Avellino and Michael Bienes.[8] Keep in mind what was going on this entire time. *Madoff was not investing the money that he received from clients.* He was depositing it in bank accounts, fabricating formal investment statements reflecting bogus rates of return, and paying current "clients" with the flow of capital coming from newer marks. Thus, as with any Ponzi scheme, he had to constantly attract fresh sources of capital in order to keep the machinery going.

At a certain point, the scheme became fully institutionalized. Its physical "store" became the famous Lipstick Building at the corner of Third Avenue and Fifty-third Street in midtown Manhattan. The nineteenth floor was the actual Store, so to speak—an accessible office for legitimate (at least in part) brokerage dealings. The eighteenth floor was the back office of BLMIS. But the seventeenth floor was the heart of the Ponzi scheme operation, where, according to the *New York Times,* "wealth went to vanish."[9]

The execution of the scheme evolved over the years. Madoff moved beyond personal connections, away from the direct solicitations that had begun to raise concerns with the Securities and Exchange Commission (SEC) and toward arm's-length advisory businesses and the fast-growing funds-of-funds industry. Through associates such as Maurice "Sonny" Cohn, Walter Noel, Sonja Kohn, and Ezra Merkin, Madoff could replenish his coffers through supposedly legitimate middlemen who set up "feeder funds" that allowed the scheme to nourish itself.

Take, for example, Noel's outfit, the Fairfield Greenwich Group (FGG), a Connecticut-based fund of funds. Noel was part of the Connecticut money culture, and FGG was one of many funds of funds that catered to wealthy investors seeking entry into lucrative, hard-to-access investment pools. FGG offered different products for different clients. The Sentry Fund was one of the notable feeder funds into Madoff's operation.

Here's how FGG described its Sentry Fund to customers:

The Fund seeks to obtain capital appreciation of its assets principally through the utilization of a nontraditional options trading strategy described as "split strike conversion," to which the Fund allocates the predominant portion of its assets. The investment strategy has defined risk and reward parameters. The establishment of a typical position entails (i) the purchase of a group or basket of equity securities that are intended to highly correlate to the S&P 100 Index, (ii) the purchase of out-of-the-money S&P 100 Index put options with a notional value that approximately equals the market value of the basket of equity securities and (iii) the sale of out-of-the-money S&P 100 Index call options with a notional value that approximately equals the market value of the basket of equity securities. The basket typically consists of between 40 to 50 stocks in the S&P 100 Index. The primary purpose of the long put options is to limit the market risk of the stock basket at the strike price of the long puts. The primary purpose of the short call options is to largely finance the cost of the put hedge and to increase the stand-still rate of return. The "split strike conversion" strategy is implemented by Bernard L. Madoff Investment Securities LLC ("BLM"), a broker-dealer registered with the Securities and Exchange Commission, through accounts maintained by the Fund at that firm. The services of BLM and its personnel are essential to the continued operation of the Fund, and its profitability, if any. The Investment Manager, in its sole and exclusive discretion, may allocate a portion of the Fund's assets (never to exceed, in the aggregate, 5% of the Fund's Net Asset Value, measured at the time of investment) to alternative investment opportunities other than its "split strike conversion" investments.[10]

So what do we have here? First, there's the description of a complicated-sounding investment strategy, which we'll revisit in a moment. Then there's the claim that Madoff will run somewhere between 95 percent and 100 percent of the money in the fund. In other words, what FGG was offering in its Sentry Fund was actually not a diversified fund of funds. It was simply a feeder into Madoff's operation. This was the listed description of the product; Madoff's role in managing the assets was in no way hidden.

Finally, there were the "returns" of the Sentry Fund. There is much hand-wringing over Ponzi schemes and other financial frauds, but it's rare that such frauds are so formalized that there is an actual track record. Figure 5.1 shows what Madoff "accomplished" via FGG's Sentry Fund. Take a moment and read the numbers, month by month, from the bottom up.

	Jan	Feb	Mar	Apr	May	Jun	Jul	Aug	Sep	Oct	Nov	Dec	Year
2008	0.63%	0.06%	0.18%	0.93%	0.81%	−0.06%	0.72%	0.71%	0.50%				4.57%
2007	0.29%	−0.11%	1.64%	0.98%	0.81%	0.34%	0.17%	0.31%	0.97%	0.46%	1.04%	0.23%	7.34%
2006	0.70%	0.20%	1.31%	0.94%	0.70%	0.51%	1.06%	0.77%	0.68%	0.42%	0.86%	0.86%	9.38%
2005	0.51%	0.37%	0.85%	0.14%	0.63%	0.46%	0.13%	0.16%	0.89%	1.61%	0.75%	0.54%	7.26%
2004	0.88%	0.44%	−0.01%	0.37%	0.59%	1.21%	0.02%	1.26%	0.46%	0.03%	0.79%	0.24%	6.44%
2003	−0.35%	−0.05%	1.85%	0.03%	0.90%	0.93%	1.37%	0.16%	0.86%	1.26%	−0.14%	0.25%	7.27%
2002	−0.04%	0.53%	0.39%	1.09%	2.05%	0.19%	3.29%	−0.14%	0.06%	0.66%	0.10%	0.00%	8.43%
2001	2.14%	0.08%	1.07%	1.26%	0.26%	0.17%	0.38%	0.94%	0.66%	1.22%	1.14%	0.12%	9.82%
2000	2.14%	0.13%	1.77%	0.27%	1.30%	0.73%	0.58%	1.26%	0.18%	0.86%	0.62%	0.36%	10.67%
1999	1.99%	0.11%	2.22%	0.29%	1.45%	1.70%	0.36%	0.87%	0.66%	1.05%	1.54%	0.32%	13.29%
1998	0.85%	1.23%	1.68%	0.36%	1.69%	1.22%	0.76%	0.21%	0.98%	1.86%	0.78%	0.26%	12.52%
1997	2.38%	0.67%	0.80%	1.10%	0.57%	1.28%	0.68%	0.28%	2.32%	0.49%	1.49%	0.36%	13.10%
1996	1.42%	0.66%	1.16%	0.57%	1.34%	0.15%	1.86%	0.20%	1.16%	1.03%	1.51%	0.41%	12.08%
1995	0.85%	0.69%	0.78%	1.62%	1.65%	0.43%	1.02%	−0.24%	1.63%	1.53%	0.44%	1.03%	12.04%
1994	2.11%	−0.44%	1.45%	1.75%	0.44%	0.23%	1.71%	0.35%	0.75%	1.81%	−0.64%	0.60%	10.57%
1993	−0.09%	1.86%	1.79%	−0.01%	1.65%	0.79%	0.02%	1.71%	0.28%	1.71%	0.19%	0.39%	10.75%
1992	0.42%	2.72%	0.94%	2.79%	−0.27%	1.22%	−0.09%	0.86%	0.33%	1.33%	1.36%	1.36%	13.72%
1991	3.01%	1.40%	0.52%	1.32%	1.82%	0.30%	1.98%	1.00%	0.73%	2.75%	0.01%	1.56%	17.64%
1990												2.77%	2.77%

Figure 5.1   Bernie Madoff's Returns, 1990–2008
Source: Fairfield Greenwich Group

Taken together, the description of the fund and the numbers are a keyhole into history's largest fraud. Several items are notable. First, when we read through the returns sequentially, their consistency is mesmerizing. Over the course of 214 months, the fund delivered positive returns 93 percent of the time. The Sentry Fund was negative in only fifteen months, and the largest loss was a mere –0.64 percent. Yet the fund was never too "hot." In only one month, early in 1991, did it return more than 3 percent. Indeed, we might think of major scams as producing the illusion of very large returns, but here the fund's annual returns are modest; after 2000, it never delivered double-digit annual returns. This was hardly a get-rich-quick scheme. Over the course of nearly eighteen years, the fund earned an annualized return of 10.6 percent, which is good but not spectacular. The fact that annualized volatility was just 2.45 percent (a *very* low number in comparison to most other assets) and that no large losses ever occurred is what's truly remarkable. The Sentry Fund's Sharpe Ratio, which refers to performance on a risk-adjusted basis, was 2.73. This is highly unusual. In context, a Sharpe Ratio greater than 1.0 is considered exceptional. Virtually no legitimate investments can achieve a figure greater than 2.0 over long stretches of time.

WHY?

So we know the key facts—what we don't know is why this took place. First, any professional investor who wanted to know that this was a fraud could have found out. One of the more interesting characters in the Madoff tale is Harry Markopolos, a stock options expert who noticed the improbable returns early on and grew consumed with uncovering the fraud. Over ten-plus years, he attempted to inform the SEC what was transpiring at the Lipstick Building, including in his December 22, 2005, submission to the SEC.[11] He detailed *thirty* red flags for why Madoff was "highly likely" to be "the world's largest Ponzi scheme."

Any regulator with even a little common sense and investing acumen would find Markopolos's points reasonable and worth further investigation, if not immediately condemning Madoff's scheme. Yet, the SEC mostly ignored Markopolos and had done so for years prior to this 2005 letter. The so-called split-strike conversion strategy mentioned in the

Fairfield Sentry description simply cannot generate these sorts of returns over long periods of time. That's true in terms of its consistent performance—"mathematically impossible," according to Markopolos—and in a technical sense because it would have been impossible to source a sufficient number of call options to execute these trades. The market simply wasn't deep enough.

Many of Markopolos's red flags didn't rely on technical knowledge of the options markets. There should have been a massive, auditable paper trail if these trades were actually taking place, but there wasn't. Madoff gave investors little access, and even less explanation for his extraordinary results. No one was welcome on the Lipstick Building's seventeenth floor. Madoff only allowed one individual to conduct audits, denying any legitimate accounting firm access to his books and records. The list goes on. In sum, Markopolos assessed that Madoff *never executed a single trade.*

So why did practiced institutional investors, as well as hundreds of untrained individual investors, make sizable, long-standing investments in Madoff when a relatively simple forensic analysis revealed so many red flags? One hypothesis is that the victims were stupid. Weren't the facts plain to see? This hypothesis doesn't hold water. Indeed, back in 1940, David Maurer addressed this head-on in *The Big Con:*

> To expect a mark to enter into a con game, take the bait, and then, by sheer reason, analyze the situation and see it as a swindle, is simply asking too much. The mark is thrown into an unreal world which very closely resembles real life. . . . Hence, it should be no reflection upon a man's intelligence to be swindled. In fact, highly intelligent marks, even though they may tax the ingenuity of the con men, respond best to the proper type of play.[12]

Ironically, the most likely victims for serious confidence games tend to be of above-average intelligence. Thus, there must be something else at work.

A FOOLISH CONSISTENCY

The scholar Ralph Waldo Emerson wrote in his classic 1841 essay *Self-Reliance* that "a foolish consistency is the hobgoblin of little minds." In his own historical circumstance, Emerson was railing against the need to act in conformity with others in the fledgling industrializing American society. As the title of his essay suggests, Emerson implored the citizens of a young America to find their own path, to embrace their private individuality over the constraints of society. Per Emerson, one should "trust thyself."

Unfortunately for transcendentalism, it appears that our brains are not wired this way. Our fast-thinking minds are always switched on, searching for recognizable patterns, which we find pleasurable. Sometimes we find them, but mostly we fabricate them. As stated in chapter 2, we see patterns in random sequences because randomness is psychologically disorienting, and we strive to avoid it. Part of this phenomenon stems from our need to control our environment. Our natural survival instincts are heightened when we don't comprehend our surroundings and we feel unsafe. Generally, given a choice between known risks and uncertainty (including the possibility that there are no risks at all), we prefer the known risks. Thus, we subconsciously see patterns in random events in order to give ourselves the illusion of control and, thus, safety.[13]

In finance, this craving for predictability is a powerful force. The emotions that always receive top billing are fear and greed—be greedy when others are fearful, and fearful when others are greedy, as the saying goes. However, predictability and consistency are just as important in the day-to-day blocking and tackling of fund investing. Professional fund investors make great hay over the importance of a consistent investment program. (As we will see in chapter 7, consistency is in fact one, perhaps the central, feature of a good investment fund.) But it, too, has a dark side.

The consistency of Madoff's returns appears to have been a powerful enabler of his Ponzi scheme. Among the victims' testimonials, collected in *The Club No One Wanted to Join,* a common theme is the appeal of consistency.[14] Per one investor, Michael De Vita:

> Over the next few years I began to diversify away from bank accounts and CDs and moved into a brokerage account. I found the results of this foray were not particularly successful, predictable or profitable. Returns varied widely from double digit annual gains to double digit losses. I was looking for something

with a reasonable and predictable rate of return. I was absolutely willing to accept limited upside gains in order to avoid a large downside risk.[15]

De Vita also commented that with Madoff, "I had exactly what I was looking for; I would gladly eschew the very large single year returns in exchange for a reliable and predictable rate of return with limited downside risk."[16] A different investor referred to Madoff as a "safe, reliable Golden Calf."[17]

Madoff was not "too good to be true." He was *just good enough all the time*. As we saw in the Fairfield Sentry Fund chart, the returns were not high. Seeing how he didn't return more than 10 percent in a year starting in 2001, it's hard to call these investors "greedy." They were simply averse to losing money and garnered some comfort from the consistency and predictability that the strategy appeared to deliver.

Of course, on one level, it does seem that the victims wanted to believe that Madoff's returns were real, despite the red flags everywhere. This was a world filled with Mulders, not Scullys. At a certain point, they took a leap of faith in the supernatural phenomenon of earning nearly riskless returns. According to Robert Trivers in *The Folly of Fools,* a wonderful study of self-deception and its impact on daily life, the idea of wanting to believe in something that isn't true has strong evolutionary roots.[18] Interestingly, Trivers's central thesis is that "self-deception evolves in the service of deception—the better to fool others."[19] We fool ourselves in order to fool others. But because explicit, conscious lying is emotionally and cognitively uncomfortable, we tend to cede this function to our subconscious.

The false narratives we tell ourselves, and then others, become a powerful source for manipulation. Indeed, it may be that Madoff himself was the ultimate expert in self-deception. As a charitable, esteemed member of the very community he secretly pillaged, he clearly employed this tactic to help sustain the fraud. While the balance between the conscious and unconscious pieces of Madoff's ruse is a matter of pure speculation, it is unlikely that all of his actions and salesmanship were based on deliberate, nefarious intentions. If they were, I guess that the tells would have been caught earlier. Purer forms of evil sometimes lurk behind the veil.

The fact that we all occasionally choose to believe things that strain credulity allows us to sidestep the least comfortable element of the Madoff saga, which is the potential culpability of the victims themselves. All return, no risk; no access to books and records; a strategy that defied any sort of industrial logic or mathematical coherence. These clues were hidden in plain sight. And there were many skeptics in the money industry who strongly, even vocally believed that something illicit was taking place inside the Lipstick Building. There were Scullys among some Wall Street bankers, blue-chip funds of funds, and other financial advisors, who saw that this situation made no sense. They chose not to believe.

So the question remains why so many did. "Another factor that made Bernie Madoff so appealing to investors was that, while many of them may have thought he was doing something not quite legal, at least he was doing it on their behalf."[20] We can only hypothesize about people's intentions here. A meaningful subset of Madoff victims did not even know they had exposure to him—they were invested in vehicles that in turn invested in other feeders into the Madoff machine. It's unfair to hold them culpable. That being said, for professional investors as well as the regulators, we cannot completely ignore the sentiment that David Maurer arrived at after a decade of studying the anthropology of ropers, marks, and big stores: "It is not intelligence but integrity which determines whether or not a man is a good mark."[21] Simply put, those professionals who wanted to know what was really going on could have found out.

The sturdy architecture of trust Madoff constructed through his consistent, predictable profile was further buttressed by the exclusivity of the enterprise, however feigned. The original *Barron's* 2001 article on Madoff was entitled "Don't Ask, Don't Tell" because one of the key sales tactics was to portray the Madoff investment pool as an exclusive fund with limited slots.[22] When investor-cum-gumshoe Harry Markopolos was attempting to sell a comparable options-trading strategy in Europe, he heard time and again about how the exclusivity of Madoff's exposure plumped its appeal. But, in retrospect, everyone was being sold the same story. Just about anyone could get access to something to which few purportedly had access.

There are few more effective ways to convince people they want something than to tell them they can't have it.[23] Madoff created the "velvet rope" effect by telling people, "I don't need your money," and then reluctantly but graciously admitting them.[24] They were then instructed to not tell anyone about their participation, intensifying the thrill of the experience as well as triggering, I'd hypothesize, the self-deception Robert Trivers describes in *The Folly of Fools*. Investors were also told that if they did reveal their participation, they'd be asked to leave the partnership. Thus, in allowing each person into the scheme, Madoff and his henchmen simultaneously ensured that they would keep mum. In other words, the con man did what con men always do first: they place confidence in you.

VERIFY, THEN TRUST

The concept of trust is complex. Heavily debated among psychologists, sociologists, and economists alike, defining and measuring trust is a slippery affair. One multidisciplinary group of scholars arrived at the following: "Trust is a psychological state comprising the intention to accept vulnerability based upon positive expectations of the intentions or behavior of another."[25] There are a couple of key elements in this definition. The first is that in order to engage in a trusting relationship, one must be willing to be vulnerable. In other words, there must be a risk of loss. Uncertainty creates the opportunity for trust, which in turn dampens uncertainty and motivates further risk taking. As such, trust is dynamic. It is not a moment in time, but an iterated affair. Second, there is the "positive expectation" that others will conduct themselves in a way that is beneficial to you, or at least not harmful.

But as we just saw, the wellspring of trust is also a cornerstone of betrayal. At some deep psychological level, this paradox is probably irresolvable. What causes us to trust others also allows them to manipulate us. Those like Madoff, with pernicious motives and abundant resources, will likely find their victims eventually. But that doesn't mean we can't develop an adaptive concept of trust that will see us through many of life's affairs, including money matters.

One starting point of establishing trust is to embed personal relationships within broader social institutions. These institutions can be norms of behavior, proscriptive rules, or concrete organizations that constrain and/ or motivate acceptable behavior. They range from "soft" to "hard" institutions. When designed and executed well, they can be effective at creating positive expectations of others—both individuals and firms. These institutions allow us to go beyond the confines of a strictly interpersonal relationship to something bigger and sturdier.

We overrate our own ability to "get" people. Perhaps apostles of body language expert Paul Eckman or denizens of the World Poker Tour can identify a "tell" that reveals true intentions, but most of us can't. The task here goes well beyond distinguishing a wink from a blink, or reading someone's body language or tone. This chapter's opening quote from former president Bush is an amusing, albeit dangerous, example of a skilled politician who, after a weekend of boating and barbecues in Maine, understood the "soul" of a ruthless political operative who subsequently revealed himself, countless times, as remarkably untrustworthy.

A well-worn phrase, born of the Cold War a generation before Putin and the younger Bush, was "Trust, but verify." At the time, the United States and the Soviet Union were engaged in a series of protracted negotiations to eliminate portions of their enormous arsenals of nuclear weapons. These were dangerous times, and as a matter of diplomacy, President Ronald Reagan supposedly used the phrase frequently. The only problem is that the phrase is backwards. We do want to trust others, but it has to be the outcome of an engagement, not the starting point.

The various social institutions that undergird trust work in different ways. Some, like laws and regulations, are constraints on behavior; they establish incentives to deter or encourage certain activities. Can we run a red light at an empty intersection? Of course, but we almost always choose not to because the anticipated punishment for doing so is sufficiently severe. In other cases, institutions are funnels for new, better, or faster information. This reduces so-called transactions costs, or the cost of doing business. The classic theory of the firm—why organizations form in the way they do—is based on this idea of information efficiencies: at some threshold of communications friction, it makes sense for unassociated parties to formally organize in order to limit the costs of transferring information.[26]

The money management business went through its first wave of institutionalization several decades ago. It was traditionally a local enterprise. Individuals and institutions alike, for the most part, entrusted their investments to bank trust departments and local financial advisors. As the industry matured, it changed quality, as increasingly large investment firms offered an array of products and services. The likes of Fidelity, Wellington, Vanguard, and Franklin Templeton developed modern business structures with a segregation of duties between those running the business and those running the portfolios. The process for buying and selling funds was professionalized. Technology was increasingly utilized to facilitate smooth transactions and provide information. Existing regulatory structures were updated and refined. And independent third-party information providers such as Morningstar and Lipper brought an unprecedented amount of insight into the industry. In other words, the traditional money management industry has established over the decades a dense network of social institutions that facilitate transparent and predictable outcomes.

One popular impression of the hedge fund industry is that it is heavily populated by undisciplined and perhaps even unethical traders.[27] For some, the industry appears to have a "wild west" quality, meaning that there are few constraints on conduct, thus devolving the possibilities for trust back toward the strictly interpersonal level. I offer a contrary view of this caricature, which is that this industry, like its older traditional fund industry sibling, has grown increasingly institutionalized. As a consequence, more robust forms of trust are now more possible.

Indeed, it's remarkable to see the somewhat parallel developments in the alternatives business in more recent years. Organizationally, the hedge fund industry has always been extraordinarily varied. Historically, much of the industry was filled with relatively small outfits, colloquially referred to as "two guys and a Bloomberg." That has changed rapidly as the industry's top firms are growing larger at a rapid pace.

For example, independent firms like Brevan Howard, Pine River, BlueCrest, and Citadel are now very large in terms of assets under management and offer an array of products. This can be one investment strategy with a few different permutations, or a true "platform" that can offer, just like mutual fund shops, a wide range of funds across many disparate strategies. In some of these product architectures, a fund's "style" is increasingly prevalent as product managers oversee a menu of tightly defined mandates.

A growing number of alternative firms are now publicly listed entities, such as Man Group, Fortress, and Och-Ziff. Other large financial institutions have made significant investments in alternative managers, either built internally or acquired. Goldman Sachs, JPMorgan, and Legg Mason are among those groups. Private equity titans like Carlyle Group, KKR, and Blackstone have made large inroads into the hedge fund space. Consolidation is rapidly taking hold in the alternatives industry, not only with hedge funds but with funds of funds as well. The maturation and consolidation of the alternatives business is bringing with it deeper forms of institutionalization. Now let's provide some further detail on this evolution.

ARCHITECTURES OF TRUST

Consider this simple but powerful fact: if Madoff had employed an independent outside group to verify the pricing of his various "funds" (or if his investors had insisted upon one), the scam could *never* have occurred. It would have been discovered the moment an objective auditor sought evidence for properly valuing the underlying securities. The same applies for any financial fraud in which the perpetrators cook their books.

A critical element of investment due diligence is the ability to independently verify the claims being made by our counterparties. Mutual funds, which are government-regulated vehicles defined by the 1940 Investment Company Act (thus often referred to as "40 Act" funds), have plenty of nominal transparency. Most notably, they're required to release full portfolios on a quarterly basis, so we can examine all of the underlying holdings. But having a full list of securities does not tell you much about how the fund manager chooses to take risk. We know what the building blocks are, but not necessarily how they are assembled. Having a large pile of bricks, wood, and other supplies in no way tells you how the house will be built or what it will ultimately look like.

Meanwhile, hedge funds have become surprisingly transparent. The press portrays them as secretive and stealthy, giving the impression that it is impossible to understand what they really do. But that's largely untrue, especially in recent years. As noted, until relatively recently the hedge fund industry lacked institutionalization. It was an immature cottage industry. No longer.

At this stage of the investment choice regime, investors can avail themselves of myriad resources to independently verify the makeup of a fund and how it works. Indeed, post-2008, the field of operational due diligence (ODD) has become one of the most important investment practices. ODD is the forensic analysis of an investment firm's "back office," meaning all of its functions with the exception of investing—trading, accounting, legal, technology, compensation, and so forth. Employing trained accountants and attorneys, higher-quality investors have long taken ODD seriously. But given the maelstrom of bad events surrounding the 2008 crisis, of which the Madoff revelation was the most prominent, now ODD is front of mind for most of the alternative investment industry. Here, lovers of checklists can rejoice! There are dozens of specific boxes to check.[28]

Much more than investment due diligence, ODD has correct answers. Do you have an independent third-party administrator strike the portfolio's net asset value (NAV)? The right answer is yes. Are your employees allowed to trade for personal gain securities in which the fund is also transacting? The right answer is no. Not every issue is completely black and white. In some instances, there are shades of gray. In others, there's not necessarily *one* right answer, but there are relatively well-accepted sets of best practices and an investment firm can choose to follow them or not.

Beyond the strictures of ODD, as alternative firms mature and mainstream, the scaffolding for a sturdier, more predictable environment, one increasingly disembodied from the charismatic leaders of these firms, is in place. Its pillars include:

Access. Before the industry went through this surge of institutionalization, it's true that many hedge fund managers were hard to access. That has changed significantly in recent years. Insofar as hedge funds remain structured as private partnerships, there will remain clearly specified regulations as to who is "qualified" to invest. That won't be changing anytime soon. However, as pension plans and endowments representing regular beneficiaries plow into alternative strategies, their staffs do have access. It's not an open door, mind you. People have jobs to do. By the same token, one can't just show up at Fidelity's office in Boston and insist on meeting the portfolio manager of the fund one is invested in. It doesn't work that way. But our ability now to interact with fund managers is unprecedented.

Transparency. For those who want to know what investments their fund managers are choosing, the availability of information is not only abundant; it's overwhelming. Information about a fund's risk profile, its underlying holdings, how it's generating profits and losses, and how it manages its operations can be acquired from the manager himself. Most funds of any significant size will also have regulatory requirements to report certain risk exposures (e.g., 13F filings). Plus, there are now firms like Measure-Risk, RiskMetrics, and other third-party data aggregators who can give further insight. If the manager isn't forthcoming, don't invest. If information was once available but no longer is, redeem.

Segregation. One of the major industry trends in recent years, especially after 2008, has been the growing interest in keeping one group's assets separate from others. Most of us typically invest in pooled vehicles in which our own assets are comingled with those of others. But when assets are comingled, our fate is partly determined by the choices of other investors, instead of the fund manager we've hired as the steward of our capital. Most pronounced for funds that trade in less liquid assets, redemptions by other investors can force the manager to make trades that might have harmful consequences for everyone. In 2008, many comingled funds were forced to either liquidate holdings at undesirable prices or put up restrictive liquidity gates on their investors. For those willing to take on the administrative burden of doing so, creating separate accounts can help solve this problem. Not surprisingly, new firms such as AlphaMetrix have stepped up with "turnkey" solutions for those seeking separate accounts.

Regulation. Finally, the alternatives business has become more regulated. Historically, hedge funds were largely unregulated investment pools. Given not only the industry's growing size but also the increased participation of workers' pensions in hedge funds, new laws such as the Dodd Frank Wall Street Reform and Consumer Protection Act of 2010 compelled hedge funds with at least $150 million in assets to register with the SEC. Other regulatory bodies such as the Commodity Futures Trading Commission (CFTC), the Financial Industry Regulatory Authority (FINRA), and state regulators have cast increasing scrutiny. All that said, the most noteworthy regulation of hedge fund structures has been in place for decades, namely, the anti-fraud provisions of the 1940 Investment Advisers Act. Even in cases where a hedge fund does not have to formally register with the SEC, which was mostly all of them until recently, they are not exempted from the laws against fraud.

Whether we think of the social institutions of trust in terms of constraints or in terms of information conduits, the alternatives industry has developed broadly and quickly. We now have many tools at our disposal to establish and grow trust. I would stress the importance of the richening information environment over the strengthening of the regulatory regime. Sunlight is often the best disinfectant—a principle that the Madoff debacle unfortunately proved too well. Yet if there is a silver lining to Madoff, it is the cultural shift that is well under way. Though difficult to quantify, it's clear that attitudes have changed. If there was once an amateurish quality to alternative managers, amateur hour is over.

Our problem isn't solved, however. Institutional constraints and efficiencies can be effective, and more institutionalization is better, all else being equal. But it doesn't cut to the deepest root of the issue: the incentives and motives of the individuals and groups we potentially partner with. Indeed, there will always be those who intend to engage in nefarious behavior. How to navigate that requires further exploration.

THE FOX'S INCENTIVE

Like Presidents Bush and Putin, we don't know what's in the hearts of our counterparts. As a result, we take steps to protect ourselves. In thinly institutionalized contexts, the burden falls heavily on the personal. We size up others on our own terms and hope that our gut is correct. In many cases, that works out fine, but as Madoff again demonstrates, the downside is massive. In more richly institutionalized settings, we have the additional benefit of established procedures, constraints, and norms. These certainly ratchet up our comfort level. But relying on a checklist remains incomplete.

Ultimately, the most critical piece of the puzzle in establishing trust is identifying a true alignment of incentives between investor and manager. The starting point here is simple: individuals are self-interested, and they respond to incentives accordingly. It's always been a central concern over whether a manager "eats his own cooking." Do they invest their own capital in the same vehicle I do? If so, then there's good reason to believe that they will make the best efforts to invest capably. A win for them is a win for me. More importantly, if I incur losses on my investment, they will too. Even here, there's no tidy algorithm to say how much of a personal investment is "enough" to spur alignment. I once advocated to invest in a fund manager who had more than $50 million of his own personal capital in the fund, and he still proceeded to act like a bonehead. I also invested alongside managers with relatively small sums at stake who acted with the utmost focus and integrity.

It is in scenarios where individual incentives are aligned that everyone is most likely to come out ahead. The problem is that a perfect alignment of incentives can never be achieved. The investor's food chain shown in figure 5.2 reveals why. The diagram shows the typical flow of assets, from end investor to fund manager. In some cases, fund investors will use an intermediary, whether it be a fund of funds, consultant, or financial advisor. In extreme cases, the investor will use a consultant to choose a fund of funds to choose fund managers who then choose securities.

The challenge is that everyone one step ahead of you on the food chain has an existential problem that you do not. For the investors, every party

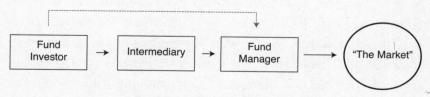

Figure 5.2   The Investor's Food Chain

in front of them on the chain is a piece of a puzzle, one element of a larger portfolio. As such, predictability is a paramount concern, so much so (as we discuss in chapter 7) that skill per se is defined by the ability to deliver consistent risk exposures. But the intermediaries and managers are ultimately concerned about their own well-being and their ability to survive. As we will see in coming pages, it is periods of crisis that exacerbate this mismatch. Thus, we are solving an optimization problem; they are solving an existential problem.

Resolving this dilemma is harder with foxes than it is with hedgehogs. Traditional managers aren't less intelligent, but they are more constrained. Within the confines of a mutual fund, there is relatively little investment or operational discretion. Not so with alternatives. Precisely because the goal of the alternative manager is to deliver positive returns without formal deference to a benchmark, they have substantial latitude during times of stress.

A focus on incentives provides insight into some of the less savory bits of the investment business, while at the same time providing some guidance for how to set and adjust our expectations for the conduct of our partners. In some cases, there is just base skullduggery. It's just bad (and/or stupid) guys doing bad things. For example, I recently noticed the example of the Simran Pre-Event Driven Activist Opportunity Fund.[29] In that case, the fund's portfolio manager was able to get a sizable investment from CalPERS, the largest US pension plan, only by lying about its total assets under management to meet a minimum threshold. How this fund passed such a prominent pension plan's due diligence effort is a little puzzling (the fund's absurd name should have been the first tip-off). I suppose that every now and then, bush leaguers make it to the pros only to be quickly revealed for what they truly are.

More serious transgressions have recently been revealed. In the past few years, US government officials have been engaged in a major sweep of firms engaged in insider trading. Several high-profile criminal actions have already occurred, and we won't be surprised to see more coming. In case after case, the theme is the same: managers taking inappropriate steps to acquire and then use material nonpublic information in order to profit. Unfortunately, the rogues' gallery includes numerous prominent investment houses, some of which have subsequently folded.[30] At Front-Point Partners, a Greenwich-based hedge fund complex that once managed billions of dollars, health care portfolio manager Joseph Skowron acquired inside information about the results of clinical drug trials that prompted him to sell his position in Human Genome Sciences, and thus avoid a $30 million loss.[31] At Diamondback, another multibillion-dollar Connecticut complex, Todd Newman was sentenced to four and a half years in prison for insider trading. As a specialist in technology stocks, Newman secretly paid for confidential, material information about two technology companies, Dell and Nvidia. Supposedly those insights allowed Newman's portfolio at Diamondback to earn an additional $72 million. Newman was in cahoots with Anthony Chiasson of Level Global, another prominent fund, who was also busted for illegally trading the same stocks. A federal court of appeals ruled that Chiasson and Newman could remain free on bail while their appeals were pending. Raj Rajaratnam, once an industry star at his $7 billion fund Galleon, was sentenced to eleven years in prison for securities fraud in stocks such as Clearwire, Akamai, and Intel.

None of these activities was the result of the "unregulated" nature of hedge funds. All of these individuals were charged with breaking laws that have been on the books for decades. These were already very wealthy individuals, earning in some cases tens of millions per year, who had no direct need for additional income. The question, then, is why.

The answer comes to back to incentives. According to Deputy US Attorney for the Southern District of New York Richard Zabel, "There's a crucible-like intensity of competition now that didn't exist [in decades past]. With hedge funds, there's a lot of capital, and they're competing ruthlessly. You have to be better every quarter or you're not going to exist. Add the tremendous incentive of great wealth, and it's not surprising that some people lack the moral fiber to resist that kind of pressure."[32]

Returning to the investor's food chain, there is indeed an incentive for some fund managers to gain an edge over others in circumstances where the line between being right and being too late is razor thin. Indeed, notice the pattern across these examples: they all occurred at funds where there was an incentive to find a *short-term* information advantage. These were all so-called data point investors, meaning that they were looking for the next marginal piece of information that would drive a stock price higher in the coming days and weeks.

Fortunately, many fund managers—both traditional and alternative—take longer-term views, and the marginal data point is not that relevant to them. What's more, even most traders engaged in a similar trading approach have stronger ethics. In fact, fraud in the hedge fund industry is perceived as much more prevalent than it actually is. It is largely a red herring. There are thousands of funds in operation. Yet only a handful, due to pronounced, perhaps perverse incentives combined with low moral fiber, cross the line.

BARBARIANS AND THEIR GATES

Finally, in the most difficult of instances to anticipate (let alone formally regulate), there are matters of judgment and ethics. To achieve trust, we make ourselves vulnerable to the actions of others on the expectation of a positive outcome, but, especially at times of heightened uncertainty, even formalized institutions and a clear set of expectations aren't always reliable guides.

Spike Lee's classic *Do the Right Thing* climaxes with a riot in the Brooklyn neighborhood surrounding Sal's pizza joint, a racial melting pot transformed into a crucible. In the film's most pointed and controversial moment, Sal's runner, Mookie, throws a trash can through the store's window. An infuriating decision for some viewers, a point of vindication for others, the question is in the title: Did he do the right thing? Of course, there's no right answer. Such is the case for all ethical quandaries that force us to grapple with our perhaps conflicting passions and interests.

So, too, with investing, where the trickiest issues are not resolved by reference to formal laws or procedures or by a tidy operational due diligence process. Such was the case with the hedge fund industry through the crisis of 2008, during which hundreds of managers told their investors that they couldn't have their money back.

By way of background, there is a long list of standard features that lawyers put into the documents that define the nature and workings of a private partnership, which is the formal structure of what is colloquially known as a hedge fund. An important issue relates to the liquidity of the fund structure itself. From the investor's point of view: When and how can I get my money back? From the fund manager's point of view: When and how do I have to redeem my investors' capital? Standard practice is to assign a periodicity to the available liquidity (e.g., monthly, quarterly, annually) as well as a notice period prior to that point at which the manager was obligated to return the funds (e.g., thirty days, forty-five days). For example, typical hedge fund liquidity would offer quarterly redemption rights, meaning investors could redeem four times per year. And the investors would have to provide forty-five days' advance notice to the manager. Thus, if you want your money back at the end of the second quarter (June 30), you need to send the hedge fund a letter indicating as much by April 15.

At the same time, standard practice was to stipulate that under certain circumstances, a fund manager could restrict liquidity—partially or entirely. The conditions for doing so could be made very specific or, as was common, quite general. Typical liquidity restriction language could refer to "adverse market conditions" that made a timely fulfillment of investor redemption requests hard to meet. Vague by design, this language allowed fund managers to request that their board of directors (the managers could not do it directly themselves in the legal context of these private partnerships) temporarily suspend liquidity. These were the so-called gates. Shut them, and no one can get out.

The years leading up to the crisis were heady times. As assets flowed into hedge funds at a breakneck speed, many investors and managers took on increasing levels of risk, including larger doses of leverage and greater comfort with owning less liquid assets. By the time 2008 came around, the industry was more vulnerable than it had been previously. The fall of Bear Stearns in March 2008 was the first shot across the bow by the looming crisis. A handful of funds, mostly all trading mortgage credit strategies, sustained major losses. Some were forced to shut down, while a limited number chose to suspend redemptions.

That episode was a prelude to the last few months of 2008, which were a jaw-dropping calamity. The global financial system approached, and barely avoided, the precipice of failure. The declaration of bankruptcy by Lehman Brothers froze client assets and triggered a bolt for liquidity. As Lehman was one of the hedge fund industry's main counterparties, the inability of clients to transact with them, especially in over-the-counter securities such as credit derivatives, quickly brought markets to a standstill. It was an incredibly anxious time, with many of the world's most sophisticated investors scrambling to save their business in a torrent that no one had ever experienced before.

Markets rely on the good-faith ability to transact when needed. As the crisis deepened daily, that ability shriveled. Everyone was watching everyone else to see what they'd do next. Up and down the food chain, investors looked to raise cash. As panic selling washed across the market, many hedge fund managers decided to gate their investors. For example, in an early December 2008 SEC filing, the Fortress Investment Group wrote that "the boards of directors and general partner of the applicable feeder funds have evaluated the most appropriate course of action to take in response to the requested redemptions in light of applicable requirements and current market conditions, and have acted unanimously to temporarily suspend pending redemptions from the fund."[33] Those who gated were among the industry's most prominent managers, including DE Shaw, Farallon, Tudor, Polygon, and Blue Bay.[34] The gating was most pronounced among those who traded credit securities—it's hard to find a prominent player in that space who did not suspend liquidity.

For some funds, there was little choice—those who had accounts with Lehman Brothers, for example. But for many there was a choice. They could redeem their investors' capital as requested, or not. The logic for gating was that being a forced seller in sharply depressed markets would crystallize losses. What's more, this forced selling would perpetuate the vicious cycle taking place in the market. From the managers' point of view, that was bad investing, and a disservice to the client. A second piece to the logic is that not all investors sought to redeem, meaning that there were two distinct constituents inside the partnership, and the fund manager would have to choose one set of interests over the other.

Did the managers who gated do the right thing? There's no correct answer. As a legal matter, they had every right to operate within the provisions of their offering documents. Of course, the First Amendment protects my right to say just about anything I please, but there are many things that I could say that would be highly imprudent. Thus, as an ethical matter the question remains. On the one hand, managers who gated showed a certain level of prudence in stabilizing their operations. In fact, in the spirit of "no good deed goes unpunished," there were numerous funds that chose not to gate on the argument that their portfolios remained liquid (these were mostly equity funds and some global macro funds) and that they had a fiduciary obligation to meet their clients' requests. Unsurprisingly, they served as ATMs to investors desperate to raise cash. Those who gated saved both their businesses and the long-term value of their clients' portfolios. Indeed, several months later, many deeply discounted assets recovered a large portion of their value.

Conversely, many industry critics argued that hedge funds took advantage of the circumstances, making a bad situation worse. From an insider's perspective, I can say that a number of managers prioritized their own interests over those of their clients. They *could* have redeemed their investors, at least partially, but they chose not to. Recall from our investor's food chain that those farther down the line are solving an existential problem distinct from yours, and many abided by that logic. In sum, the institutionalization of the fund industry has had many salutary effects. Ultimately, however, there must be an alignment of interests among counterparties to ensure win-win outcomes. In some cases, despite the best of intentions, that is unattainable.

TRUST IS HAVING CONFIDENCE that others will treat you as you hope they will. That source of hope stems from the richness of the connections that bind us together. Many have observed, however, that our ties have loosened of late. Per social scientist Robert Putnam, "During the first two-thirds of the [twentieth] century, Americans took a more and more active role in the social and political life of their communities—in churches and union halls, in bowling alleys and clubrooms, around committee tables and card tables and dinner tables . . . then, mysteriously and more or less simultaneously, we began to do all those things less often."[35]

As Putnam famously wrote, we are increasingly "bowling alone." A provocative 2012 essay by Ron Fournier and Sophie Quinton entitled "In Nothing We Trust" sets out more recent data that our faith in schools, government, and churches is on the decline. Most recently, George Packer hammers the point home in *The Unwinding* that our social institutions are fraying.[36] The richness of civil society is under assault. This is highly consequential for those seeking to achieve acceptable outcomes from the experts we choose to make important decisions for us.

Broadly speaking, the trust deficit has certainly widened with our financial institutions. This is particularly the case for banks, which have become some of the weakest strands in our social fabric, the result of decades of degradation. Their actions in the run-up to the crisis and its aftermath have made matters worse. For example, contrary to the conventional wisdom that it was massive amounts of leverage that sank the banks in 2008, William Cohan argues that the crisis stemmed from a fundamentally changed set of incentives among financial executives. After all, the most basic tenet of causal logic is that you can't explain change with a constant, and evidence suggests leverage ratios actually did not climb considerably from previous decades into the mid-2000s.[37] They had been elevated for many years.

What did change were incentives. Firms such as Goldman Sachs had long been private partnerships, in which senior partners were forced to make substantial capital commitments to their ventures. This served as a welcome check on excessive risk taking given how much money senior management had on the line. As these firms became publicly listed, the governors on risk were reduced and in some cases eliminated. The early 2000s saw a number of questionable practices, especially in structuring debt securities for unwitting customers.[38] JPMorgan's lack of oversight in the recent "London Whale" controversy and the ongoing LIBOR scandal, which will arguably turn out to be the largest price-fixing scheme in history, will aggravate matters further.

It's easier to generalize about banks than to do so about money managers. Still, as we can see with foxlike investors who maintain the legitimate ability to change course abruptly, achieving trust goes beyond having the right policies and procedures in place. To be sure, buttressing certain institutions can help considerably. Recall that the Madoff affair would never have happened in the presence of an independent group charged with verifying the portfolio's value. But beyond that, trust is a dynamic concept, and maintaining it requires us to adapt to changing, uncertain conditions.

THE DEVIL(S) YOU KNOW

If I'd had more time, I'd have written a shorter letter.

—Mark Twain

CARTOGRAPHERS DON'T MAKE LIFE-SIZE MAPS FOR A REASON. LIKE-wise, inquisitive fund investors don't transcribe every detail of what a manager does. There's a difference between being comprehensive and providing perspective. The goal of manager due diligence is to understand the relevant features of an investment. We're aiming to set expectations and then adapt those expectations in a dynamic market context.

This isn't easy. Portfolio managers and those who research them tend to get mired in endless detail, to lose the proverbial forest for the trees. The challenge is to transform the deluge of data into useful information, to separate signal from noise. Or according to Einstein's first law of work: "Out of clutter, find simplicity."

Because we are loss averse, what we want to know is: What can go wrong? And what are the consequences if it does? In the world of complex investments, it is hard to simplify—to get at the core of what could go wrong. Try as we might, we have limited intellectual capacity for processing numerous variables and the shifting causal relationships among them. Here we see the value of placing method over content. We need an approach that can abstract from the endless detail of modern markets and get at what really matters.

This chapter delivers a framework to efficiently build expectations across the foundational investment risks that underlie every portfolio. It features five dimensions: *concentration, directionality, leverage, illiquidity,* and *complexity.* This simplifying, common vocabulary allows us to think more clearly about what can go wrong; virtually any investment due diligence effort can be structured around these five dimensions.

THE MOST INTERESTING MAN(AGER) IN THE WORLD

I love those Dos Equis beer ads about "the Most Interesting Man in the World." That suave, handsome gentleman is gifted and privileged beyond compare. Maybe somewhere out there is also the Most Interesting Man (or Woman) in Fund Management. This person wouldn't necessarily fly to Colombia for morning coffee, have inside jokes with complete strangers, or ace a Rorschach test, but he or she would be consistently smarter than the thousands of other savvy portfolio managers analyzing the same markets all day, every day.

Unfortunately, that's unlikely, despite the countless people claiming to know the trajectory of a stock, bond, commodity, or currency better than the next guy. On a more regal plane, visions of guys like Jim Simons of Renaissance, Paul Singer of Elliot Associates, Seth Klarman of Baupost, or Ray Dalio of Bridgewater might come to mind, which is reasonable. Those gentlemen and a few others like them have built powerful, outstanding investment companies and have served their clients well. Perhaps they can even ace a Rorschach test.

As a practical matter, however, it's nearly impossible to sustain a statistically significant edge over others at this stage in the evolution of data-soaked global markets. Yet the world of finance continues its intense quest for an informational advantage, no matter how slim, and this can prompt unethical behavior, as we've seen with hedge funds like SAC, Galleon, FrontPoint, Diamondback, and Level. Superior results, when we see them, are more likely to stem from a differentiated (and in many cases, more extreme) risk profile than any insider edge.

We generate return by taking risk. We outperform by taking risks that are different in size or scope from others. In investment due diligence, there are five risk dimensions worth investigation:

✓ Concentration: How many bets are you making? How big are those bets?

✓ Directionality: Are you long, short, or neutral to your chosen market?

✓ Leverage: Will you reach your objective based on the inherent return of your underlying securities or do you need borrowed capital to do so? To what extent is the portfolio vulnerable to the demands of its creditors?

✓ Illiquidity: How easily and cheaply can you buy securities? How deep is your market? Is the manager's ability to exit a bad investment impaired? Is the manager capable of satisfying redemptions from the fund?

✓ Complexity: How many return drivers are embedded in your investment program? How many ways can things go wrong?

Here's the rub: Each of these five factors is a source of *both* outperformance and blowup risk. Note that the distinction between mutual fund and hedge fund is irrelevant in this discussion. This is a singular framework to think about underlying investment risk, regardless of the package it comes in. So let's walk through the five dimensions of the prism and explore their implications for manager due diligence, keeping in mind that our goal here is not to over-fit everything we see to these factors, just like the cartographer is typically not looking to use a bigger piece of paper to make a better map. The goal is to understand more with less.

THE RISK PRISM

Each of the five risk dimensions varies in magnitude (figure 6.1). The idea is basic: the farther out investors are on any one axis, the more of that risk they are undertaking; the closer they are to the center, the smaller the risk and the more likely they are to make or lose nothing. (To be very clear, that's in terms of absolute returns, not returns relative to a benchmark.) As levels of risk and return are positively correlated, the farther out one moves on each or all of the dimensions, the more likely it is that the fund will endure massive losses—or generate enormous, peer-beating, and career-making returns.

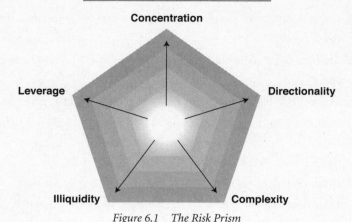

Figure 6.1   *The Risk Prism*

Concentration

The portfolio feature most emblematic of the money industry's knack for salesmanship and storytelling is concentration, or the number and size of the "bets" in one's portfolio. Generally, in due diligence, we often spend more time on a manager's favorite ideas or picks that exemplify his process than on anything else.

There are no formal thresholds for what constitutes a big bet; it's context dependent. Like pornography, it's hard to define, but you know it when you see it. For an equity fund, it might be a 15 percent position in Apple, while for a bond fund it might be a 9 percent position in the debt of some packaging company. And funds vary in their tolerance for big positions. While you occasionally see a fund consisting of mostly chunky positions, it is more common to see a portfolio with a handful of bigger positions and then a long "tail" of smaller, less impactful positions.

To see a stark difference in concentration, contrast a quantitative equity fund and an activist equity fund. Most investments with a quantitatively driven process will look for fine-grained inefficiencies over large data sets. Whether those models focus on earnings momentum, balance sheet quality, free cash flow, low valuations, or some other factors, these funds tend to hold hundreds of positions with the goal of iteratively scalping small inefficiencies, accumulating meaningful amounts of alpha in the process. These firms grow out of both the traditional (e.g., Chicago Equity

Partners, First Quadrant, Numeric, DFA, InTech, and BGI) and alternatives industries (e.g., AQR, PDT, Two Sigma, and Renaissance). These funds all have diversified portfolios.

Activist funds are exactly the opposite. These are the big swingers, fund managers who show up on CNBC and garner newspaper headlines by buying huge positions in companies and often ruffling feathers with company management, with whom they typically disagree about how the company should be run. They see enormous untapped value in the company's stock but believe that in order to unlock it, it's necessary to make big changes to the company, often over the complaints of incumbent management. Magnate Carl Icahn has epitomized the activist ethos for years, taking meaningful stakes in dozens of companies, including Time Warner, Motorola, Lear, Biogen, and Herbalife. Other examples would be Eddie Lampert of ESL Investments, Dan Loeb of Third Point, Bill Ackman of Pershing Square, Warren Lichtenstein of Steel Partners, Bruce Berkowitz of Fairholme, David Einhorn of Greenlight, and Chris Hohn of TCI.

These individuals are among the most articulate and charismatic money managers on the planet. It is easy to be swayed by their convictions, not only because they are glib, but also because they are smart and conduct detailed and sophisticated financial analyses. They'll often produce hundreds of pages of research justifying their largest positions.

As compelling as the stories and data are, however, let's not lose sight of two points. First, despite the copious and compelling research, all of these investors are sometimes wrong, with large economic consequences for their investors.[1] Second, in every instance, there are other highly informed individuals who believe exactly the opposite of these activists.

Take the 2010 row over St. Joe, a Florida land development company. Publicly and stridently, two of the fund industry's best known stars took diametrically opposed positions. Bruce Berkowitz, whom Morningstar named its fund manager of the decade, was long the company's stock, while David Einhorn of the prestigious Greenlight Capital was short it.[2] Einhorn publicly argued that St. Joe's undeveloped land parcels were worth far less than the company believed, and suggested that the company was knowingly misstating the land values—a serious allegation. Berkowitz disagreed, believing company management to be trustworthy and the stock significantly undervalued. In these sorts of cases, with highly qualified voices on either side of the argument, you cannot know who will end up being correct.[3] (As of mid-2013, the company was still in business, but it's stock was about 40 percent below its 2010 peak when the disagreement surfaced, and 80 percent below its all-time high in 2005.)

Concentration matters because it raises the stakes for being right or wrong. Whether or not a hyperdiversified quant fund is correct on any individual pick is not that relevant; most positions are a very small percentage of the portfolio, so whether they double or halve is barely consequential. But whether Einhorn or Berkowitz is ultimately correct about St. Joe is very meaningful to anyone invested with Greenlight or Fairholme. The simple math for any concentrated position makes that clear: A 20 percent position that tanks 50 percent not only lops off 10 percentage points of return that's hard to recover; it also can destabilize an entire investment firm owing to angry investor calls, bad press, and (most critically) asset outflows. One or two bad bets can sink an entire fund. Despite being the largest hedge fund launch in European history in 2006, Jon Wood's SRM lost nearly all its assets and investor support after a small number of massive bets in the likes of Northern Rock and Countrywide Financial went awry in 2007 and 2008.

Big bets are the stuff of headlines, the most sensationalistic of the five risk dimensions. Who is buying what is the focus of virtually all investment newsletters and blogs. It would be rare for a portfolio manager to brag about how much leverage he is employing or how complex his strategy is, but not at all odd to tout his favorite positions. Popular CNBC programs like *Fast Money* and *Mad Money* are all about picking the right stock and then betting big.

Concentration in a fund's top positions is plain to see, but equally big, less transparent bets are often not. In four of the five risk dimensions (complexity being the exception), there are *veiled risks* that require extra diligence and ingenuity to uncover. In the case of concentration, there are underlying bets that are less immediately visible than parking 20 percent of your fund's assets in the stock of Pfizer or Verizon. A fund may limit its position sizes but at the same time take large bets on specific risk factors. A fund may have hundreds of positions, none individually large, but still be taking just one or two big bets—in other words, engaging in *false diversification*. How? Think of it this way. We may have hundreds of underlying positions, but if the performance of most of those positions is itself driven by the same underlying risk, then false diversification is afoot.

Take so-called style bets, the kind that stem from Morningstar's Style Box. If we look inside each of the nine equity style boxes, we see that the average fund is highly diversified in terms of the number of holdings, but at the same time highly correlated to the relevant index (e.g., large-cap value to the Russell 1000 Value Index). To some extent, funds will deliver the underlying "beta" of their targeted market segment.

Without using too much technical language, let's touch base quickly on the concept of beta, the most important technical concept in investing. Beta measures the stock's sensitivity to aggregate market movements, the amount that any single security or an entire portfolio is expected to move as the market moves. For instance, if a particular stock (or portfolio) has a beta of 1.0, then it is expected to move in perfect synchronicity with the market. A stock (or portfolio) with a beta of 2.0 is expected to move exactly twice as much as the market does. In that case, if the market rose 3 percent, you should expect that stock to gain 6 percent, as it's twice as sensitive to aggregate market movements. Conversely, a stock (or portfolio) with a beta of 0.5 should move up only 1.5 percent in that context.

Buying a diversified mid-cap growth fund will largely deliver mid-cap growth beta. There might very well be stock-picking "alpha," but the largest percentage of the total return stream is the beta of the underlying market.[4] The details of the underlying stock positions, how they're picked, what worked and what didn't, are less relevant than the fund's beta profile. The analysis of hedge funds, which don't abide by a specific benchmark, is driven by the exact same logic. Although absolute return vehicles, or hedge funds, are sometimes referred to as "skill-based" investments, their returns are driven, to some extent, by underlying beta exposure. For instance, in the most populated hedge fund strategy, long/short equity, *all* those vehicles have an underlying exposure to the equity markets in which they invest. What determines the size of that bet connects us with the next category in our risk prism.

Directionality

Of the risk prism's five dimensions, directionality is probably the easiest to wrap one's brain around. Is a fund's portfolio long or short its target market, or something in between?

In the popular nomenclature, when you're long, you're a bull; when you're short, you're a bear. With traditional investments, investors are exclusively long, meaning that they own a fund consisting of stocks or bonds (or both) and hope that those securities appreciate in value. Traditional funds do not short securities, nor do they hold cash balances in excess of small amounts needed for smooth trading. Historically, nearly all mutual funds were long-only investments, although that's changing. ETFs have traditionally been long-only as well, but in recent years, fund companies have offered a wide array of choices that can be partly or fully short targeted markets. Figure 6.2 sets out some basic numbers for how to think about long positions and short positions in a portfolio context.

In the simplest illustration, take a fund with a $100 investment. The standard long-only investment would then invest that same amount in the market: no more, no less, save for a minor cash position to minimize trading friction. Thus, to use the nomenclature, the fund is 100 percent long ($100 \div 100$), 0 percent short, thus 100 percent "net" long ($100 - 0 = 100$).

Alternative vehicles are not constrained that way. Foxlike investors can be flexible in how they position their portfolios depending on their bottom-up view on individual securities or top-down view on the market. A common strategy among conservative hedged equity funds would be to invest most but not all of their capital (leaving some "dry powder") and

	Typical Mutual Fund	Typical Hedged Equity Fund	Typical Market Neutral Fund	Typical Activist Fund	Typical Short-Only Equity Fund
Long Exposure	100	90	200	75	0
Short Exposure	0	50	200	0	60
Net Exposure	100	40	0	75	−60

Figure 6.2   Long and Short Styles of Investing

then build a book of short positions somewhat smaller than the long book, making for a fund with a "long bias." With a hypothetical $100 investment, the fund manager would buy $90 worth of stocks and short $50 worth of stocks. Thus, the fund is 90 percent long (90 ÷ 100), 50 percent short (50 ÷ 100), and 40 percent net long (90 − 50 = 40). This basic arithmetic works with any inputs.

The classic market neutral fund, in order to achieve its eponymous objective, builds two equally sized long and short books. The net effect is that the fund has from limited to no market exposure. The activist funds that grab headlines with their bold stances tend not to short. They usually focus on companies they believe to be deeply undervalued. In order to mitigate risk, they'll hold larger cash stakes. There are also "short-only" funds that are exclusively bearish on individual securities or the market overall. Because of the volatility and structural challenges involved with shorting, these funds also tend to hold a fair bit of cash.

The directionality of an investment is on a dial, not a switch. Managers can run from completely long to completely short and every notch in between. This perspective helps clarify a few key points. While the media may draw bright lines between hedge funds and mutual funds, reality is grayer. One of the great myths of alternative investments is that they are idiosyncratic, uncorrelated investments; that hedge fund investing should isolate the skill of the portfolio manager and downplay the impact of the market's direction. But in fact, all alternative vehicles are directionally positioned to some extent. They take directional bets on stocks, bonds, commodities, or some other asset class. True market neutrality is almost impossible to achieve.

Rather than refer to all alternatives as "hedged," we should regard the choice set as highly varied. Distressed debt is a classic alternative strategy that is primarily long only, or at least very long biased. When a company does poorly or goes bankrupt, its balance sheet is likely restructured, creating new debt and equity issues that could be deeply undervalued if the firm navigates the restructuring process skillfully. Some of the most prominent blue-chip hedge funds, such as Appaloosa, Redwood, Silver Point, Canyon, and Oaktree, engage in this type of strategy. While the investments these firms make are idiosyncratic, they are also highly directional, and their returns can have a strong relationship to certain equity and debt markets. Likewise, some of the classic activist funds, such as Icahn, TCI, and Steel Partners, are accessible only through a private limited partnership (in other words, a hedge fund vehicle), yet are highly directional. While their specific holdings might have idiosyncratic qualities, each holding plus the portfolio overall—to the extent that it is directional—means that the returns it generates will have a healthy amount of beta.

That's even more true for emerging markets hedge funds. These alternatives might hedge some, but technically, it's difficult to short in these markets. Once upon a time I was responsible for Asian investments for a large investment firm. We only invested in hedge fund structures on behalf of our clients. Because India was one of the markets of interest to us, I surveyed the available choices. There weren't many, since India remains an immature market in terms of foreign access, so I spent considerable time researching largely unknown names like Monsoon, Orange, Horizon, and Voyager, all based in Mumbai. Each of these vehicles was effectively long only but charged hedge fund fees and forced investors to lock up their capital for extended periods. Meanwhile, there were plenty of mutual funds that offered similar exposure for a fraction of the fees and daily liquidity—Matthews and Templeton among them. Across the board, the returns to all of these Indian funds, like emerging markets funds more generally, are strongly infused by beta to those markets, regardless of the legal structure in which the fund is delivered.

As with concentration, the extent of directionality can also be veiled. With more complex strategies that trade derivatives or employ sophisticated "relative value" techniques, determining how long or short a fund is can be a challenge. Even simple, nominal exposures like those set out in figure 6.2 can get more complicated. In 2007, for example, there were some peculiar crosscurrents in global markets. As mentioned in chapter 3, the global banking industry had lurched into the early stage of the crisis that peaked the following year, while China and other emerging markets were delivering astounding growth rates and equity market performance. Global energy and commodity stocks in particular benefited. Not unlike investors who saw the dislocation between small-value and large-growth stocks earlier in the decade, a number of cunning fund managers had the insight and flexibility to attack this opportunity.

From the perspective of understanding directional risk, these funds appeared to be running at a low net exposure. To give a caricature, a fund could run identically sized long commodities and short financials positions and appear to be positioned as market neutral, suggesting that the fund was largely immune to swings in the market. That was hardly the case here: if Chinese demand for oil and copper began to slow while the US and EU authorities ameliorated their banking issues, a fund positioned for the opposite would get clobbered. In fact, 2007 did see financials do poorly and energy issues do well, meaning that, on the surface, some funds looked to be genius stock pickers when in fact they were not. Instead, they had made two savvy but distinct market calls. This disconnect between different parts of the same portfolio is sometimes referred to as "basis risk." It can apply not only to sectors, but also to geography, market capitalization, and other factors. It sometimes makes the evaluation of investment choices especially tricky.

Leverage

Financial leverage makes the size of your investment bigger. It magnifies the sensitivity of an investment to market events, creating higher highs and lower lows. Levered investments are more volatile. The most common form of leverage is borrowed money. The mechanics of these arrangements vary, but the end result is generally the same. The size of a portfolio can be increased by borrowing money while maintaining the same initial investment, or equity. To use a simple example, an investor may have $100 of equity and then borrow an additional $50. This investor can then purchase $150 of securities. In this situation, the equity in this portfolio will have a magnified sensitivity to the performance of the underlying investments.

Let's tweak the previous table to illustrate the math on leverage. See that in figure 6.3 the bottom row has been changed from "net exposure" (directionality) to "gross exposure" (leverage). Now the arithmetic is to add the long and short exposures to arrive at total exposures. The typical mutual fund is not levered. If I invest $100, I receive $100 of market exposure. In a typical conservative hedged equity fund, the manager may run an under-levered long portfolio (investing only $90 of the available $100)

	Typical Mutual Fund	Typical Hedged Equity Fund	Typical Market Neutral Fund	Typical Activist Fund	Typical Short-Only Equity Fund
Long Exposure	100	90	200	75	0
Short Exposure	0	50	200	0	60
Gross Exposure	100	140	400	75	60

Figure 6.3   Levered Styles of Investing

and also short $50. In sum, the fund's total gross exposure is $140. In other words, the fund is levered 1.4 times.

With our original example of having $100 in equity and then borrowing an additional $50, let's suppose that the underlying investments increase 10 percent over the course of the next year. If this portfolio did not use any leverage, its value would increase in line with the value of the underlying investments. However, by using leverage, the equity of the portfolio will increase by 15 percent minus the cost of borrowing the additional $50.

Using leverage is all well and good provided that your bets are paying off. If not, leverage will magnify your losses. That's why it's risky. Using our example, see what happens if the portfolio's underlying assets decrease 10 percent rather than increase 10 percent. If the portfolio is unlevered, the equity will decrease 10 percent, in line with the underlying assets. However, if the portfolio is levered, the equity will decrease by 15 percent as well as suffer the cost of financing the additional $50.

Leverage entails taking on a liability from a creditor and becoming a debtor. Of course, this is not a risk-free proposition; creditors have rights, and they take measures to protect their risks. Generally, as a levered portfolio suffers losses, debtors are required to post more collateral, known as a margin call. If the debtor is not able to satisfy this demand, creditors have the right to seize the underlying assets or take other measures to protect themselves. This limits the size of the loss that a levered fund can withstand without the creditors' stepping in.

Leverage increases the cost of being wrong. It increases your vulnerability to unforeseen market events as well as the goodwill of your creditors. What types of securities are being levered is central to the story. The less inherently volatile a security is, the more amenable it is to applying leverage (and the more likely it is that a bank will lend against it).

Take the extreme example of US Treasuries versus frontier market equities. The monthly price volatilities of the two asset classes are very different. High-quality government bonds have limited volatility, while the stocks from countries like Bangladesh, Nigeria, and Peru are extremely volatile. Purchasing those bonds with leverage is not particularly dangerous, but buying the stocks would be. The math is simple. If we put down, say, 20 percent to purchase exposure to the MSCI Frontier Markets index, we would effectively have a 5x levered position. Our small equity investment would be supporting a large amount of assets. Just a short bout of extremely bad returns in frontier markets would wipe out our investment entirely. And even before we got to that point, we would surely have already received margin calls from our lender.

Traditional strategies are unlevered, while many alternative strategies tend to use some to achieve their desired return targets (although some use none). For instance, convertible bond arbitrage is a classic alternative strategy that aims to extract an inefficiently priced call option that's embedded in the convertible security. That is done by buying the convertible bond and then shorting the equity that the bond is convertible into. When executed properly, this effectively hedges away any exposure to the equity and isolates the value of the potentially mispriced option. Because the equity volatility is hedged, the strategy is amenable to several turns of leverage, depending on the specifics of the securities and the temperament of the portfolio managers. Another strategy, fixed income arbitrage, tends to use even greater amounts of leverage insofar as it tends to focus on scalping small inefficiencies among fixed income securities. On the one hand, the returns of convertible and fixed income arbitrage would be very modest if leverage were not employed. On the other, the greater the use of leverage, all else being equal, the greater the chance of trouble. Thus, the use of leverage for these strategies becomes a balancing act between the two extremes.

Liquidity

Liquidity is the ability to easily purchase or sell a security. For securities, especially the stocks of most big companies such as Apple, General Electric, and Caterpillar, liquidity generally is not an issue. There are readily available buyers and sellers near, or at, the current market price, transactions costs are low, settlement is quick, and once existing orders are filled, new ones return to the market. Yet this is not the case for many other securities.

Think about selling your home. Unlike when selling a publicly traded stock, there are likely no readily available buyers, there is little in the way of market pricing besides comparable transactions, any interested buyer will have to start his or her due diligence from scratch, transactions costs are high, the time to settlement is lengthy, and there are many contingencies in the process. We all know of homes that sold only after a seemingly endless string of potential buyers, in many cases years after the sellers intended to sell them.

The same concept applies to certain financial assets. Modern finance has created a slew of securities that have some or all of the following properties: complexity, small size, limited or no public disclosure of information, limited trading and price discovery, limited broker/sponsor support, and complex settlement. The more of these characteristics an investment has, the more illiquid it probably is. As investors painfully realized in 2008–2009, the market for many of the more exotic products that had been created—such as collateralized debt obligations, asset-backed commercial paper, and auction-rate securities—was extremely limited. Many of these securities were idiosyncratic structures that were small to begin with. Trading relied on the broker/dealer network of banks that transacted in these types of products. Holders of these securities quickly realized that only a limited number of buyers fully understood them and that the dealer community could quickly stop committing capital to facilitate trading.

As we evaluate fund managers, we need to ask ourselves: Is this portfolio sufficiently liquid that the manager has the flexibility to transact without creating undue market frictions? Can the manager trade relatively freely? With listed equities, liquidity can be more easily assessed, as there is readily available information on trading volume, bid/ask spreads, and market depth. But as a fund dips further into small and especially micro-cap stocks, liquidity issues will increasingly rear their heads. Outside of equities, liquidity can quickly become a major problem. With debt and other securities that rely on dealer markets to provide pricing and bridge counterparties, we don't have the luxury of the information that formal exchanges provide.

Ultimately, liquidity is the ability to change your mind. A fund manager who sees a great bargain in the distressed debt of some energy or consumer company but then reruns the numbers and realizes they were wrong is unlikely to be able to sell that debt even if he wants to, except perhaps at a loss. If that fund's underlying investors want their money back and the manager is compelled to redeem them, he ends up as a "forced seller." Without liquidity, there is little flexibility.

An old saw about liquidity is that you can have as much of it as you want—until you really need it. In other words, liquidity can be illusory. By definition, liquidity is a social concept—the only one of the five that meets this definition. The other four are existential features of the fund. They would exist, without modification, even if it were the only fund in existence. Liquidity is tricky to plan for since it sometimes relies on quirks that are easy to miss. One of these quirks is the "crowdedness" of any particular trade. In one notorious example, the German auto company Volkswagen briefly became the largest company in the world by market capitalization because a group of European and US fund managers were forced to rapidly buy back their short positions in the stock after it was revealed that rival Porsche was massively accumulating Volkswagen stock. Prominent investors all making the same bet were caught by surprise and were unable to exit the trade before they lost billions of dollars.[5]

Finally, one other major, often hidden problem is afoot. In addition to the potential illiquidity of a fund's underlying investments, investors must be wary of a potential mismatch of the fund's assets (market investments) and liabilities (capital from investors). This is the risk that a manager cannot return capital to investors when they want it back. Liquidity is a social phenomenon, yet the motivations of others are often inscrutable. As such, we must assess whether the liquidity terms of an investment make sense relative to the liquidity of the underlying instruments. There's a reason that mutual funds with daily liquidity only truck in easy-to-trade securities, mostly stocks and bonds. With illiquid positions in areas like distressed debt, bank loans, and private placements, it's appropriate to ask investors to lock up their money for long periods of time.

The crisis of 2008 painfully demonstrated how badly asset-liability mismatches can hurt investors and managers alike. Indeed, it was greatly exacerbated by them. Effectively screaming "fire" in a crowded movie theater, investors who immediately demanded their capital back in the summer and fall of 2008 triggered a rush to the exits, creating a vicious cycle. Some well-meaning fund managers needed to restrict liquidity as a result. At the same time, other, less ethical fund managers took the opportunity to gate investors when it was not necessary. In 2013 there are still some fund managers who have not returned capital to investors.

Complexity

The fifth and final dimension to the risk prism is complexity. This dimension ties to our distinction between foxes and hedgehogs. When we choose experts, we can opt for those with constrained capabilities or those with a more flexible approach. The more comfortable we are making our own asset allocation and market timing decisions, the more we will rely on hedgehogs. The more we are overwhelmed by what to do, the more we will rely on foxes.

We've already seen in the four other dimensions of the risk prism that money managers can extend themselves in ways that amplify the rewards and costs of being right or wrong. With this notion of complexity, we can capture other dimensions of choice: specifically, the wherewithal and ability to adapt to changing circumstances.

Modern finance has a fetish for complexity.[6] The global banking system has embraced several extreme forms, not least of which was the frantic structuring of illiquid credit instruments leading up to the 2007–2008 crisis. It's not clear in retrospect whether the buyers of these credits fully appreciated the risks they were taking, nor if the investors who gorged themselves on these structures did. Certainly it seems that some of the major banks have not learned their lesson, if JPMorgan's 2012 "London Whale" episode is any indication. The bank lost at least $6 billion due to trades structured and advocated by one of its main traders, Bruno Iksil.

According to a 2013 US Senate report, Iksil's complex, derivative-heavy credit bets were vetted by JPMorgan's senior risk and investment officers, including the head of the Chief Investment Office, Ina Drew. Iksil delivered a presentation to his colleagues, advocating support for his making "the trades that make sense." But according to an investigation by the US Senate, the detailed explanation of the sensible trades was so complex and used so much jargon that "even the relevant actors and regulators could not understand." In fact, Ina Drew "told the Subcommittee that the presentation was unclear, and she could not explain exactly what it meant."[7] JPMorgan lost billions on a series of transactions that apparently even some insiders couldn't understand.

There are several specific forms of complexity we must consider when choosing investment experts. I'll briefly discuss three:

✓ Multiple moving pieces
✓ Allocation
✓ Innovation

Moving pieces. In many instances, portfolio managers will take bets that have a number of moving pieces—rather than being simply long or short a particular security. I recall that prior to the 2008 crash, a number of hedge fund managers took great interest in toll road companies due to their steady cash flow and "utility-like" quality. A favorite name was Autostrade, an Italian firm that collected tolls and ran concession stands on national highways. While the thesis was straightforward, the stock had more volatility than one might expect from a true utility, thanks to peaking interest in infrastructure companies globally. Thus, many traders constructed elaborate "baskets" of securities that were long Autostrade, but then short futures on the Italian market as well as some other infrastructure stocks, thus "stripping out" distinct, undesired market risks. In another example, a manager could buy the stock of an energy company going through some sort of company-specific restructuring but then short oil futures, creating a stub value of the company independent of the commodity price.

There are myriad other forms of relative value trading. The popular "carry trade" uses the proceeds of a short sale of one asset to fund the purchase of others. This is especially popular among currency traders, who buy currencies with higher yields and short currencies with lower yields, thus capturing the spread between the two. A very popular carry trade has been shorting the lower-yielding Japanese yen and going long the higher-yielding Australian dollar. With "pairs trading," equity traders will go long and short two companies in the same industry, thus stripping out the industry exposure and isolating the relative mispricing between the two. Think Dell versus Hewlett Packard or Visa versus MasterCard.

These sorts of trades are clever, though sometimes too clever by half. Underlying all of them is the assumption of a predictable relationship among the constituents of the trade. Unfortunately, the markets often don't cooperate with this assumption. In the carry trade, there is the risk that the higher-yielding currency devalues, or that during times of stress, there is a "flight to safety" to the lower-yielding currency. A smoothly operating carry trade can blow up quickly. Basket trades are intellectually interesting, but what sometimes happens is that the portfolio manager hedges away nearly all of the risk, which means the position neither profits nor loses much. With these trades, the possibility of getting two or more things wrong, not just one, is always prevalent.

Allocation.   A second element of complexity is the ability to reallocate capital among different strategies; it is a hallmark of unconstrained portfolio management. I was recently reviewing a hedge fund with capabilities to invest up and down the corporate capital structure, everything from bank loans and bonds to convertibles and equity. Sometimes referred to as "capital structure arbitrage," this is a popular hedge fund strategy. Under that headline, this is the list of the strategies the fund claims to pursue: arbitrage, carry, value, capital structure, synthetic put, long volatility, credit, event-driven, optionality, and macro hedge. Three things to note: One, this is a long list of strategies. Two, the definitions of these strategies do not abide by some industry glossary, so a major part of the due diligence must center on defining what each is. Three, it will be very difficult to establish clear expectations for how this fund will invest my money.

Multi-strategy funds have become increasingly popular over the last decade as it became clear that having fewer tools in the tool kit is not a good plan for long-term business viability—as we saw in chapter 4's discussion of merger arbitrage. Some of the gargantuan multi-strategy firms that are now preeminent in the hedge fund industry, such as Elliot,

Och-Ziff, or Highbridge, pursue a remarkably broad set of strategies. This is a double-edged sword. On the one hand, having a high degree of flexibility gives one more existential safety in navigating tough markets. But on the flip side, the investor's task in setting and managing expectations for the fund will grow harder with the increasing degrees of freedom. Take a classic multi-strategy event fund that can pursue merger arbitrage, distressed debt, and special situation equity strategies. First, we must endeavor to understand whether they are effective within each bucket. But then we must consider whether they are skilled at efficiently allocating capital *across* the buckets.

Innovation.   A third form of complexity is innovation. This is adaptation in its purest form: an institutionalized mandate to research in order to identify new ways of extracting value in the market. Some firms rely on the tried and true—for example, those adhering to classic value investing spelled out in Benjamin Graham and David Dodd's *Security Analysis* (of which Warren Buffett is the most prominent disciple). What those investors look for in a stock today is the same as it was decades ago. It doesn't change; there is no innovation.

But others engage in primary research on how to identify and capitalize on market inefficiencies in new and creative ways. For example, one of the world's prominent hedge funds, Winton Capital, devotes extraordinary resources to scientific research on how markets work. Among other efforts, it sponsors the research of many professional mathematicians at the Oxford Science Park in England on the belief that "robust statistical research provides the richest and most reliable source of information on market behavior."[8] The goal is to develop complex algorithms to identify profitable opportunities. Winton is not alone—there are many other investment firms in both the alternative and traditional fields with a comparable commitment to not only primary research but advanced technologies that can accelerate the pace and complexity of trading strategies.

If a major premise of a fund's "edge" is its commitment to continuously update models and methods, it becomes virtually impossible for any outside investor to keep pace with the velocity of innovation, thus making expectations management very difficult. Indeed, a critical element for firms committed to innovative research is confidentiality. They rarely let you peek inside the models, so you're ultimately going on faith. More broadly, we must assess the balance that our experts try to strike between discipline in an underlying investment approach and an opportunistic evolution of the approach.

GENIUSES, COWBOYS, AND THE COST OF BEING WRONG

Now let's revisit our "Most Interesting Manager in the World" from earlier in the chapter. Imagine a scenario where a fund manager avoids any of these exposures. The resulting portfolio would have several hallmarks:

- ✓ Diversified
- ✓ Market neutral
- ✓ Unlevered
- ✓ Highly liquid
- ✓ Simply executed

The manager's risk profile would resemble the smaller black pentagon in the top picture in figure 6.4. He would be taking very little investment risk. While this sounds very safe, it implies an impossible mission: the fund's portfolio manager would need a consistent informational advantage over the thousands of other portfolio managers trying to do the same thing with comparable access to the same Bloomberg terminals, company management, competitors, customers, suppliers, and all other forms of publicly available information. This expert would be a Genius.

The opposite of the Genius is a scary character. He would employ an opaque strategy to go long a small number of illiquid, leveraged positions. He is a Cowboy. Cowboys are heroes or losers, and not often much in between. The sprawling pentagon in the bottom of figure 6.4 reflects the extensive risks he is taking. This could very well produce the best results around. But it's more likely to blow up and take much of his investors' capital along with it.

Situated between the Genius and the Cowboy is the practical, everyday reality of the modern money management industry. Managers have to take certain portfolio risks to outperform, and it is the top job in manager

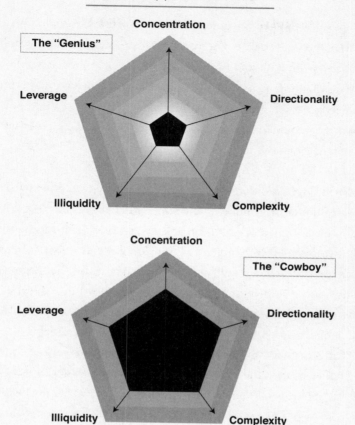

Figure 6.4   *Geniuses versus Cowboys*

research to identify what risks are being taken. The farther out on an axis an expert extends himself, the more he is vulnerable to both the risks and the benefits of that dimension.

We can ascribe nearly every *investment-related* (i.e., not fraud-related) fund manager blowup to excesses along these dimensions. Sometimes pushing the envelope along one axis might be enough to get the fund in trouble, but more often it's the combination of two or more extreme risks that does it.

Leverage + Illiquidity

Arguably the most toxic brew in investments is a combination of leverage and illiquidity. One can lever liquid securities without there being much likelihood of a problem as long as those securities aren't too volatile. If that's true, then the chance of a margin call and forced selling is unlikely. Conversely, owning illiquid issues is not a big deal as long as they are not bought on margin and as long as the fund's structure has an appropriate match between assets and liabilities. When the two factors collide, however, the chance of trouble increases considerably. This can be seen in some of money management's most notable disasters.

Long-Term Capital Management.   As has been well documented, LTCM was one of the most prominent and successful hedge funds of the 1990s, owing to an all-star cast of fund managers, such as John Meriwether, as well as two Nobel Prize winners, Myron Scholes and Robert Merton, as advisors. Indeed, Scholes and Merton won the prize for their expertise in derivatives in 1997, the year before the derivative-laden LTCM lost billions for investors and required a major intervention by some of the world's largest banks in order to avoid broader financial market contagion.

LTCM's primary strategy was fixed income arbitrage that looks for small inefficiencies in the bond market and then applies generous leverage to earn sizable gains. Their hunting ground was primarily in the debt of the highest-rated sovereigns in Europe, the United States, and Japan. However, LTCM's strategy quietly infused a fair amount of potential illiquidity into the mix by trading so-called off-the-run issues. Explained simply, a newly issued thirty-year bond would be considered an on-the-run issue, while the thirty-year bond that was issued six months ago, thus having a remaining maturity of 29.5, would be off the run. There are typically very small price discrepancies between such holdings, and the correlation between them tends to be extremely high.

In addition to fixed income arbitrage, LTCM also engaged in other sorts of trades such as statistical arbitrage, all of which were of relative value in nature and employed complex mathematical formulas to construct. For instance, there are so-called dual share class trades when a large company has issued stock in different jurisdictions. Because these classes reflect the value of the same overarching entity, they should trade at similar values. To the extent they don't (for whatever reason), there is an arbitrage opportunity. LTCM had a dual share class trade in Royal Dutch Shell, for example.

LTCM was wildly successful—until it wasn't. Given the pedigree and network of its principals, the fund had raised billions of dollars in assets and then generated very good performance for several years. At the start of 1998, the fund had $4.7 billion in equity capital and borrowed $124.5 billion.[9] Thus it was levered twenty-five times. That is a lot of leverage. Furthermore, recall that liquidity is a slippery concept because it is a moving target—it changes all the time in response to the live supply-and-demand dynamics in the marketplace.

The Russian debt default and ruble devaluation in the late summer of 1998 were the proximate drivers of LTCM's undoing. The Russian default prompted a global scramble for the highest-quality, most liquid assets. This "flight to safety" went heavily into US Treasury bonds, whose prices spiked. The problem for LTCM was that in extracting small discrepancies in the sovereign bond market, it was long off-the-run bonds and short on-the-run bonds. When the market plowed into liquid on-the-run Treasuries, LTCM was forced to cover their shorts at the same time their less-liquid long positions were more difficult to exit. Across several other less liquid positions (it also had direct exposure to emerging markets, including Russia), the highly levered LTCM was forced to sell positions at the worst moment.

A vicious cycle ensued. By September 25, 1998, LTCM's equity capital was approximately $400 million, a drop of more than 90 percent from just months earlier. But because the firm still held more than $100 billion in liabilities, it was effectively 250 times (!) levered for a time, until it was bailed out by several global investment banks. Interestingly, merely one year later, John Meriwether and some of the same LTCM partners were able to raise a significant amount of capital to run a similar strategy, but with the promise of doing so with less leverage.

Amaranth. While the circumstances for LTCM and Amaranth, a Greenwich-based hedge fund, were quite different, the outcome was the same: a massively levered illiquid bet on relative value trades blew up a well-regarded, multibillion-dollar enterprise. Founded by Nick Maounis, Amaranth had its roots in convertible bond arbitrage. Over time, it took on more of a multi-strategy profile, bringing on more capabilities in order to run a more robust business platform.

Energy trading eventually became Amaranth's claim to fame. Brian Hunter, the head of that business though only in his early thirties, had made some wildly successful trades, such as in 2005, when he was correctly bullish on the price of natural gas, if only due to the unanticipated impact of Hurricane Katrina. He supposedly earned upwards of $100 million that year.[10] In 2006, Hunter traded what is known as a calendar spread, which is a relative value bet between two time points on the same commodity futures price curve. Specifically, Hunter was long "winter" natural gas futures and short "non-winter" natural gas futures on the belief that gas prices would increase beyond market expectations during the cold months, but then decline into the warmer months. For example, he was long March 2007 futures and short April 2007 futures. Amaranth made this an unusually large bet, representing a significant percentage of the global market in natural gas futures. Thus, not only did this render liquidity risk "imprudently" high, but Hunter applied a significant degree of leverage to plump its returns.[11] Thus, the cost of being wrong was magnified enormously.

Around mid-2006, Amaranth's total assets under management were north of $9 billion, making it an industry bellwether with its offices situated in a modern, secluded trading compound in a nondescript Greenwich office park. When the firm's calendar spread trade began to fail, however, the firm quickly struggled. The weather did not cooperate with Hunter's expectations for a colder winter, which would have meant more demand and higher prices. As natural gas prices began to fall in early September 2006, the anchor to Amaranth's bet unraveled. Hunter expected the spread between the winter and non-winter futures to widen, but they actually narrowed. As the losses mounted, the extreme amount of leverage employed amplified the losses and drew in the firm's creditors, who demanded more collateral. Nor could Amaranth sell out of its positions. Given the size of the bet, there were few counterparties with whom the firm could have transacted. The position was illiquid.

In just a few weeks' time, the firm lost approximately $4.9 billion on the energy trade alone, about half the fund's value. Amaranth was subsequently compelled to find outside buyers to rescue the distressed energy portfolio. JPMorgan and Citadel stepped in and bought portions of the book at a significant discount, thus pushing losses for Amaranth toward $6 billion. The firm was irreparably damaged and ultimately folded.

In these examples, it's clear that the combination of excessive leverage and illiquid investments can produce bad results. Further, in both cases and others, it's noteworthy that the trades were complex relative value positions. Illiquidity and leverage combined are bad enough, but when applied to baskets of securities where a presumed correlation among them must persist in order to be successful, the brew gets even more toxic. Oftentimes, these relative value positions are considered safe because of their low realized daily volatility. But what is seen does not illuminate the potential for violent "tail" events triggered by extreme unforeseen events. Third, it's clear that this combination of risks can get out of control quickly. In both cases, the fund was in good shape until it suddenly went out of business, despite having supposedly world-class operations.

CURIOUS INCIDENTS

There's a moment in the Sherlock Holmes story "Silver Blaze" in which the ingenious hero cracks the case at hand by observing what did *not* happen. As the case of the eponymous missing horse unfolded, a Scotland Yard detective pressed Holmes's logic for why the horse was soon to be discovered, prompting Holmes's reference to "the curious incident of the dog in the night-time," meaning the guard dog that was stationed near the horse's stable. The puzzled detective was confused as "the dog did nothing in the night-time." Replied Holmes: "That was the curious incident."

Many dogs don't bark. Non-events are all around us, infinite in number and thus difficult to consider. Stories where nothing much happens aren't that interesting, so we focus on those where something does. Because we don't think statistically, we systematically overestimate the relevance of realized occurrences.

While I believe this risk prism can help one to make better investment decisions, we must also remember the core principle that method supersedes content. All the cautionary tales in this chapter show the dire consequences of extending oneself along one or more of the risk dimensions. There's only one nagging problem: Most of the funds that extend themselves along the dimensions of the prism don't blow up.

There is a cardinal sin in the empirical sciences known as "selecting on the dependent variable." It basically means you look at outcomes and then work backwards to figure out the factors causing those outcomes. The main problem this causes is "selection bias" or "sample bias." In my casual reading, books on business success, such as the kinds that distinguish great from good companies, are notorious culprits. Many case studies of management and business success select on the dependent variable—they focus only on what worked!

So, too, with investing. *When Genius Failed*, Roger Lowenstein's tale of Long-Term Capital Management, is a wonderful book. It should be required reading for anyone in finance. But it shouldn't lead us to conclude that all highly leveraged funds that also invest in illiquid securities are destined to implode. For one thing, leveraged illiquidity is the underpinning of almost all private equity, yet "blowups" in those funds are rare, largely because they are structured with multiyear liquidity terms that create the appropriate asset-liability match. Among hedge funds, many traders who engage in convertible bond arbitrage mix leverage and illiquidity on a daily basis. However, most of those funds don't blow up. In general, there are thousands of funds, but only a handful deliver extreme results.

Where I think the prism can be handy in anticipating problems is to focus on degrees or tendencies in manager risk profiles. First, funds that exhibit extremes along just one dimension likely have a limited chance of disaster. I have come across some wildly complex strategies that don't rate much on the other dimensions. In my experience, these strategies tend to end with a whimper instead of a bang, as what they're doing is moving around a lot of pieces in the portfolio but not actually taking on much risk. They are too clever by half. Likewise, a fund that is highly directional may have big price swings, but absent other elements, it's unlikely to wildly outperform or underperform. Second, it's the combination of risks that is the real source of trouble. But even there, it's up to the diligent analyst to understand the specific calibration of risks at work in that particular strategy. It is here that more detailed and technical understandings of the many investment strategies come into play; these are critical in understanding why some firms with excessive risk profiles blow up while other comparable peers do not—which is the formulation of the proper research question at hand.

Finally, much of investing, like life generally, changes on the margins. It is incremental. The extremes will always catch our eye, but it's the smaller things that matter on a day-to-day basis. The process of adapting our expectations to a manager's dynamic risk profile will have an incremental quality to it. In that process, we should avoid if at all possible the fallacy that the case at hand will necessarily take on the properties of the group or type with which it is affiliated. For as we know, many dogs don't bark.

TRUE-TO-SCALE MAPS are accurate but unusable. So is overly detailed and lengthy investment research. In offering a parsimonious model of investment risk, I have suggested shortcuts we can use to understand the potential sources of loss or gain with any particular money manager—traditional and alternative managers alike.

These are the five dimensions that we use to form investment expectations. If the fund is concentrated, its big bets will drive performance. If the fund is directional, expect returns to be highly correlated to its target market. If the fund is excessively levered relative to the norm for that strategy, expect it to do spectacularly well or blow up, or both. If the fund is illiquid and lacks investment terms that match assets to liabilities, there will eventually be a big problem. If it's complex, you are unlikely to be able to form clear expectations.

Thus far, I've given short shrift to the quest for an informational advantage, to the entire field of fundamental security analysis, the bedrock foundation on which much of the investment industry rests. Indeed, the Most Interesting Manager in the World would not have to take any of these risks. He or she would be consistently smarter or more creative than others. While for all practical purposes, this manager does not exist, there still remains the question of whether or where managers add skill or "alpha." In the next chapter, we address that topic head-on.

PARSING LAKE WOBEGON

*Promises are the uniquely human way of ordering the future, making
it predictable and reliable to the extent that this is humanly possible.*

—Hannah Arendt

NESTING

Storyteller Garrison Keillor famously described the fictional hamlet of
Lake Wobegon as a place where "all the women are strong, all the men
are good looking, and all the children are above average." Of course, not
everyone can be above average, but that doesn't stop most of us in the
real world from thinking we're better at many things than we actually are.
Behavioralists have copiously documented the human disposition toward
overconfidence; in fact, they often call it the "Lake Wobegon effect."

This condition is very much in evidence in the world of fund management and in investing generally. In a career devoted to picking winners,
I can't think of a single instance when a portfolio manager I was interviewing didn't tell me that he was better than the rest. The claim could be
made in a matter-of-fact sort of way, but ultimately what investment firms
trumpet is their "edge." Of course, it would be silly not to. Who claims that
they're average at their job? Yet the numbers don't—and can't—add up. By
definition, the average manager is average. In nonfictional places, half of
everyone is below average.

But mathematical truisms don't define human interactions. How
we adapt to uncertain and dynamic circumstances does. So how best to

evaluate the skill of the experts we choose? My experience suggests that the satisfaction we get from our investments does not directly or proportionally map onto conventional measurements of skill. Funds with great performance might garner little notice, while those with average numbers can be very satisfying to their customers. "Alpha," the Greek letter that is industry shorthand for skill, is only part of the story.

Why is that? The answer I propose might be the most unorthodox claim made in *The Investor's Paradox:* that, when evaluating financial experts, *skill is as much a social outcome as an individual achievement.* I am not suggesting that we replace conventional treatments of alpha, but that we supplement them with a concept that is more encompassing and more reflective of the actual practice of hiring and firing fund managers.

We can see this nested understanding of skill in Figure 7.1. From the outside working in, popular convention is to focus on some measured outperformance against a specific benchmark. The statistics may be basic or complex, but the question is simple: Did you beat your bogey? Outperformance comes and goes for most fund managers. Trying to consistently "beat the market" is an extreme challenge. But investors do (or should) have high expectations for the *consistency* of the approach their experts take, and the consequent results. There are plenty of examples where a manager underperforms, yet the investor is actually satisfied with the outcome because it squares with what was expected. Thus, in this deeper sense, *skill is the ability to meet expectations.*

But as we've seen throughout the book, those expectations don't come out of thin air. Setting, refining, and updating expectations is hard work. It is interactive, based on the necessarily messy dialogue between client and expert. As a result, skill is as much a subjective phenomenon as it is an objective, financial measurement. Skill becomes the ability to fulfill one's promises. At this social level, we supplant statistical measures with a type of game theory in which all parties strive to find equilibrium. This is much closer to what really happens in the world of fund investing: dialogue among self-interested parties under conditions of uncertainty. That dialogue might fail at times as a result of investing missteps or poor communication. But it can also create the context for investors to "satisfice." In many instances, investors will stick with the experts who are good enough,

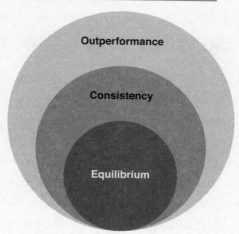

Figure 7.1   Nested Forms of Skill

but by no means the best, at what they do. Switching out of a stable equilibrium and undergoing the costs of searching for something better is often not worth it.

ALPHA(BET) SOUP

It's reasonable to ask whether experts are good at their jobs. We do it every day with meteorologists, doctors, judges, and many others. In finance, there is simple math we can do to gauge alpha: just look at the fund manager's performance relative to an appropriate benchmark. Suppose a traditional long-only fund invests broadly in global stock markets. Its bogey would most likely be the MSCI World Index. If for the relevant period, say 2012, the index was up 15.83 percent and the fund in question was up 16.50 percent, then the fund generated 67 basis points of alpha. There are fabulously complicated statistical methods for calculating skill, but this back-of-the-envelope exercise is the mental model investment people use on a day-to-day basis.

The academic literature on skill is vast, especially as it relates to luck among stock pickers.[1] Basically, the question at hand is whether "active management" works, or if markets are sufficiently efficient that few (or no one) can trump the sum wisdom of all other investors—"the market"—over time.

In the long-only world of security selection, the evidence is not encouraging. Early work by William Sharpe, Jack Treynor, and Michael Jensen started the deluge of skepticism toward active management.[2] For example, Jensen argued that a sample of mutual funds from the mid-1940s to the mid-1960s was not only unable on average to predict security prices better than a "buy-the-market-and-hold" (recall that index funds did not exist in the early postwar era), but also failed to demonstrate that any single fund could outperform a randomly generated portfolio. (This is not so dissimilar from Philip Tetlock's finding that political experts weren't better than dart-throwing chimps.) And when you consider that he looked at underperformance *gross* of fees, fee-paying investors' shortfalls were that much larger.

A critical blow against the argument for active management arrived a couple of decades later, when Chicago economists Eugene Fama and Kenneth French published "Common Risk Factors in the Returns on Stocks and Bonds." Rather than simply look at manager skill relative to broad market beta, they introduced two other factors—valuation and market capitalization—to potentially explain why some managers outperformed a naïve market bogey. They found that bets on "style" frequently masqueraded as skill. To make matters worse, Mark Carhart introduced one additional factor—momentum—that accounted for a good portion of what little alpha remained. There are certainly other studies that show pockets of traditional stock-picking skill.[3] However, most support the original findings.[4]

The study of skill in the world of hedge funds is a murkier task, but one that has attracted an increasing level of academic scrutiny. Are the managers of hedge fund strategies skillful? The debate is intense, but a review of the literature suggests a qualified yes. In a 2011 study of approximately 8,400 hedge funds from 1995 through 2009, Roger Ibbotson, Peng Chen, and Kevin Zhu conclude that across time and by strategy, these offerings have consistently delivered statistically significant alpha.[5]

Figures 7.2 and 7.3 provide the authors' main findings. Figure 7.2 presents their data on the mix of alpha and beta across eight popular alternative strategies. For example, over a fifteen-year period, the average gross return for long/short equity funds was approximately 14 percent. Net of fees, those funds on average returned 10 percent, of which just more than half can be attributed to "systematic beta." By systematic beta, the authors are referring to what amount of performance can be attributed to the markets for stocks,

	Pre-Fee Return (%)	Fees (%)	Net of Fee Returns (%)	Alpha (%)	Systematic Beta (%)
Convertible Arbitrage	10.76	3.35	7.41	2.79	4.61
Emerging Market	12.51	3.70	8.81	4.66	4.15
Equity Market Neutral	10.34	3.27	7.08	2.86	4.21
Event Driven	11.91	3.58	8.33	3.94	4.39
Fixed Income Arbitrage	9.72	3.14	6.57	2.91	3.67
Global Macro	11.08	3.42	7.67	2.54	5.13
Long/Short Equity	13.99	4.00	9.99	4.79	5.20
Managed Futures	7.79	2.76	5.03	0.57	4.46
Short-Biased	1.17	1.50	−0.34	1.91	−2.25
Overall Equally Weighted	*11.13*	*3.43*	*7.70*	*3.00*	*4.70*

Figure 7.2   *Alphas, Betas, and Costs by Hedge Fund
Strategies, January 1995–December 2009*
Source: Robert G. Ibbotson, Peng Chen, and Kevin X. Zhu (2011), "The ABCs of
Hedge Funds: Alphas, Betas, and Costs," Financial Analysts Journal, *67 (1), 20.*

	Post–Fee Return (%)	Alpha (%)	Systematic Beta (%)
1998	−3.78	−15.28	13.33
1999	25.54	7.32	17.16
2000	1.19	6.40	−5.03
2001	2.02	10.62	−8.22
2002	1.09	10.29	−8.57
2003	18.50	12.42	5.40
2004	7.87	2.93	4.86
2005	8.51	4.67	3.71
2006	12.53	3.18	9.09
2007	11.52	4.72	6.41
2008	−16.74	6.38	−22.17
2009	19.25	7.78	10.44

Figure 7.3   *Annual Hedge Fund Alphas and Betas*
Source: Robert G. Ibbotson, Peng Chen, and Kevin X. Zhu (2011), "The ABCs of
Hedge Funds: Alphas, Betas, and Costs," Financial Analysts Journal, *67 (1), 21.*

bonds, and cash. In other words, slightly less than half of those returns are attributable to the skill of the manager—which is considerably higher than the traditional stock-picking vehicle.[6] The overall data, displayed in the bottom row, show that over this fifteen-year period, more than one-third of total net of fee returns is attributable to manager skill.

Figure 7.3 looks at the same data from a different angle. It aggregates all the strategies into one pool and looks at the persistence of alpha year over year. With the exception of 1998, we can see that "hedge funds" broadly defined produced substantial levels of alpha relative to total returns.

One nice feature of these data is that they cast a very realistic light on the nature of hedge fund returns. As we've seen, some folks believe that alternative investments are a completely different animal from traditional investments. But these data clearly demonstrates that hedge fund returns have a meaningful beta component to them. Across the spectrum from traditional to alternative investments, all funds feature some degree of market beta—the key question is how much.

THE MIRAGE MIRAGE

The debate over whether hedge funds are worth it, given their cost, complexity, and controversy, has been raging for years. Not only do the data presented in the previous section provide some evidence of skill; the comparative performance versus standard asset classes appears to be attractive, as shown in figure 7.4. In the eighteen years of data compiled by the Centre for Hedge Fund Research at Imperial College London, the composite of hedge fund strategies delivered higher returns than stocks, bonds, and commodities with considerably lower volatility than stocks and commodities (though not bonds), thus generating better risk-adjusted returns versus each of these major asset classes.

Some critics vehemently disagree that investing in hedge funds is worthwhile. In John Bogle's latest book, *The Clash of the Cultures,* the index fund pioneer extends his long-standing criticism of hedge fund managers as undisciplined, fast-trading speculators. He even aligns the

	Hedge Funds	Global Stocks	Global Bonds	Commodities
Annualized Average Returns	9.07%	7.18%	6.25%	7.27%
Annualized Standard Deviation of Returns	7.20	15.72	3.95	22.47
Annualized Sharpe Ratio	0.76	0.23	0.68	0.16

Figure 7.4   *Hedge Fund Performance Compared to Primary Asset Classes, 1994–2011*
Source: http://www.kpmg.com/KY/en/Documents/the-value-of-the-hedge-fund-industry-part-1.pdf

rise in prominence of hedge fund managers with the moral decline of Western society. In *The Hedge Fund Mirage,* a more serious polemic that has garnered much attention, Simon Lack states his thesis in the volume's opening sentence: "If all the money that's ever been invested in hedge funds had been put in treasury bills instead, the results would be twice as good."[7] Whatever outperformance one might see from some hedge funds is "too good to be true." Lack launches a broadside against the industry: hedge fund managers keep most of their funds' profits while leaving their investors with little to nothing; hedge fund investing is suboptimal to traditional methods; and if a hedge fund loses money, it has "broken its promise" to investors.

While the book is largely anecdotal, Lack does offer up some hard data, which are damning taken on face value. Yet his analysis is almost completely wrong. Take his bold opening claim: that US Treasuries have been a much better investment than hedge funds. To support this, he relies heavily on an academic study by Ilia Dichev and Gwen Yu that takes a statistically informed look at the real experience of hedge fund investors.[8] They conclude, reasonably, that such investors earn returns that are unsatisfactory. But they also state, in the abstract of their article (i.e., right up front), that hedge fund returns during the sample period "are only marginally higher than the risk-free rate as of the end of 2008." In other words, hedge funds *beat* T-bills over time, not lagged, let alone by half.

The more peculiar twist underlying Lack's primary argument, something he also adopts from Dichev and Yu, is the reliance on what are known as "dollar-weighted returns" versus "time-weighted returns." Though technical, the distinction is important. Time-weighted returns reflect a simple buy-and-hold approach to investing. Take any stock, bond, mutual fund, ETF, or hedge fund. If its value today is 100 and a year from now it is 120, its time-weighted return is 20 percent. Simple. Dollar-weighted returns are more complicated, as they incorporate the timing and magnitude of our investments. They are the returns earned by *investors,* not those that accrue to a particular *investment.* In other words, a fund's value may climb from 100 to 120 over the course of a year, but that doesn't mean we make our full allocation to it at 100. If we didn't buy the fund until it hit 118, then we didn't earn 20 percent; we earned 1.7 percent.

There is no more basic lesson in finance than to "buy low, sell high." Unfortunately, most of us don't act that way consistently. For a number of reasons, we often do exactly the opposite. We might get excited about good performance and want to join in on a "winning" trade; by the same token, we feel unsettled buying something that is struggling and defer investing at depressed valuations. But here's the rub: If I buy a high-quality but volatile mutual fund like Fairholme after seeing fabulous past returns, then lose faith and sell after poor returns in 2011, only to subsequently miss a huge rebound in 2012, *my* results are awful, but Fairholme's are not. That's on me, not on portfolio manager Bruce Berkowitz. The same logic, which Lack ignores, applies to all investment types, including mutual funds. The actual returns that investors receive on their long-only investments are far less than the headline rate of return.[9]

While Lack's analysis is off the mark, I would suggest that there are indeed some very serious problems with a statistically based analysis of something called skill. First, the definitions themselves are misleading. Hedge funds aren't an asset class. Thus, broad debates about whether "they" are valuable are meaningless. That serious institutional investors continue to define part of their allocation strategy in terms of hedge funds or alternatives reflects the fact that we're still in the early stages of the debate.

A second, more granular problem is that relying on hedge fund databases to say something meaningful about the skill of the underlying managers is also irrevocably flawed. Why is that? It's because the available data provide no information about any particular fund's idiosyncratic risk profile. The major hedge fund data providers offer performance data for funds categorized by strategy type, such as "event driven," "macro," or "hedged equity." Yet those strategy labels don't create the kind of clean comparisons we find among funds categorized in the same Morningstar Style Box.

Take the "event-driven" category. Broadly defined, this is a group of funds that look to profit from various forms of corporate activity, such as a merger or bankruptcy. But we wouldn't know how each fund in that category actually does without doing direct due diligence on each offering. Whether the fund invests in equities or bonds; in the United States or globally; through directional or arbitrage styles—the database offers none of that information. Likewise among long/short equity funds, those database categories will include funds that run with directional exposures that vary widely. Thus, when much of academia relies on these data sets (even when correcting for various statistical biases), it shows some ignorance of how alternative fund managers actually work. The available data force us to rely on returns-based analysis rather than risk-based analysis.

Third, even when a flexible manager outperforms his or her peers or a benchmark, we don't necessarily know why. With fully invested traditional investments, we reasonably assume that security selection is the key driver of returns, but even in that case a manager can run more concentrated portfolios or can take meaningful relative sector bets. By contrast, Foxlike investors are all over the place. Depending on their mandate, they not only pick individual securities, but can potentially rotate across different sectors, countries, or market cap bands; switch among different asset classes; and engage in market timing by changing net exposure, gross exposure, or both.

WHAT TO EXPECT WHEN YOU'RE EXPECTING

New York Yankees pitcher Lefty Gomez once famously quipped that "I'd rather be lucky than good." It's a keen insight because much of what we experience in life is in fact driven by luck or circumstance, not by active skill. Luck matters. It matters more than we might want to admit, not just in terms of the big lottery of one's station in life, but in all the day-to-day things that matter—the friends we have, the schools we attend, the jobs we get, the accomplishments we realize.

That said, the balance of importance between luck and skill can vary considerably according to the domain in which we're operating. Can you be wrong on purpose? This is the fascinating question posed by Michael Mauboussin in his contribution to the debate over skill versus luck in human endeavors.[10] The answer varies widely across settings, calling into question when the notion of skill is even meaningful. Where you cannot be wrong deliberately, luck prevails. Activities in which you can make mistakes if you choose to are skill-rich endeavors. In the classic statistical exercise of picking balls out of an urn, assuming the balls are uniform in quality except that some are red while others are blue, nothing but luck determines which color ball is chosen. On the opposite end of the spectrum is chess. Obviously, one can choose to make boneheaded moves that would cause one to lose the game quickly. It is a skill-rich endeavor.

Investing has a strong degree of luck associated with it. You can certainly lose nearly every chess game you play, but can you build a portfolio that consistently loses money? The answer is probably not, as some of the risks you choose are bound to be favored by the market from time to time. Think of our Cowboy from chapter 6. Certainly a bold risk taker can put his fund in a position to blow up, but it is also not hard to imagine that leveraged, illiquid, directional, concentrated portfolios can do fabulously well for a stretch. In luck-rich endeavors, it is prudent to pay as much, if not more, attention to the consistent execution of process as to the outcome.[11]

Yet it's not even a foregone conclusion that experts can stick to their knitting and deliver what's expected. Here we come back to our distinction between hedgehogs and foxes. Those who know "one big thing" shouldn't be that hard to figure out, as they have limited flexibility in what they can do. We can be pretty sure that in nature, a hedgehog under attack will roll up into a ball. Foxes are less predictable.

This perspective is more useful for making good investment decisions than are conventional statistical notions of alpha. For one thing, the notion that one can build a portfolio around experts who regularly best the competition is tenuous. Not only does performance chasing not work, but we've already seen overwhelming data showing that the world's top professional fund pickers are not particularly good at picking funds. Second, the principle of diversification is built around the idea of assembling a group of role players who collectively produce something better than what any of them could have produced individually. Whether in money management, business, or sports, it is the interaction of different pieces that typically builds the best outcome. A team of Michael Jordans sounds intriguing, but there's a reason why the NBA All-Star Game is usually so clunky. Likewise, it's very hard to build a theory of portfolio construction for a basket of star managers.[12]

For money managers, the ability to deliver a predictable risk profile is situated between the consistency of outcomes (which we can't expect in luck-rich scenarios) and the consistency of process. In our nested treatment of skill, let's look at a couple of examples that highlight the centrality of consistency in choosing the right experts.

The Skill of a Hedgehog

The ability to be consistent is itself a skill and should not be taken for granted, even in what appear to be the simplest of situations. In the world of managed funds, arguably the simplest choice is an exchange-traded fund, or ETF. As data in chapter 3 showed, the ETF business has exploded in size in recent years as investors seek out supposedly simpler solutions to their portfolio problems. Thus, we would think that it won't take long to build our expectations for an ETF. By definition, they track a predefined market segment. In one form of granularity or another, it is entirely the "beta" of that segment. In the realm of investing, this should be as easy as it gets.

Many ETFs do indeed meet these expectations. The most popular ETF, the S&P 500 SPDR, tracks the performance of the S&P 500 nearly perfectly. Through mid-2013, the SPDR lagged the actual S&P 500 by just a few basis points on rolling five-, ten-, and fifteen-year look-back periods. That's exactly what it's supposed to do.

Yet others don't. Most notably, leveraged and inverse ETFs have been notorious disappointments. Leveraged ETFs aim to amplify the performance of the particular index or market segment they track, while inverse ETFs aim to provide investors with the opposite of the performance of that segment. A leveraged inverse ETF combines both features, basically shorting the target market and using leverage to do so. The ETF producers will use some combination of derivative securities to achieve this performance.

The performance of a number of these leveraged and inverse ETFs has been wildly off the mark, clearly violating the reasonable expectations of their customers. Take the ProShares Ultra S&P 500 (SSO), for example, which aims to double the performance of the S&P 500. On any one day, it might achieve that return target. For example, on May 6, 2013, the S&P 500 gained 0.19 percent while SSO gained 0.44 percent. That's roughly accurate. However, over longer periods of time, the fund doesn't come close to doubling the performance of the S&P 500. Over the previous five years through that same date, the S&P 500 gained 4.98 percent per year while the "levered" ETFs gained just 1.34 percent on an annualized basis. Meanwhile, the ProShares UltraShort S&P 500 (SDS) aims to return twice the inverse of the market. It is a levered short fund. Even more egregiously than its sister product SSO, SDS declined at an annualized rate of –25.8 percent over the past five years. The back-of-the-envelope math is that SDS should have lost about 10 percent per year (twice the inverse of the S&P 500). There are plenty of other examples, especially from more esoteric markets.[13]

What gives? There's a clear explanation for this apparent aberration. Certain levered and inverse ETFs reset their net asset value on a *daily* basis, meaning that the returns on SSO, SDS, and the like are not subject to compounding. This objective of daily tracking is actually reflected in the fine print of these vehicles' prospectuses. Though the explanation is clear, the spirit of the outcome is still unsettling. In fact, this is a violation of expectations sufficiently egregious that the SEC has stepped in to protect unwitting consumers. "[W]e believe individual investors may be confused about the performance objectives of leveraged and inverse exchange-traded funds (ETFs)."[14]

The Skill of a Fox

If setting expectations for supposedly simple vehicles is tough, then gauging what to expect from experts who enjoy substantial flexibility will be even more so. Let's look at the case of hedged equity funds over recent years. There have been literally thousands of these vehicles at one time or another. The differences across them can appear bewildering. However, in my experience, we can broadly generalize about how a majority of these funds work. Contrary to the reputation of hedge fund managers as hyperactive traders, it is much more common to see these experts demonstrate a fidelity to detailed, fundamental research. Your average long/short equity manager is not going to talk to you about technical market analysis and daily trading patterns. Instead, the conversation will almost always focus on company-specific fundamentals: earnings, cash flow, balance sheet, company management.

There will be some key factors that do vary. The most notable is how directional a hedged equity manager chooses to run. Some will be very long biased, thus not very different from mutual fund managers focused on the same markets. Others will run with a more neutral exposure, meaning that their long and short portfolios are of roughly equal size. As mentioned in chapter 6, the gamut of exposures hedge funds choose to run is quite wide. Relatedly, some managers will dial their net exposures and leverage up or down in response to certain variables, such as the level of market volatility or certain macroeconomic data. Finally, the holding period for stocks will vary. Some will focus on the nearer term while others will look to own their stocks for years.

Even with these variables, the general focus and execution of the hedged equity strategy has not changed since it was first executed several decades ago. The central exercise is to own "good" companies trading cheaply and short "bad" companies trading rich. Even taking into account variable amounts of net and gross leverage, hedged equity funds tend to do well when there is a divergence in performance between those "good" and "bad" companies. This is almost always true. It is the strategy's profile, or what I would call the hedged equity style. What does change over time is the market environment for executing this strategy. So what we might casually observe to be skill can actually be just a style of investing that happens to be in favor.

The vacillating performance of the hedged equity strategy bears this out. During the 2000–2002 bear market, many hedged equity vehicles performed well due to the large performance dislocation between different segments of the stock market, one that was driven by "bottom-up" company fundamentals, more so than macroeconomic "top-down" forces. In the years before the 2000 crisis, large-cap growth stocks such as those in technology and telecom traded on extremely high valuations. Smaller-cap companies in "old economy" sectors like industrials were in reasonably healthy shape and their stocks were attractively valued. As evidenced in chapter 3, there was thus a massive dislocation between opposite corners of the equity market. For some who made sizable bets *too early* on this dislocation—long small-value stocks and short large-growth stocks—the outcome was disastrous, best evidenced by the unwinding of Julian Robertson's Tiger Fund. But for those who were able to hold on and let fundamentals run their course, the rewards were sizable.

While it's a gross generalization that the typical long/short equity fund was long value stocks and short growth stocks, this was true for a meaningful subset of the group. Surely, some managers executed much better than others during this period, producing a wide dispersion of returns among hedged equity offerings. But the foundational cause of many hedge funds' success during this period was the environment more so than being smarter. The hedged equity style was in favor. Indeed, when the market rebounded in 2003, many hedged equity funds struggled. Yet it's not as if these managers became stupid between 2002 and 2003. Instead, fundamentally oriented hedge equity funds can falter in so-called junk rallies when lower-quality companies outperform higher-quality issues.

Contrast the TMT bubble to the crash of 2008, when the impact of style versus skill was just as germane. This was an extreme bear market, but very different from that of 2000–2002. Unlike the earlier period, the 2008 episode was a global liquidity crisis with little historical precedent. It was not a crisis mainly premised on shaky corporate fundamentals. While some companies did perform much better in 2008, this was less important than the global stampede out of nearly all risk assets. In many instances, whatever could be sold was, regardless of fundamentals. Perversely, because higher-quality issues were more liquid during the crisis, the better stocks and bonds were actually sold more rapidly than the junk, in order to raise cash and play defense.

This was a macro driven market. Making matters worse, when regulators stepped in during the fall of 2008 to temporarily outlaw the short selling of certain securities, especially financial stocks, alternative fund managers were whipsawed, forced to cover their shorts—shorts that would have performed extremely well. There was considerable hand-wringing among investors and the media about how hedge funds performed during 2008. People who set their expectations for the performance of hedged equity funds in 2008 based on what they thought they had observed in 2000 were sorely disappointed, as will always be the case when we conflate style and skill in the managing of expectations.

Hedged equity funds provided another head-scratcher for investors in 2011. That year was a weak but positive spell for traditional equities, as the S&P 500 gained 2.1 percent. During the same stretch, the HFR Hedged Equity Index dropped 8.4 percent. What happened? Figure 7.5 helps us make sense of it by presenting month-over-month returns for that year.

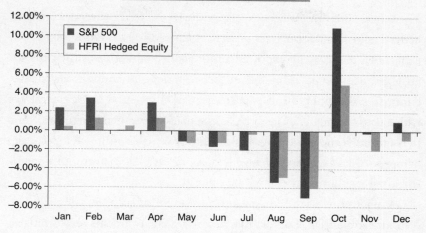

Figure 7.5   Too Clever: Long-Only Equity vs. Hedged Equity in 2011
Source: HFR

Following on a good spell of market performance in 2009 and 2010, many investors grew comfortable that we had returned to a more "normal" market in 2011. In the first quarter, markets were up nicely, and hedged equity funds, as one would expect, also made positive gains (though less so because of their hedged nature).

Hedged equity funds tend to *invest* according to fundamentals, but *trade* with a momentum bias, meaning that they will let their winners ride. Thus, net exposures tend to drift up in positive markets. By the same token, many (though certainly not all) will sell into weakness, reducing overall risk exposures. Recall that foxlike investors don't like to push their luck in dangerous situations; instead, they retreat and retool for the next attack. Most of the industry was justifiably gun-shy after the 2008 crisis, so the tendency to ride winners and sell losers was heightened post-crisis.

By the second quarter of 2011, the average hedged equity fund had begun to extend its risk profile. Unfortunately, when springtime volatility hit, these funds were poorly positioned, thus losing about the same as the market during May and June. In fact, 2011 has become emblematic of so-called risk-on, risk-off markets, meaning that, independent of corporate fundamentals, liquidity flowed in and out of the market rapidly and unpredictably. Ironically, for hedge funds often seen as "traders," this volatile trading environment was a nightmare.

When volatility spiked to extraordinary levels in the late summer, hedged equity funds, on average, were clobbered. Despite running hedged exposures, the strategy captured most of the market downturn in August and September. Gun-shy and bruised, hedged equity funds further trimmed risk—only to miss the sharp market rebound in October, after which they extended risk again. Alas, the market was mixed in the last couple of months and the average hedged equity vehicle continued to struggle. Whipsawed and damaged, hedged equity funds in 2011 featured some of the worst results the strategy could offer.

A big umbrella is a lifesaver during a severe storm. On sunny days, it's a cumbersome stick. Context matters. Some environments are conducive to appearing skillful, while others are not. Skill (or lack thereof) is often mistaken for style. Sometimes that style will be in favor and other times it will be out of favor.

To the extent that our experts appear to have veered from their usual style, one of two things has occurred. Either the manager has violated our expectations, or we have set our expectations incorrectly. As has been a theme throughout, this exercise gets harder in proportion to the flexibility the experts are afforded. Recall our first law of manager due diligence from chapter 4. It grows increasingly difficult to work with managers who have larger degrees of freedom in their investment program. The managers with the most extreme flexibility are the most likely to disappoint us because the gap between expectations and outcomes is likely to be widest. Foxes hunt, but not always in the way we anticipate.

We are then left with the deepest challenge of all, which is forming expectations in the first place. Where do expectations come from? A key consideration of any social activity is the intentionality of the subjects. Why did they do what they decided to do? Statistical analyses of investment performance do not address the fact that sentient beings can always make one choice over another. This is a particular challenge for choosing foxlike experts. Intentions matter, and getting at their source cannot be reduced to a statistical exercise. As we form expectations for how our experts will serve us best, we must try to understand their intentions and how they may change over time and circumstance.

GORILLAS IN OUR MIDST

How do we get to know others? There are some for whom answering that question is a lifetime passion.

Several decades ago, famed paleontologist Louis Leakey dispatched a young woman named Jane Goodall to the Gombe Stream region of Tanzania to research its indigenous chimpanzee culture. There was no way of knowing that this first visit in 1960 would spur one of the most revolutionary research efforts ever conducted in primatology and anthropology.

In order to truly understand this foreign culture, Goodall inserted herself into jungle living. On and off for nearly a half century, she observed and documented the daily routines of the chimps. She lived near them, got to know them, and opened a window into a world that no one had seen before. Many consider her greatest finding to be that apes build and use tools in their daily life. Previously, we had believed that humans were alone in their use of tools. Yet Goodall directly observed, for example, how the chimps would curl up a leaf in order to extract edible insects from their nests. Personalizing the chimps with names rather than numbers or other clinical ID tags, Goodall beautifully captured the "interpersonal" dynamics of Gombe. This passage from *Through a Window* shows the granularity of observation that Goodall brought to bear in describing Goblin, the group's dominant male:

Nine minutes after he had first moved, Goblin abruptly sat up and, almost at once, left his nest and began to leap wildly through the tree, vigorously swaying the branches. Instant pandemonium broke out. The chimpanzees closest to Goblin left their nests and rushed out of his way. Others sat up to watch, tense and ready for flight. The early morning peace was shattered by frenzied grunts and screams as Goblin's subordinates voiced their respect or fear. A few moments later, the arboreal part of his display over, Goblin leapt down and charged past me, slapping and stamping on the wet ground, rearing up and shaking the vegetation, picking up and hurling a rock, an old piece of wood, another rock. Then he sat, hair bristling, some fifteen feet away. He was breathing heavily. My own heart was beating fast. As he swung down, I had stood up and held onto a tree, praying that he would not pound on me as he sometimes does. But, to my relief, he had ignored me, and I sat down again.[15]

Aggressive, jealous, moody, generous, elated. These were the emotions of the jungle, as human as what we see in our own conclaves. And it was Goodall's prolonged commitment to observation and engagement that allowed her to truly capture the deep rhythms of that particular culture and identify the relationship between stimulus and response in a complex social setting.

The jungles of Gombe are not so different from the skyscrapers of Hong Kong or the doorways of Mayfair. When I first read the passage above, it immediately occurred to me that we could replace Goblin with any number of portfolio managers I've met and Goodall with one of the fund's team members. I know of a mutual fund manager who walked around his trading desk gripping a baseball bat that he continuously tapped into his other palm. I know of screaming arguments among co-portfolio managers that destroyed the partnership. I know of profanity-laden calls from furious investors to their fund managers, and of managers who gave it back in kind. Gombe, indeed.

These spectacular events are rare, however, and are less important than the "normal" day-to-day routine. Where does our understanding of social settings come from? We all want to understand the behavior of our subjects and to be able to anticipate the relationship between stimulus and response in a noisy social setting. But while anthropologists can literally camp out and observe, no one is camping out at a fund manager's office. For professional fund pickers, there is the opportunity for so-called site visits during which we can directly interview the staff as well as generally observe the culture of the office. But there are limits to this engagement in terms of time, resources, and patience—we typically have a few hours at most to directly observe a firm's local rhythms.

Thus, in the real world of fund research, we're back to the process of interacting with the experts themselves or with their representatives, such as marketers or product specialists. Admittedly, we know from the studies cited in chapter 2 that the interview process is flawed.[16] But we work with what we have when it comes to setting expectations. Fortunately, we are not necessarily resigned to a onetime interaction. When well executed, it's actually a cycle.

THE GHOST OF CLIFFORD STREET

This book opened with a brief tale about one of the worst manager interviews I've ever conducted. I stumbled my way through it, embarrassed myself along the way, but have tried to draw some lessons from it and other poor showings. When you do the same task thousands of times, you're bound to make mistakes. And while I would certainly like a mulligan on some of them, I do feel I was able to glean some key elements of a sound process. For professional fund pickers and financial advisors who have access to portfolio managers, these are sound tips for effective interviewing. For individual investors without such access, these tips still give some useful direction for interacting with whatever sort of financial expert you're looking to hire.

Be Prepared

This is basic but important. Nowadays there is an enormous amount of information available about our potential investments. As mentioned in chapter 5, the money management industry has grown increasingly institutionalized. The hedge fund industry in particular has taken enormous steps to provide increasing levels of access and transparency. For those who are qualified to receive the information, there are mountains of data potentially available about what risks a fund takes, what its performance record is, how the portfolio managers make decisions, and how they manage their operations. What's more, you don't need to get everything from the fund manager directly. Through the SEC, third-party information providers, and the Internet, there's a lot you can triangulate with. And always Google your subject—it's amazing what you can find.

It's incumbent on the fund investor to seek out and study that information, which then becomes the grounding for the conversation. Once armed with information, prepare for a dialogue in which you can learn what's most important to you, fully appreciating that no interview ever goes perfectly according to script. I once had the head of manager research for one of the world's largest investment consultancies insist that the proper method of preparation was to send a complete list of questions to the portfolio manager several days ahead of time on the argument that he could fully prepare to answer. I disagree. The fund manager is ultimately trying to sell you his product, and giving him all of your questions ahead of time lessens the chance of an engaged dialogue and increases the chance of a more tightly spun sales pitch.

If you cannot prepare to do due diligence on an investment because of a lack of available information, that's a major tip-off that the fund manager is going to be tough to work with. In my experience, fund managers are never friendlier or more accessible than when they are soliciting your business. So if they play tough at the beginning, it's only going to get worse after they have your money.

Pose Questions, Not Answers

While the interview process is best structured as an open conversation, that doesn't mean the exercise should serve primarily as an opportunity for the investor to wax poetic about markets or other topics. This is something I used to do a fair bit, and I still see it with many analysts. In fact, the more experienced they are, the more likely it is that they will use the interaction as an opportunity to voice a well-earned opinion. The analyst will start with a long preamble that sets the table for a question that usually ends up being something like "What do you think of the opinion I just offered?" This is not the right way. As much as possible, ask one question at a time. Don't phrase questions as answers. Try not to give a manager a set of choices but instead pose open-ended questions. Shape the conversation for your own purposes but do not determine its outcome by asking leading questions.

It's impossible to advise on the appropriate content for the questions. It is completely driven by circumstances. But as we mapped in chapter 4, there are only four core questions that define manager research: Can I trust you? What do you do? Are you good at your job? Are you the right fit for me? And even these four quickly reduce to one. The question of fit is one we should really ask of ourselves, knowing our own portfolio objectives. And questions on trust and skill can be triangulated through a variety of questions, data collection, and other investigations.

So we're down to the one. There's a famous Talmudic story about a man who asked Rabbi Hillel if he could explain the entire Torah while standing on one leg. Hillel's reply referenced the Golden Rule: "What is hateful to you, do not do to your neighbor: that is the whole Torah while the rest is commentary." The same structure applies to manager research. The one question I've asked over and again for more than a decade is: "What do you do?" While never phrased that bluntly, the spirit of the question is always the same. If you are reasonably well trained in finance and fully prepared for the conversation, the rest should truly result in a constructive conversation.

A couple other notes on content. Probably the two most popular questions asked of managers are "What is your edge?" and "What are your best ideas?" The former is a reasonable question that we do want the answer to, while the latter often drums up good stories. Unfortunately, both questions can lead us down the wrong path. These are "softball" questions, basically asking an expert to tell you how he skilled he is. Further, as a matter of interviewing protocol, when we ask sequential questions, we tend to follow the string that has formed and find it hard to divert. Thus, if the conversation starts with basically "How smart are you?," it probably won't veer far from that.

The more foxlike an investor, the more what we really need to know is his methods for adaptation. As discussed in chapter 4, there are (often implicit) rules for improvisation, and to the extent a manager is going to "make it up" as he goes along, we need to probe as much as possible. The manager is probably not fully articulate about this, which is to be expected, but this is where the skill of the interviewer comes in. Structure the conversation in a way that enables the manager to best address this critical facet.

Listen

A boss of mine was once fond of saying that we were given "two ears but just one mouth" for a reason. Listening is one of the most underappreciated skills we have. It's something we actually have to work at to be better. This is certainly an area where I've appreciated some good coaching. In particular, the practice of active listening is critical. Contrary to an aggressive interrogatory approach, the highest and best use of an interviewer is to put the portfolio manager in a position to best represent all of the relevant expectations about his program. Active listening can make that more likely. Thus, you should not only pay close attention to what is being said (and not said), but on key points repeat back to the subject what has been said. This not only confirms what you've heard. The act of repeating will increase both your comprehension and your retention. And chances are the manager will take it as a sign of respect that you're paying such close attention (as few do). You are providing him with an opportunity to articulate his approach and establish expectations. Active listening works.

Be Stupid

In the early to mid-1990s, Nick Leeson, a derivatives trader for Barings Bank, one of the UK's oldest and most august investment banks, made a series of unauthorized trades that grew larger and larger in size. When the Kobe earthquake roiled Asian markets in early 1995, Leeson's bet at the time that Japanese market volatility would stay low went horribly wrong. Despite not knowing these trades existed, Barings was still on the hook for covering more than $1 billion in losses, which it didn't have. Almost overnight, Barings was insolvent. According to Leeson's memoir, "Luckily for my fraud, there were too many chiefs who would chat about it at arm's length but never go further. And they never dared ask me any basic questions, since they were afraid of looking stupid about not understanding futures and options."[17]

No one wants to look stupid. It's not only embarrassing; it creates professional risk. Nonetheless, there are ways to embrace intellectual honesty without jeopardizing one's career. There are smart kinds of stupid. Think of TV detective Columbo, whose modus operandi was to take a modest, unassuming approach. By asking a string of simple questions he was able to piece together a fact pattern that solved the crime.

In my own career, I've seen some skilled interviewers probe complex topics by asking a very clear string of simple but pointed questions. In fact, at one of the firms I worked for we were able to avoid one of the largest hedge fund blowups in history by asking some very basic questions about some puzzling derivatives exposure that made very little sense, at least on the surface. By pointing to one number on a page and asking "Please explain this number to me," my colleague was able to Columbo his way to understanding the impending train wreck.

Personally, I think some of the best interviews I've conducted were the result of my saying to the portfolio manager at some point, "I don't understand what you are saying. Can you explain it again?" This is humbling, but that's not necessarily a bad thing. Doubt, ignorance, and mistakes are all sources of wisdom.[18] As we saw in Philip Tetlock's study of experts, those who were willing to admit mistakes were much more likely to be better forecasters. Further, you do learn something about your subjects by seeing how they respond. On balance, those who take the opportunity to educate rather than condescend will be better partners.

THE FIELD OF DREAMS

Speaking of those partners, nearly all of our attention throughout this book has been on the tasks of the fund investor. Yet in conducting more effective investment due diligence, it takes two to tango. Fund managers are as responsible for how well due diligence goes as are the allocators. In my experience, that's not something that many portfolio managers want to hear. I've heard countless complaints about investors who are merely "box checkers" and generally aren't able to "get" what they're doing. There is an element of arrogance in this, for sure. Fund managers, whether traditional or hedge, rarely lack confidence. The funny thing is, so many fund managers I've met—intelligent, charismatic, and wealthy as they might be—rarely take the time to understand what the person across the table is trying to accomplish.

The common mindset among fund managers, ranging from the smallest emerging manager to ones already overseeing billions in capital, is the same as Kevin Costner's character in *Field of Dreams:* "Build it and they will come." If the fund delivers good returns and runs a reasonably stable business, then investors should flock to it. Sometimes that works—never underestimate the investing public's disposition to chase performance and a good story. My recollection of the years between 2003 and 2007 is of a free-for-all: fund managers with little to no portfolio management experience were able to raise vast sums of money in a short period of time. Many of those funds are now out of business. Indeed, the problem is that hot money departs from a cooled-off manager just as quickly as it flows in. Even if it were possible to outperform consistently, which it isn't, this is not the recipe for a stable business. Moreover, in the post-2008 era, it has gotten even harder as market volatility has raised career risk up and down the fund-investing food chain.

In light of how difficult it is for most funds to attract assets in our current era, portfolio managers can employ some of the prescripts in *The Investor's Paradox* to grow their businesses more effectively. For as much as they complain about the "box checkers" that take hours of their time asking endless questions, they themselves tend to be quite poor at explaining what they do and generally front an elevated sense of value added that is rarely justified by the evidence. There are tactical measures managers can take to accommodate their customers, such as ease of access and transparency. But the deeper task is to fully engage in the conversation with investors. For experts in finance but not necessarily communications, this can be hard to do.

Ultimately, managing expectations is a two-way street. Precisely because of their flexibility, alternative fund managers have the harder challenge. Their prerogative to change stripes over the course of time and circumstance is the source of increasing appeal to many investors. But what are the manager's "rules of improvisation"? How have they adapted in the past and how do they expect to do so in the future? There are no precisely correct answers to these questions. While that may be frustrating to some who crave that precision, the fact is that satisfaction stems from our expectations being met, and expectations are an inexorably social phenomenon.

WHEN TRAVELING TO UNKNOWN PLACES, we need not only maps. We need translators, too. As we seek more complicated solutions to difficult investment problems, we increasingly turn to investors with flexible investment programs. To evaluate these managers, we do not have the same easy benchmarks that are available in traditional fund investing. Thus, understanding what managers do and whether they've accomplished their objectives is a function of dialogue that is complex and iterative. Skill is ultimately a negotiated equilibrium among multiple parties. It isn't just received from afar, like a package at the door. Instead, for those who adopt an adaptive mindset toward fund investing, the chance for success is remarkably high, thus making, somewhat ironically, the promise of Lake Wobegon less illusory than mathematics would suggest.

8

LESS

You get what you get and you don't get upset.
—Sarah Portnoy, Age 6

FROM CLUTTER TO SIMPLICITY

Albert Einstein had three "rules of work" that guided his daily effort:

- ✓ Out of clutter, find simplicity.
- ✓ From discord, find harmony.
- ✓ In the middle of difficulty lies opportunity.

Though I can't possibly know, I suspect that these were aspirations as much as rules, rising from the clutter, discord, and difficulty of his professional tasks. I also suspect that the search for simplicity in a world of clutter topped this list because it is the gateway to solving so many problems of modern life. Finally, I suspect that Einstein saw these rules as a blueprint for a satisfied life, for himself as well as for every future reader of these rules, well beyond the confines of the office.

Getting from more to less is hard work. Simple doesn't mean easy. Sometimes you'll wonder if it's even worth it. In wealthy postindustrial societies, process enhancement and efficiency gains are thin elixirs. They make things better, but they don't quench any deeper thirst. Still, simplification is a reasonably noble goal across the many complex choice regimes in our professional and personal lives. The world of investments, like those of health, education, commerce, and leisure, has marched relentlessly toward overabundance and complexity. *The Investor's Paradox* has aimed to diagnose the historically specific problem facing investors and then offer some suggestions to help navigate it.

The global investor class faces a nested problem. At one level, we crave more options to help us feed, house, and educate our children; be charitable in our communities; and retire comfortably. Yet when we get more options, we are less likely to achieve those goals. At another level, overwhelming, complex choice steers us to rely on intelligent, charismatic, and opportunistic experts. But those experts, increasingly abundant and accessible, are likely to disappoint. Seek the fox, but be careful what you wish for. At times, it feels as if we can't win.

I have attempted to pull back the curtain on the modern money management industry and give some advice on how to make better investment decisions. While the framework I've delivered is all-encompassing, much of our focus has been on alternative investments because of their growing prominence and tendency to inspire confusion. I have tried to communicate that among this controversial set of experts, there is no all-knowing master of the universe pulling the strings; rather, there is something very human, flawed, and knowable that any serious interlocutor can understand. This insight is both empowering and deflating: empowering in that we can now master what we once thought indecipherable; deflating because it would be nice if someone really did have all the answers.

There are countless investments available to us, each with countless features. If we try to enumerate the details of each and map their relationships, we will surely miss the forest for the trees. I have argued that the problem of investing is a problem of choice, and problems of choice can be solved. Especially when the environment is complex, we must appreciate the myriad challenges to making good decisions—the biases and quirks that influence us, many of which operate unconsciously. And in particular, when choosing to work with dynamic experts whom we need to help us get where we want to go, we must engage in a repeated process of adaptation to multiple forms of change—in our experts, in our environments, and in ourselves.

Luckily, only a few foundational questions truly matter in this quest: trust, risk, skill, and fit. This book has addressed primarily the first three. The topic of fit raises difficult questions about where our preferences come from—why we want the things we want. A robust answer to that deep question is beyond the scope of this work. That's not to say that we can't move beyond the experts and the environment and shift the lens inward. I thus conclude with a couple of points about ourselves.

MIRROR, MIRROR

In any endeavor, we typically learn through reflecting on our mistakes. Investing is no different, which is why the bulk of what's written about the "masters of money" is unhelpful because it lionizes the winners, gives short shrift to their mistakes, and pays no attention to traders who are average or worse. Understandably, no one wants to read a book about losers.

Indeed, the genesis of this book was a basic thought exercise on how I might do my job better. It started with an Excel spreadsheet: I made a list of due diligence experiences in which I thought I could have done better. I then looked for patterns in those errors. Were there certain types of funds, strategies, portfolio managers, market opportunities, business platforms, and so forth that seemed to attract or repel me? Were my analyses—and my gut—ultimately right or wrong? I surveyed the literature on fund investing in the hope of finding guidance in this process, but I didn't find anything particularly helpful.

As I looked for patterns, an inchoate version of the risk prism detailed in chapter 6 emerged. I realized that thinking about good and bad decisions in a vacuum, without reference to broader theory, was pointless. I had tentatively concluded, from my many mutual fund and hedge fund due diligence sessions, that most funds most of the time are not delivering alpha through better security selection. There was *always* someone above average—that temporary resident of Lake Wobegon—but they usually didn't stay there for long. Hence the question in my fledgling mental model at the end of chapter 6: Do you prefer Geniuses or Cowboys? While great stock pickers or "moneymakers" with an "edge" remain the obsession of some fund analysts, for me it became increasingly clear that broader risk considerations mattered a lot; in fact, they mattered more. In that vein, what I saw was that I tilted consistently toward concentrated, directional managers: managers who took big bets on a handful of names. I liked the conviction and the apparent deep research that lay behind it. In the halcyon days between 2003 and 2007, this bias proved prescient and enriching; in 2008 it was disastrous.

This exercise started with both a spreadsheet and a basic question: What counts as a mistake? There are at least a couple of different ways to think about this. First, scientists distinguish between "type 1" and "type 2" errors, more colloquially known as *errors of commission* and *errors of omission*. A type 1 mistake is when you make a decision—take action—and end up being wrong. For instance, when an investment "blows up" (loses most or all of its value) or turns out to be a fraud, the error can destroy whole firms and careers. A type 2 error, on the other hand, would be to decline to invest in something that ends up being a great success. Your reason for passing may have been legitimate, but it's hard not to feel regret. However, it's rare that type 2 errors get you fired. Missed opportunity may sting, but it almost never cripples.

Second, there is an even subtler difference between a mistake and a bad outcome. The question is whether the observed outcome falls within our range of reasonable expectations. A bad outcome is something that falls within that range but is not one we necessarily want. For example, in 1999, 2003, or 2009, a conservatively positioned stock fund returned far less than its more aggressive peers. This is a bad outcome but not a mistake. The manager was *supposed* to underperform.

As a manager's degrees of freedom increase, it becomes harder to distinguish between a mistake and a bad outcome. Take the example of an emerging market (EM) equity hedge fund. Because of optimism toward EMs and the technical challenge of shorting certain EM stocks, few funds in this niche actually hedge much. They tend to run with a long market bias, often with net market exposure north of 50 percent. The logic for setting expectations in this bare-bones case isn't that difficult. If EM equities gained 40 percent and a fund tends to run 50 percent net long, then we should anticipate, all else being equal, a gain of approximately 20 percent. In 2008, the MSCI EM Equity Index lost 53.1 percent. According to Morningstar, the average diversified emerging markets mutual fund lost 54.4

percent, suggesting that the returns of the typical long-only EM vehicle consist of almost entirely beta. Meanwhile, the average EM hedge fund, according to HFR EM Global Index, dropped 30.9 percent. If we assume no stock-picking alpha, then this result implies an average net exposure of ~ 58 percent (i.e., 30.9% ÷ 53.1%), which sounds about right. These 2008 results are awful from an absolute return perspective, but they are bad outcomes, *not mistakes.*

Let's now complicate this example. EM equities are volatile. Not only can they can tank quickly, they tend to be highly correlated when they do so. That correlation stems from the impact of "top-down" factors such as growth trends, interest rate levels, political change, or commodity prices—as opposed to "bottom-up," company-specific factors—that drive all security prices similarly. There is relatively little idiosyncratic risk in each security. Thus, almost all EM hedge funds incorporate top-down analysis; none is a purely bottom-up stock-picking vehicle. EM funds will also adjust their leverage and net market exposure to reflect the bullish or bearish views on the overall economy.

So now the portfolio manager has set our expectations that he has three tools in his tool kit: stock selection, adjusting net exposure, and adjusting leverage. The latter two are different forms of market timing. Returning to 2008, we might be led by the three-tool portfolio manager to expect that he can take cover when storm clouds form on the economic horizon. He can take any number of defensive precautions, such as shorting more stocks, lowering net exposure, or moving more of the portfolio into cash.

So with this additional information, was my choice to invest in this average EM hedge fund a mistake, or can I chalk it up to a bad outcome? Did the manager meet my expectations? The answer to the latter is probably not, but the extent of the mistake depends on the details of the conversation with the manager, as well as the raw numbers. As covered in chapter 7, skill is determined through a social process as much as it is by statistical analysis.

For example, I once researched a London-based emerging markets equity hedge fund whose managers touted their market-timing ability more than their stock-picking ability. They invested only in large-cap EM stocks and admitted that they did not have much edge in issues like Petrobras or Ping An; perhaps on the margin they could find an edge. But they did firmly believe that their investment process could anticipate the big swings EMs are known for. Based on savvy market calls and deft portfolio positioning, this fund earned *positive* returns in 2008 and then decent positive returns during the rebound in 2009. That's a great outcome.

Returning to the average EM hedge fund manager referenced at the start, what were my expectations of his top-down ability compared to his stock-picking edge? It is much more common that equity fund managers sell their security-selection abilities than their knack for market timing. Thus, I would want to know if the portfolio manager accurately represented his market-timing ability, if I could evidence that ability in the past, or if my disappointment in a 30 percent loss was the result of unrealistic expectations based on weak due diligence. The logic of this exercise can be applied generically across any form of manager research.

Mistakes are unavoidable. But self-awareness and intellectual honesty are worthy goals. First, they are achieved by appreciating the impact that natural biases have on good decision making. Among some of the other biases discussed in chapter 2, hindsight and confirmation biases are especially germane. We all have the tendency to play Monday morning quarterback. Once we know the outcome of an event, we can create a narrative for why it was going to happen that way. We do this all the time, but it is not a rigorous method of analysis. We also tend to seek out information that confirms our hypotheses. It feels better to be right than to push harder to figure out if we actually might be wrong. But entertaining competing hypotheses and collecting data appropriately (meaning not selectively choosing data that support your case) are the keys to sound decision making.

Second, think through your specific investment biases. Using the risk prism can help formulate some hypotheses on your own dispositions. As mentioned, for a long while I liked managers who took large, concentrated bets but ran liquid books light on leverage. This predisposed me to a certain type of manager; I liked one type of Cowboy. I once had a very bright colleague who loved complexity: He liked intricate puzzles and wanted to hire managers who arrived at nuanced solutions to complex problems. He liked Geniuses.

None of these tilts is right or wrong. Recall that absent any of the five dimensions of the risk prism—directionality, concentration, illiquidity, leverage, and complexity—an investor has to be consistently better informed than other highly intelligent, aggressive traders. But who these days, operating within the boundaries of the law, is always smarter than others? Hardly anyone. Thus, we pick our poison. Generally, almost every mistake—and every success—will be driven by at least one of these five generic elements.

Finally, measurement inspires management. If you're a serious investor, you should keep track of everything you do—conversations, meetings, hirings, firings, and any other "touches." Make an annual scorecard of your type 1 and type 2 errors. Look for patterns; identify your biases. Explore alternative explanations for why your predictions of success worked or failed. Remain intellectually honest.

A tidy algorithm for success will not emerge from keeping track of your predictions, but something positive likely will, if only self-awareness. The bad news about good intentions in the field of manager research is that it can take a long time to accumulate enough evidence to know if you are right or wrong. Unlike that in domains such as meteorology or anesthesiology, the temporal disconnect between decision and outcome is extreme. But we have to play the hand we're dealt.

THE BEAUTY OF GOOD ENOUGH

Nearly a quarter century ago, in 1990, a then relatively unknown economist named Paul Krugman penned a book called *The Age of Diminished Expectations*. He argued that in a period of generally rising wealth, problems related to indebtedness and income inequality would undermine future prosperity. As its title suggests, Krugman saw these growing headwinds as sources of caution in otherwise bountiful times. The book hardly had an alarmist tone, however. It predicted no imminent calamity; it merely pointed out some of capitalism's internal tensions. These did come home to roost, but not until seventeen years later.

One can imagine an identically titled book being published today with a far more ominous sense of concern. The problems Krugman diagnosed then look positively tame compared to our current ones. Notwithstanding a sharp rise in global equity markets over recent years, we are still beset by structural headwinds that won't abate soon. The New Normal framework, in a nutshell, is that a large, sustained deleveraging cycle has negative consequences for growth and unemployment. The consequences of an unprecedented, massive expansion of the monetary base are unknown, but the potential for sharply rising inflation, and perhaps the onset of stagflation, is real. And widening economic inequality never bodes well for growth or social stability. The likelihood that we will relive the stretch of double-digit returns of the 1980s and 1990s is slim.

This is, indeed, the true age of diminished expectations. Or at least it should be. Optimism bias and our tendency toward overconfidence make us hopeful about the future. And that's not a bad thing. To operate otherwise would be depressing. To ratchet down our expectations for ourselves and our children feels wrong. We want better. We want more.

But wanting something does not mean you're going to get it. As has been the consistent theme of *The Investor's Paradox,* disappointment necessarily results when reality defies aspirations. We are left with a Goldilocks dilemma of sorts. If we expect too much of markets and the experts we hire to navigate them, we will incur not only emotional disappointment but also the more practical stressor of missing our financial goals. Expect too little and we will necessarily underachieve by taking too little risk. Getting it just right is the trick.

Broadly speaking, many investors have not recalibrated their expectations to reflect new financial realities. This mismatch is most visible among US pension plans. The current state of defined benefit plans is dire, in no small part because declining interest rates have pushed liabilities significantly higher. Overseeing trillions of dollars in assets, many of these plans now face severe funding shortfalls. For instance, a 2013 study of the top one hundred US corporate plans by consultant Towers Watson revealed a $295 billion gap between what the funds owed their workers and how much the funds were able to pay out.[1]

In order to meet this challenge, pensions have made Herculean assumptions about what their investment portfolio will earn. Based on a set of assumptions for the long-term return of different asset classes, many plans assume a roughly 8 percent annualized rate of return. This number crisply captures the lofty expectations of some of the world's largest investment pools. For example, in 2012 the largest US pension scheme, CalPERS, trimmed its 7.75 percent assumed rate of return to 7.5 percent. The Illinois

Teachers' Retirement System continues to assume an 8.5 percent return. Other states and municipalities have stuck to targets between 8 percent and 8.5 percent.

Basic math is not kind to these assumptions. In a back-of-the-envelope example, assume that a pension plan has a 40 percent allocation to fixed income and a 60 percent allocation to equities. Also assume that, in the current environment, a high-quality bond portfolio will return 3 percent, meaning a 1.2 percent contribution to the plan's returns. If the overall target return is 8 percent, then the remaining 6.8 percent would have to be achieved by earning 11.3 percent on the stock portfolio. That is well in excess of the historical risk premium offered by stocks. We can work the math around in a number of different ways—allocate more to equities, assume a higher return on bonds—but it will remain extremely difficult to meet expectations.

Although the crisis is well-known, it's not clear how to resolve it. The obvious solution—lowering the target rate—creates other problems. Foremost among them, it increases the size of the liabilities. Alternatively, the plan can increase its contributions (which it can't afford) or decrease benefits (which is politically untenable).

Or they can find a different path by choosing better or different money managers. Hence the aggressive push by pensions into alternative investments.[2] It is understood that bonds won't return much and equities, though potentially lucrative, are highly unpredictable—thus the search for a third way, for something "alternative." Here we come full circle to what we should expect from alternatives. I think it's safe to say that serious confusion remains. Some continue to believe that hedge funds aim to "beat the market." For instance, a spokesman for CalPERS said in August 2012, "There is a premium that goes with investing in alternative investments because they typically are a little bit riskier, but higher return."[3] Other prominent voices look at them differently, stressing their volatility-dampening effect.[4]

I subscribe to the latter perspective based on the simple observation that hedge funds hedge. Most alternative strategies should underperform in up markets and outperform in down markets. Their appeal is the potential to capture more market upside than downside, thus making for attractive risk-adjusted returns. This is compelling, but hardly controversial—or at least shouldn't be. Neither saints nor sinners, hedge funds and those operating them can be truly known only through hard work. Manager due diligence may be an oddball vocation, but its value is profound.

Fortunately, many of us don't have the intractable balance sheet of a pension plan. Nonetheless, we all still face a similar dilemma because the challenge to traditional stock and bond investments is manifest. We, too, are searching for something different. Not surprisingly, money management firms are responding with large menus of new choices. Alternatives are going mainstream. I hope that I have convinced you that we each have it in our power to make sense of them, to form reasonable expectations and to update them accordingly.

Our last word is Nobel laureate Herbert Simon's most famous word: satisfice. It is unlikely that our investment portfolios will return anything close to what they did in decades past. If we are surprised to the upside, that's fantastic. If we find that resolving the investor's paradox is not necessary, and that this book is superfluous, it means that most of us are wealthier than we might have anticipated. That's a good outcome.

But I think it unlikely. In turbulent times, therefore, I believe that true investment success starts with ourselves. We struggle to overcome our built-in biases, look to experts to help solve problems, and hope to eventually find the right path forward. If that path involves choosing the "best" managers and trying to "beat the market," we will fail. If we take sober stock of the problems each of us—as individuals or institutions—is trying to solve, the chance of success grows considerably. Professor Simon codified the somewhat commonsense notion that we find ways to get by. And sometimes what's good enough is just perfect.

NOTES

CHAPTER 1

1. Barry Schwartz (2004), *The Paradox of Choice: Why More Is Less,* New York: Harper Collins.
2. Sheena S. Iyengar and Mark R. Lepper (2000), "When Choice Is Demotivating: Can One Desire Too Much of a Good Thing?" *Journal of Personality and Social Psychology,* 79 (6), 995–1006.
3. Alexander Chernev (2003), "When More Is Less and Less Is More: The Role of Ideal Point Availability and Assortment in Consumer Choice," *Journal of Consumer Research,* 30 (2), 170–183; Rainer Greifeneder, Benjamin Scheibehenne, and Nina Kleber (2010), "Less May Be More When Choosing Is Difficult: Choice Complexity and Too Much Choice," *Acta Psychologica,* 133, 45–50; David G. Mick, Susan M. Broniarczyk, and Jonathan Haidt (2004), "Choose, Choose, Choose, Choose, Choose, Choose, Choose: Emerging and Prospective Research on the Deleterious Effects of Living in Consumer Hyperchoice," *Journal of Business Ethics,* 52 (2), 207–211; Barry Schwartz (2000), "Self-Determination: The Tyranny of Freedom," *American Psychologist,* 55 (1), 79–88; Schwartz (2004), *The Paradox of Choice*; Avni M. Shah and George Wolford (2007), "Buying Behavior as a Function of Parametric Variation of Number of Choices," *Psychological Science,* 18 (5), 369–370. The contrary position is stated in Benjamin Scheibehenne, Rainer Greifeneder, and Peter M. Todd (2010), "Can There Ever Be Too Many Options? A Meta-Analytic Review of Choice Overload," *Journal of Consumer Research,* 37 (3), 409–425; and Benjamin Scheibehenne, Rainier Griefender, and Peter M. Todd (2009), "What Moderates the Too Much Choice Effect?" *Psychology & Marketing,* 26E (3), March, 229–253.
4. A seminal work in the traditional rational choice approach to choice is Kenneth J. Arrow (1963), *Social Choice and Individual Values,* 2nd edition, New Haven, CT: Yale University Press. The behavioral approach was pioneered by Amos Tversky and Daniel Kahneman. Their research and insights are captured in Daniel Kahneman (2011), *Thinking, Fast and Slow,* New York: Farrar, Straus and Giroux. Kahneman and Tversky, along with Sheena Iyengar and Barry Schwartz, have been my strongest influences for developing this book's behavioral perspective.
5. Sheena Iyengar (2010), *The Art of Choosing,* New York: Twelve Books, 7.
6. Ibid., 10.
7. Ibid.; Robert Trivers (2011), *The Folly of Fools: The Logic and Self-Deception in Human Life,* New York: Basic Books, 22–23; Dan Gardner (2011), *Future Babble: Why Expert Predictions Are Next to Worthless and You Can Do Better,* New York: Dutton, 134.

8. Ellen Langer and Judith Rodin (1976), "The Effect of Choice and Enhanced Personal Responsibility for the Aged: A Field Experiment in an Institutional Setting," *Journal of Personality and Social Psychology,* 34, 191–198; Ellen Langer and Judith Rodin (1977), "Long-Term Effects of a Control-Relevant Intervention with the Institutional Aged," *Journal of Personality and Social Psychology,* 35, 897–902. Cf. Daniel Gilbert (2006), *Stumbling on Happiness,* New York: Random House. See also Richard Schulz (1976), "Effects of Control and Predictability on the Physical and Psychological Well-Being of the Institutionalized Aged," *Journal of Personality and Social Psychology,* 33, 563–573.

9. Schwartz (2004), *The Paradox of Choice,* 2.

10. The suggestive power of these advertisements has been labeled by some as "disease mongering" by pharmaceutical companies to create or grow markets for treatment by convincing people that they are sick. For example, the reported incidence of restless leg syndrome (RLS) appears to have skyrocketed once drug companies began to advertise cures. See Steven Woloshin and Lisa M. Schwartz (2006), "Giving Legs to Restless Legs: A Case Study of How the Media Helps Make People Sick," *PLoS Medicine,* 3 (4), e170, DOI, 10.1371/journal.pmed.0030170.

11. John Tierney (2011), "Do You Suffer from Decision Fatigue?" *New York Times,* August 17. Some studies show that individuals spend three to four hours per day resisting desire—not doing something they "really" want to do (e.g., eat, sleep, purchase).

12. Sheena S. Iyengar, Gur Huberman, and Wei Jiang (2004), "How Much Choice Is Too Much? Contributions to 401(k) Retirement Plans," in *Pension Design and Structure: New Lessons from Behavioral Finance,* ed. Olivia S. Mitchell and Steve Utkus, Oxford: Oxford University Press, 83–95. See also Gary R. Mottola and Stephen P. Utkus (2003), "Can There Be Too Much Choice in a Retirement Savings Plan?" Malvern, PA: Vanguard Center for Retirement Research: Vanguard Group Inc. On the various ways in which plan sponsors can shape the choices of their participants, see James J. Choi, David Laibson, and Brigitte C. Madrian (May 2004), "Plan Design and 401(k) Savings Outcomes," National Bureau of Economic Research Working Paper 10486, www.nber.org/papers/w10486.

13. Eugene F. Fama (January 1965), "The Behavior of Stock Market Prices," *Journal of Business,* 38 (1): 34–105; Eugene F. Fama (1970), "Efficient Capital Markets: A Review of Theory and Empirical Work," *Journal of Finance,* 25 (2), 383–417.

14. Not surprisingly, there are now a proliferating number of funds that will assemble a portfolio of underlying ETFs for investors for an extra fee in addition to the pass-through costs of the ETFs themselves.

15. Investment Company Factbook, www.icifactbook.org/fb_ch2.html.

16. Sarah N. Lynch (2013), "U.S. SEC Prepares for Hedge Fund Advertising Blitz," Reuters, September 17; Timothy Spangler (2013), "Who's Afraid of Hedge-Fund Advertising?" *The New Yorker,* www.newyorker.com/online/blogs/news-desk/2013/08/whos-afraid-of-hedge-fund-advertising-1.html.

17. Richard Grinold and Ronald Kahn (1999), *Active Portfolio Management: A Quantitative Approach for Producing Superior Return and Controlling Risk,* New York: McGraw-Hill.

18. There's a wonderful *Calvin & Hobbes* comic strip in which Calvin throws one of his typical temper tantrums demanding a toy that he had never heard of previously; but now that he had heard of it, it was something he "must have."

19. This begins to bridge us into the question of whether our own preferences are exogenously or endogenously derived, a heavy issue that will loom above various parts of the narrative but one that we will not resolve in these pages.

20. Alexander Chernev (2003), "Product Assortment and Individual Decision Processes," *Journal of Personality and Social Psychology,* 85 (1), 151–162; Chernev (2003), "When More Is Less and Less Is More," 170–183.

21. Iyengar and Lepper (2000), "When Choice Is Demotivating," 996.

22. John T. Gourville and Dilip Soman, "Overchoice and Assortment Type: When and Why Variety Backfires," www.rotman.utoronto.ca/bicpapers/pdf/04-08.pdf.

23. The standard literature on investing is mostly about picking stocks or bonds, building portfolios, or other areas of personal finance. It doesn't provide much direction for choosing the right funds. There is a vast academic finance literature that focuses primarily on the narrow question of whether fund managers have investment skill. There are a few how-to guides on fund selection that are mostly checklists of the positive attributes we would like our managers to have. And there is a journalistic literature on so-called market wizards, which tells wonderful tales of investment prowess. While each of these literatures has its strengths and weaknesses, it's fair to say that they each pay short shrift to the behavioral complexities of choice, disregard the historical and social context within which we make investment decisions, and rigidly divide the world into either traditional or alternative categories.

24. Barbara E. Kahn and Jonathan Baron (1995), "An Exploratory Study of Choice Rules Favored for High Stakes Decisions," *Journal of Consumer Psychology,* 4 (4), 305–328; Robert B. Cialdini (2008), *Influence: Science and Practice,* 5th edition, New York: Pearson.

CHAPTER 2

1. Higher-profile perma-bulls such as Goldman Sachs's Abby Joseph Cohen are a prominent example.

2. James K. Glassman and Kevin A. Hassett (1999), *Dow 36,000: The New Strategy for Profiting from the Coming Rise in the Stock Market,* New York: Times Business, 3.

3. Sheena Iyengar (2010), *The Art of Choosing,* New York: Twelve Books, 260.

4. On this paradox, see Barry Schwartz (1994), *The Costs of Living: How Market Freedom Erodes the Best Things in Life,* New York: W.W. Norton. On the choice to delegate to an expert, see Richard DeCharms (1968), *Personal Causation: The Internal Affective Determinants of Behavior,* New York: Academic Press; Edward Deci and Richard M. Ryan (1985), *Intrinsic Motivation and Self-Determination in Human Behavior,* New York: Plenum; Shelley E. Taylor (1989), *Positive Illusions: Creative Self-Deception and the Healthy Mind,* New York: Basic Books; Miron Zuckerman, Joseph Porac, David Lathin, R. Smith, and Edward L. Deci (1978), "On the Importance of Self-Determination for Intrinsically Motivated Behavior," *Personality and Social Psychology Bulletin,* 4, 443–446.

5. Kathryn Schulz (2010), *Being Wrong: Adventures in the Margin of Error,* New York: HarperCollins; Joseph T. Hallinan (2009), *Why We Make Mistakes: How We Look Without Seeing, Forget Things in Seconds, and Are All Pretty Sure We Are Way Above Average,* New York: Broadway Books; Dan Gardner (2011), *Future Babble: Why Expert Predictions Are Next to Worthless and You Can Do Better,* New York: Dutton; David H. Freedman (2010), *Wrong: Why Experts Keep Failing Us—And How to Know When Not to Trust Them,* New York: Little Brown and Company; Nate Silver (2012), *The Signal and the Noise: Why So Many Predictions Fail—But Some Don't,* New York: Penguin Press; Iyengar (2010), *The Art of Choosing;* Gary Klein (2011), *Streetlights and Shadows: Searching for the Keys to Adaptive Decision Making,* Cambridge, MA: MIT Press; Daniel Kahneman (2011), *Thinking, Fast and Slow,* New York: Farrar, Straus and Giroux; Malcolm Gladwell (2005),

Blink: The Power of Thinking Without Thinking, New York: Little Brown and Company; Barry Schwartz (2004), *The Paradox of Choice: Why More Is Less*, New York: Harper Collins.

6. Philip Tetlock (2005), *Expert Political Judgment: How Good Is It? How Can We Know?*, Princeton, NJ: Princeton University Press, Kindle edition. The claim is not that Tetlock invented the field of expert decision making, but it is among the most comprehensive and methodologically sophisticated. James Shanteau claims that the earliest study of expert decision making was in the judging of the quality of grain; cf. H.D. Hughes (1917), "An Interesting Corn Seed Experiment," *Iowa Agriculturalist*, 17, 424–425. James Shanteau (1992), "The Psychology of Experts: An Alternative View," in *Expertise and Decision Support*, ed. G. Wright and F. Bolger, New York: Plenum, 11–23.

7. Zvi Gitelman, ed. (2000), *Cultures and Nations of Central and Eastern Europe: Essays in Honor of Roman Szporluk*, Cambridge, MA: Harvard Ukrainian Research Institute.

8. Tetlock (2005), *Expert Political Judgment*, Kindle edition, location 1098.

9. Ibid., location 1102.

10. Michael Snyder (2010), "Say What? 30 Ben Bernanke Quotes that Are So Stupid that You Won't Know Whether to Laugh or Cry," *Economic Collapse Blog*, December 6, http://theeconomiccollapseblog.com/archives/say-what-30-ben-bernanke-quotes.

11. Edmund L. Andrews (2008), "Greenspan Concedes Error on Regulation," *New York Times*, October 23, www.nytimes.com/2008/10/24/business/economy/24panel.html?_r=0.

12. Michael Lewis (2010), *The Big Short: Inside the Doomsday Machine*, New York: W.W. Norton & Company.

13. Nassim Nicholas Taleb (2007), *The Black Swan: The Impact of the Highly Improbable*, New York: Random House.

14. David N. Dreman and Michael A. Berry (1995), "Analyst Forecasting Errors and Their Implications for Security Analysis," *Financial Analysts Journal*, 30–41. A similar argument is presented in Michelle R. Clayman and Robin A. Schwartz (1994), "Falling in Love Again: Analysts' Estimates and Reality," *Financial Analysts Journal*, 66–68. For a contrarian view, see Lawrence D. Brown (1996), "Analyst Forecasting Errors and Their Implications for Security Analysis: An Alternative Perspective," *Financial Analysts Journal*, 40–47.

15. William F. Sharpe (1966), "Mutual Fund Performance," *Journal of Business, Supplement on Security Prices*, 39 (January), 119–138; Jack L. Treynor (1966), "How to Rate Management Investment Funds," *Harvard Business Review*, 43 (January–February); Michael C. Jensen (1967), "The Performance of Mutual Funds in the Period 1945–1964," *Journal of Finance*, 23 (2), 389–416; Eugene F. Fama and Kenneth R. French (1993), "Common Risk Factors in the Returns on Stocks and Bonds," *Journal of Financial Economics*, 33, 3–56; Mark M. Carhart (1997), "On Persistence in Mutual Fund Performance," *Journal of Finance*, 52 (1), 57–82.

16. Amit Goyal and Sunil Wahal (2008), "The Selection and Termination of Investment Management Firms by Plan Sponsors," *Journal of Finance*, 63 (4), August.

17. Arleen Jacobius (2012), "New Mexico Fund Marks Progress, Plots More Reform," *P&I Research Center*, November 26, www.pionline.com/article/20121126/PRINTSUB/311269972.

18. Benoit Dewaele, Hugues Pirotte, Nils Tuchschmid, and Erik Wallerstein (2011), "Assessing the Performance of Funds of Hedge Funds," Midwest Finance Association 2012 Annual Meetings Paper, available at SSRN 1929097.

19. This finding of lack in skill among most fund pickers is in no small part why the fund of funds industry now appears to be in decline. As investors question the value add of hedge funds themselves, they have grown even more skeptical of the allocators who have generally not added value above and beyond their added level of fees. Christine Williamson (2012), "Asset Gap Widens as Hedge Funds of Funds Slide," September 17, www.pionline.com/article/20120917/printsub/309179981.

20. Dewaele (2011), "Assessing the Performance of Funds of Hedge Funds."

21. Paul E. Meehl (1986), "Causes and Effects of My Disturbing Little Book," *Journal of Personality Assessment,* 50 (3), 370–375; Michael A. Bishop and J.D. Trout (2002), "50 Years of Successful Predictive Modeling Should Be Enough: Lessons for the Philosophy of Science," *Philosophy of Science,* 69, September, S197–S208; Robyn Dawes, David Faust, and Paul E. Meehl (1989), "Clinical versus Actuarial Judgment," *Science,* 243, March, 1668–1674.

22. Robyn M. Dawes (1979), "The Robust Beauty of Improper Linear Models in Decision Making," *American Psychologist,* 34 (7), July, 571–582.

23. Tetlock (2005), *Expert Political Judgment,* Kindle edition, 172.

24. Ola Svenson (1981), "Are We All Less Risky and More Skillful Than Our Fellow Drivers?" *Acta Psychologica,* 47 (1981), 143–148.

25. David Dunning and Justin Kruger (1999), "Unskilled and Unaware of It: How Difficulties in Recognizing One's Own Incompetence Lead to Inflated Self-Assessments," *Journal of Personality and Social Psychology,* 77 (6), December, 1121–1134; Shelley E. Taylor (1989), *Positive Illusions: Creative Self-Deception and the Healthy Mind,* New York: Basic Books.

26. Robert Trivers (2011), *The Folly of Fools: The Logic and Self-Deception in Human Life,* New York: Basic Books, 15.

27. Dominic D.P. Johnson and James H. Fowler (2011), "The Evolution of Overconfidence," *Nature,* 477 (7364), 317–320.

28. Trivers (2011), *The Folly of Fools.*

29. Cf. Werner F.M. De Bondt (1991), "What Do Economists Know about the Stock Market?" *Journal of Portfolio Management,* 17 (2), 84–91.

30. Thomas Gilovich, Robert Vallone, and Amos Tversky (1985), "The Hot Hand in Basketball: On the Misperception of Random Sequences," *Cognitive Psychology,* 17, 295–314.

31. Simcha Avugos, Jorn Koppen, Uwe Czienskowski, Markus Raab, and Michael Bar-Eli (2013), "The 'Hot Hand' Reconsidered: A Meta-Analytic Approach," *Psychology of Sport and Exercise,* 14 (1), 21–27; Michael Bar-Eli, Simcha Avugos, and Markus Raab (2006), "Twenty Years of 'Hot Hand' Research: Review and Critique," *Psychology of Sport and Exercise,* 7, 525–553. Per the latter, "The empirical evidence for the existence of the hot hand is considerably limited."

32. Cf. Trivers (2011), *The Folly of Fools,* 23–24.

33. Daniel Kahneman and Amos Tversky (1984), "Choices, Values, and Frames," *American Psychologist,* 34, reprinted in Kahneman (2011), *Thinking, Fast and Slow,* 433–448.

34. There are some noteworthy exceptions where the payoff is actually asymmetric in the opposite direction—the potential for loss far outweighs that for gains. The best example of this is merger arbitrage, where the upside potential is small and the downside is big, but the likelihood of the deal closing is estimated to be so high that the *probability-adjusted* payoff is attractive across a diversified portfolio of such bets.

35. Amos Tversky and Daniel Kahneman (1973), "Availability: A Heuristic for Judging Frequency and Probability," *Cognitive Psychology,* 5 (2), 677–695.

36. Florida Museum of Natural History, "International Shark Attack File: ISAF Statistics for the World Locations with the Highest Shark Attack Activity (2001–2012)," www.flmnh.ufl.edu/fish/sharks/statistics/statsw.htm; Randy Kreider (2012), "Dangerous Rip Currents Claim Lives at Florida Beaches," *ABC News,* June 18, http://abcnews.go.com/Blotter/dangerous-rip-currents-claim-lives-us-beaches/story?id=16542337.

37. James Spedding, Robert Leslie Ellis, and Douglas Denon Heath, ed. (1858), *The Works of Francis Bacon,* vol. 8, sections XLVI–XLVII, 79–80, Boston: Taggard and Thompson. Quote found in Raymond S. Nickerson (1998), "Confirmation Bias: A Ubiquitous Phenomenon in Many Guises," *Review of General Psychology,* 2 (2), 175–220.

38. Cf. Nickerson (1998), "Confirmation Bias."

39. Carole Hill, Amina Memon, and Peter McGeorge (2008), "The Role of Confirmation Bias in Suspect Interviews: A Systematic Evaluation," *Legal and Criminological Psychology,* 13, 357–371; S.M. Kassin, C.C. Goldstein, and K. Savitsky (2003), "Behavioural Confirmation in the Interrogation Room: On the Dangers of Presuming Guilt," *Law and Human Behaviour,* 27, 187–203.

40. E. Jonas, S. Schulz-Hardt, D. Frey, and N. Thelen (2001), "Confirmation Bias in Sequential Information Search after Preliminary Decisions: An Expansion of Dissonance Theoretical Research on Selective Exposure to Information," *Journal of Personality and Social Psychology,* 80, 557–571.

41. Kahneman (2011), *Thinking, Fast and Slow,* 203.

42. While the biases-and-heuristics literature has become wildly popular thanks to scholars such as Daniel Kahneman and journalists such as Malcolm Gladwell, a lesser-known school of thought called naturalistic decision making (NDM), led by social psychologist Gary Klein, demonstrates that across many real-world scenarios, our ingenuity overcomes our biases. To summarize NDM's motivation and mission: "Instead of trying to show how people do not measure up to ideal strategies for performing tasks, we have been motivated by curiosity about how people do so well under difficult conditions." Gary Klein (1998), *Sources of Power: How People Make Decisions,* Cambridge, MA: MIT Press, 1–2.

43. Isaiah Berlin (1953), *The Hedgehog and the Fox: An Essay on Tolstoy's View of History,* New York: Simon & Schuster, 3.

44. Tetlock, *Expert Political Judgment,* Kindle edition, location 225.

45. Ibid., location 1566–1568.

46. The political implications of this sentiment are far larger than quotidian issues of punditry. Recall that menacing line from Yeats's "The Second Coming" (1921) where he writes that when we are in a world of chaos, "The best lack all conviction, while the worst / Are full of passionate intensity." At ripe moments in history, allegiance to individuals knowing one big thing can have dire consequences.

47. Shanteau (1992), "The Psychology of Experts," 11–23; R. M. Hogarth (1981), "Beyond Discrete Biases: Functional and Dysfunctional Aspects of Judgmental Heuristics," *Psychological Bulletin,* 90, 197–217.

48. H. Murphy and R. L. Winkler (1977), "Can Weather Forecasters Formulate Reliable Forecasts of Prediction and Temperature?" *National Weather Digest,* 2, 2–9; Klein (2011), *Streetlights and Shadows.*

49. Kahneman (2011), *Thinking, Fast and Slow,* 242.

50. There is nothing "black box" about this; on any day, a hedge fund manager could give you a rough value, but because of certain accounting nuances plus exposure

to underlying securities themselves that aren't marked to market price on a daily basis (e.g., distressed debt), the number wouldn't be that meaningful.

51. Neal Roese (2005), *If Only: How to Turn Regret into Opportunity,* New York: Broadway Books, Kindle edition, location 111.

52. On a similar point that objectively better outcomes can produce subjectively worse evaluations of those outcomes, see Sheena S. Iyengar, Rachael E. Wells, and Barry Schwartz (2006), "Doing Better but Feeling Worse—Looking for the 'Best' Job Undermines Satisfaction," *Psychological Science,* 17 (2), 143–150.

53. "[W]hat the brain expects to happen in the near future affects its physiological state. It anticipates, and you can gain the benefit of that anticipation. The tendency of Alzheimer's patients not to experience placebo effects may be related to their inability to anticipate the future." Trivers (2011), *The Folly of Fools,* Kindle edition, location 1349.

54. See Jonah Lehrer (2009), *How We Decide,* New York: Houghton Mifflin Harcourt, as well as Wolfram Schultz (1998), "Predictive Reward Signal of Dopamine Neurons," *Journal of Neurophysiology,* 80 (1), July, 1–27.

55. Schwartz (1994), *The Costs of Living.*

56. Herbert A. Simon (1955), "A Behavioral Model of Rational Choice," *Quarterly Journal of Economics,* 69 (1), 99–118.

57. Barry Schwartz, Andrew Ward, John Monterosso, Sonja Lyubomirsky, Katherine White, and Darrin R. Lehman (2002), "Maximizing versus Satisficing: Happiness Is a Matter of Choice," *Personality and Social Psychology,* 83 (5), 1178–1197; Barry Schwartz (2009), "The Maximization Paradox: The Costs of Seeking Alternatives," *Personality and Individual Differences,* 46 (5–6), 631–635.

CHAPTER 3

1. Thomas Kuhn (1962/1970), *The Structure of Scientific Revolutions,* Chicago: University of Chicago Press, 93 (1970, 2nd edition, with postscript).

2. The philosophical grounding for this perspective comes from institutional economics (e.g., Douglass North [1981], *Structure and Change in Economic History,* New York: W.W. Norton), economic sociology (e.g., Mark Granovetter [1985], "Economic Action and Social Structure: The Problem of Embeddedness," *American Journal of Sociology,* 91 [3], 481–510), and behavioral economics (e.g., Kahneman and Tversky [1974], "Judgment Under Uncertainty: Heuristics and Biases," *Science,* 185 [4157], pp. 1124–1131).

3. Investment Company Institute (2012), *Investment Company Fact Book: A Review of Trends and Activity in the U.S. Investment Company Industry,* 52nd edition, Washington, D.C., ICI.

4. Peter Bernstein (1992), *Capital Ideas: The Improbable Origins of Modern Wall Street,* New York: Free Press, 264.

5. Ben S. Bernanke, "The Great Moderation," speech delivered at the Meetings of the Eastern Economic Association, Washington, DC, February 20, 2004, www .federalreserve.gov/boarddocs/speeches/2004/20040220/.

6. James H. Stock and Mark W. Watson (2003), "Has the Business Cycle Changed and Why?" *NBER Macroeconomics Annual 2002,* ed. Mark Gertler and Kenneth Rogoff, Cambridge, MA: MIT Press, 17, 159–230.

7. Ibid., 161.

8. Robert Pozen and Theresa Hamacher (2011), "Most Likely to Succeed: Leadership in the Fund Industry," *Financial Analysts Journal,* 67 (6), 1–8.

9. Quoted by John C. Bogle (1997), "The First Index Mutual Fund: A History of Vanguard Index Trust and the Vanguard Index Strategy," www.vanguard.com/bogle _site/lib/sp19970401.html.

10.　See www.fundinguniverse.com.

11.　Burton Malkiel (1973), *A Random Walk Down Wall Street,* New York: W.W. Norton; Paul Samuelson (1974), "Challenge to Judgment," *Journal of Portfolio Management,* 1 (1), 17–19; and Charles D. Ellis (1975), "The Loser's Game," *Financial Analysts Journal,* 31 (4), 19–26. For a wonderful tour through the academic and industry advances of this time, especially the rise of modern portfolio theory, the efficient markets hypothesis, and the rise of passive asset management (indexing), see Bernstein (1992), *Capital Ideas,* in which he nicely lays out the sweep of ideas of Harry Markovitz, William Sharpe, Eugene Fama, Paul Samuelson, and others and their implications for the modern investment management industry.

12.　See www.fundinguniverse.com.

13.　In 2003, the then CEO of Janus, Mark Whiston, commented in an interview with the *New York Times*: "When it comes to the business side of mutual funds, distribution is paramount. . . . It's no different in mutual funds than it is at [Procter and Gamble]." See also Brian Portnoy (2003), "A Checklist for Fund Shopping," February 18, 2013, http://news.morningstar.com/articlenet/article.aspx?id=86581.

14.　Eugene F. Fama and Kenneth R. French (1993), "Common Risk Factors in the Returns on Stocks and Bonds," *Journal of Financial Economics,* 33 (1), 3–56.

15.　In a parallel effort, the modeling of bond portfolio returns also advanced its own "three factor" model by accepting the improved explanatory power of including a bond's credit quality as well as its maturity.

16.　For a history of the index fund, see Bernstein (1992), *Capital Ideas,* 247–249.

17.　William H. Gross (2012), "Cult Figures," *PIMCO,* pimco.com/en/insights/pages/cult-figures.aspx; Jeremy J. Siegel's *Stocks for the Long Run: The Definitive Guide to Financial Market Returns & Long Term Investment Strategies,* now in its fifth edition, was first published in 1994.

18.　Though causing barely a ripple in the surging tide of 1998's equity market, the Russian debt default and the ensuing troubles at LTCM did course through a large portion of the then-nascent hedge fund industry.

19.　"Julian Robertson," Wikipedia, http://en.wikipedia.org/wiki/Julian_Robertson.

20.　Joseph A. Schumpeter (1942), *Capitalism, Socialism and Democracy,* London: Routledge.

21.　"Asset class," *Investopedia,* www.investopedia.com/terms/a/assetclasses.asp.

22.　The "alternatives" bucket often includes both hedge funds and private equity. The latter is a distinct type of illiquid investment and is not the subject of this book.

23.　Kuhn (1962/1970), *The Structure of Scientific Revolutions.*

24.　Simon Lack (2012), *The Hedge Fund Mirage: The Illusion of Big Money and Why It's Too Good to Be True,* New York: Wiley, 79.

25.　David Swensen (2000), *Pioneering Portfolio Management: An Unconventional Approach to Institutional Investment,* New York: Free Press.

26.　Pensions & Investments (2005), "Number of Hedge Fund Startups in 2004 a Record," *Pensions & Investments,* February 3, www.pionline.com/article/20050203/reg/502030716.

27.　Angelo Gordon, Citadel, Highfields Capital, Renaissance Technologies, Brevan Howard, AQR Capital, DE Shaw, JPMorgan/Highbridge, SAC Capital, Cheyne Capital, Atticus, ESL Investments, Lone Pine, Tudor, Gartmore, Avenue Capital, Farallon, Moore Capital, Soros, GLG Partners, Bridgewater, Fortress, Och-Ziff, Barclays Global Investors, Lansdowne Partners, Caxton Associates, Goldman Sachs Asset Management, Perry Capital, BlueCrest Capital, Man Group/AHL, Marshall Wace, Sloane Robinson, The Children's Investment Fund. "100 Hedge

Funds to Watch," *Financial Times,* http://media.ft.com/cms/02fd5a42-f338-11db
-9845-000b5df10621.pdf.

28. Perhaps the only notable product development was the so-called target fund, a
turnkey asset allocation vehicle based on a target retirement date. Thus if I were
to purchase today a "Target 2030" vehicle, the fund would be heavily tilted toward
stocks today, and then reallocate to fixed income investments as the target date
approached.

29. "Complete ETF List," *Master Data,* http://masterdata.com/HelpFiles/ETF_List
.htm.

30. Andrew W. Lo (2012), "Reading About the Financial Crisis," *Journal of Economic
Literature,* 50 (1), 151–178.

31. Jeremy Grantham (2013), "Investing in a Low Growth World," *GMO Quarterly
Letter,* www.gmo.com/websitecontent/GMO_QtlyLetter_1Q2013.pdf.

32. Carmen M. Reinhart and Kenneth S. Rogoff (2009), *This Time Is Different: Eight
Centuries of Financial Folly,* Princeton, NJ: Princeton University Press, Kindle edition, location 576.

33. Mohamed El Erian (2009), "A New Normal," PIMCO Secular Outlook (May),
www.pimco.com/EN/insights/pages/secular%20outlook%20may%202009%20
el-erian.aspx.

34. Robert J. Gordon (2012), "Is U.S. Economic Growth Over? Faltering Innovation
Confronts the Six Headwinds," NBER Working Paper No. 18315 (August), www
.nber.org/papers/w18315.

35. Ibid., 1.

36. James Montier (2013), "The Purgatory of Low Returns," *GMO Quarterly Letter,*
(July), 6–19, www.gmo.com/websitecontent/GMO_QtlyLetter_ALL_2Q2013.pdf.

37. Bill Gross (2011), "Family Feud," *PIMCO Investment Outlook* (December), www
.pimco.com/EN/insights/pages/family-feud.aspx#.

38. Citi Prime Finance (2012), Institutional Investment in Hedge Funds: Evolving
Investor Portfolio Construction Drives Product Convergence, http://icg.citi.com
/icg/global_markets/prime_finance/index.jsp.

39. Juliet Chung (2012), "Fidelity Offers Hedge-Fund Access via Arden Tie," *Wall
Street Journal,* December 6.

40. Citi Prime Finance (2013), The Rise of Liquid Alternatives & the Changing Dynamics of Alternative Product Manufacturing and Distribution, http://icg.citi
.com/icg/global_markets/prime_finance/index.jsp.

41. Kuhn (1962/1970), *The Structure of Scientific Revolutions,* 10.

CHAPTER 4

1. Sheena Iyengar (2010), *The Art of Choosing,* New York: Twelve Books, 213.

2. Daniel Kahneman (2011), *Thinking, Fast and Slow,* New York: Farrar, Straus and
Giroux.

3. Edward Chancellor (1999), *Devil Take the Hindmost: A History of Financial Speculation,* New York: Farrar, Straus and Giroux; Charles Mackay (1841), *Extraordinary Popular Delusions and the Madness of Crowds,* London: R. Bentley; Roger
Lowenstein (2001), *When Genius Failed: The Rise and Fall of Long-Term Capital
Management,* New York: Random House; Michael Lewis (1989), *Liar's Poker: Rising through the Wreckage on Wall Street,* New York: W.W. Norton, and (2011) *The
Big Short: Inside the Doomsday Machine,* New York: W.W. Norton.

4. Gregory Zuckerman (2009), *The Greatest Trade Ever: The Inside Story of How
John Paulson Defied Wall Street and Made Financial History,* New York: Broadway
Books.

5. Scott Patterson (2009), *The Quants: How a Small Band of Math Wizards Took Over Wall St. and Nearly Destroyed It,* New York: Crown.

6. Karl Pearson (1892), *The Grammar of Science,* London: J.M. Dent & Sons, Ltd., 16.

7. David Hume (1748), *An Enquiry Concerning Human Understanding,* 2nd edition, ed. Eric Steinberg, Indianapolis, IN: Hackett, Kindle edition, location 849.

8. Ibid., location 739.

9. Richard Feynman (2001), *The Character of Physical Law* (Messenger Lectures, 1964), Cambridge, MA: MIT Press.

10. See Stephen Van Evera (1997), *Guide to Methods for Students of Political Science,* Ithaca, NY: Cornell University Press.

11. Robin Goldstein et al. (2008), "Do More Expensive Wines Taste Better? Evidence from a Large Sample of Blind Tastings," *Journal of Wine Economics,* 3 (1), 1–9.

12. Whether luxury items produce higher customer satisfaction is an interesting question. The preponderance of studies shows a positive correlation between price and quality ratings for a large majority of 1,200 product markets. Cf. Gerard J. Tellis and Birger Wernerfelt (1987), "Competitive Price and Quality under Asymmetric Information," *Marketing Science,* 6 (3), 240–253.

13. Jonah Lehrer (2010), *How We Decide,* New York: Houghton Mifflin Harcourt.

14. Christine Benz (2007), *Morningstar Guide to Mutual Funds: Five Star Strategies for Success,* 2nd edition, New York: Wiley; John C. Bogle (2009), *Common Sense on Mutual Funds: Fully Updated 10th Anniversary Edition,* New York: Wiley.

15. Atul Gawande (2011), *The Checklist Manifesto: How to Get Things Right,* New York: Metropolitan Books.

16. Recall the young woman in the George Clooney film *Up in the Air* who engineered a question and response flow chart for efficiently firing employees. It's not a stretch to imagine engineering manager due diligence in a similar manner.

17. Gary Klein (2011), *Streetlights and Shadows: Searching for the Keys to Adaptive Decision Making,* Cambridge, MA: MIT Press.

18. The sources for Viking, Lone Pine, Tiger Global, and Maverick, and Third Point can be found at the searchable site of the Securities and Exchange Commission: www.sec.gov/edgar/searchedgar/companysearch.html.

19. An early classic study of our limited cognitive capacity is George A. Miller (1956), "The Magical Number 7, Plus or Minus Two: Some Limits on Our Capacity for Processing Information," *The Psychological Review,* 63, 81–97.

20. Secretary Colin L. Powell, Opening Remarks before the Senate Governmental Affairs Committee, September 13, 2004, www.fas.org/irp/congress/2004_hr /091304powell.html.

21. Martha Lagace (2009), "Kind of Blue: Pushing Boundaries with Miles Davis," *Working Knowledge,* April 13, http://hbswk.hbs.edu/cgi-bin/print/6096.html.

22. "*Kind of Blue,*" Wikipedia, http://en.wikipedia.org/wiki/Kind_of_Blue.

23. "Jazz Quotes," *A Passion for Jazz,* www.apassion4jazz.net/quotations7.html.

24. Klein (2011), *Streetlights and Shadows.*

25. Gary Klein (1998), *Sources of Power: How People Make Decisions,* Cambridge, MA: MIT Press.

26. Klein (2011), *Streetlights and Shadows,* 88.

27. Colm O'Shea in Jack D. Schwager (2012), *Hedge Fund Market Wizards: How Winning Traders Win,* New York: Wiley, xv.

28. Gaurav Jetley and Xinyu Ji (2010), "The Shrinking Merger Arbitrage Spread: Reasons and Implications," *Financial Analysts Journal,* 66 (2), 54–68.

29. Hedge Fund Research. Hedge Fund Research.com.

CHAPTER 5

1. David W. Maurer (1940), *The Big Con: The Story of the Confidence Man and the Confidence Game,* Indianapolis: Bobbs Merrill, 1.
2. Ibid., 103.
3. Ibid., 286.
4. "*The X-Files,*" Wikipedia, http://en.wikipedia.org/wiki/The_x_files.
5. Erin Arvedlund (2009), *Too Good to Be True: The Rise and Fall of Bernie Madoff,* New York: Portfolio; Diana B. Henriques (2011), *The Wizard of Lies: Bernie Madoff and the Death of Trust,* New York: Times Books/Henry Holt.
6. Arvedlund (2009), *Too Good to Be True,* 28.
7. Ibid., 49.
8. Ibid., 26
9. Diana B. Henriques and Alex Berenson, "The 17th Floor, Where Wealth Went to Vanish," *New York Times,* December 14, 2008, www.nytimes.com/2008/12/15/business/15madoff.html?pagewanted=all&_r=0.
10. Fairfield Greenwich Group (September 2008), *Fairfield Sentry, Ltd. Fact Sheet.*
11. Harry Markopolos (2011), *No One Would Listen: A True Financial Thriller,* with Frank Casey, Hoboken, NJ: Wiley.
12. Maurer (1940), *The Big Con,* 103.
13. Robert Trivers (2011), *The Folly of Fools: The Logic of Deceit and Self-Deception in Human Life,* New York: Basic Books, 24.
14. Erin Arvedlund, ed. (2010), *The Club No One Wanted to Join: Madoff Victims in Their Own Words,* Andover, MA: Doukathsan Press.
15. Ibid., 102.
16. Ibid., 104.
17. Ibid., 167.
18. Trivers (2011), *The Folly of Fools.*
19. Ibid., Kindle edition, location 258.
20. Arvedlund (2009), *Too Good to Be True,* 119.
21. Maurer (1940), *The Big Con,* 103.
22. Erin E. Arvedlund (2001), "Don't Ask, Don't Tell: Bernie Madoff Is So Secretive, He Even Asks His Investors to Keep Mum," *Barron's,* May 7.
23. Robert B. Cialdini (2008), *Influence: Science and Practice,* 5th edition, New York: Pearson.
24. Arvedlund (2009), *Too Good to Be True,* 159.
25. Denise M. Rousseau, Sim B. Sitkin, Ronald S. Burt, and Colin Camerer (1998), "Not So Different After All: A Cross-Discipline View of Trust," *Academy of Management Review,* 23 (3), 393–404.
26. Ronald Coase (1937), "The Nature of the Firm," *Economica,* 4 (16), 386–405. Cf. Oliver Williamson (1985), *The Economic Institutions of Capitalism: Firms, Markets, Relational Contracting,* New York: Free Press.
27. John C. Bogle (2012), *The Clash of Cultures: Investment vs. Speculation,* New York: Wiley.
28. Randy Shain (2008), *Hedge Fund Due Diligence: Professional Tools to Investigate Hedge Fund Managers,* New York: Wiley.
29. "SEC Charges Chicago-Based Investment Adviser with Defrauding CalPERS and Other Clients," April 18, 2013, www.sec.gov/News/PressRelease/Detail/PressRelease/1365171514754#.UgIg-5Jwrl4.
30. "Ex-Level Global Analyst Says He Tipped Boss, Level Global, SAC," November 15, 2012, www.finalternatives.com/node/22114; Jenny Strausberg, Michael

Rothfeld, and Susan Pulliam, "FBI Sweep Targets Big Funds," *Wall Street Journal,* January 19, 2012, http://online.wsj.com/article/SB1000142405297020446 8004577168450897919374.html; Patricia Hurtado (2013), "Ex-Diamondback Manager Gets 4 1/2 Years in Insider Case," May 2, www.bloomberg.com/news /print/2013-05-02/ex-diamondback-manager-gets-4-1-2-years-in-insider-case .html; Patricia Hurtado (2013), "Chiasson Seeks Leniency from Court Citing Charitable Work," May 1, www.bloomberg.com/news/2013-04-30/chiasson -says-charitable-works-merit-non-guideline-prison-term.html; Michael Rothfeld, Susan Pulliam, and Chad Bray (2011), "Fund Titan Found Guilty," *Wall Street Journal,* May 12, http://online.wsj.com/article/SB10001424052748703864 204576317060246641834.html.

31. Azam Ahmed (2011), "Former FrontPoint Manager Pleads Guilty to Insider Trading," *New York Times,* August 15, dealbook.nytimes.com/2011/08/15/former -frontpoint-manager-pleads-guilty-to-insider-trading/.

32. Quoted in James B. Stewart (2012), "In a New Era of Insider Trading, It's Risk vs. Reward Squared," *New York Times,* December 7.

33. Fortress Investment Group LLC (2008), US SEC Form 8-K, December 3, www .sec.gov/Archives/edgar/data/1380393/000119312508247037/d8k.htm.

34. "Hedge Funds Lock the Gates" (2008), *New York Times,* March 6, http://dealbook .nytimes.com/2008/03/06/hedge-funds-lock-the-gates/; David Walker and Phil Craig (2008), "Hedge Funds Slam 'Gates' on Their Edgy Investors," *Wall Street Journal,* October 27, http://online.wsj.com/article/SB122507308891970983.html; Alistair Barr (2010), "Hedge Funds Try New Way to Avoid Big Redemptions," *Market Watch,* June 10, articles.marketwatch.com/2010-06-10/industries/30680 521_1_hedge-funds-redemptions-fund-firm; David Enke (2008), "Hedge Funds Retaining Investors through Gates, Restrictions, Fee Concessions," *Seeking Alpha,* December 9, http://seekingalpha.com/article/109816-hedge-funds-retaining-inv estors-through-gates-restrictions-fee-concessions; Joseph Checkler (2008) "Hedge Fund Withdrawals Accelerate," *Wall Street Journal,* December 8, http:// online.wsj.com/article/SB122868561280086255.html; Lawrence Cohen and Thomas M. Griffin (2008), "A Run on Hedge Funds: Redemption Strategies and Responses," December 30, www.finalternatives.com/node/6474; Louise Story (2008), "Hedge Funds Are Bracing for Investors to Cash Out," *New York Times,* September 28, www.nytimes.com/2008/09/29/business/29hedge.html?_r=0.

35. Robert Putnam (2001), *Bowling Alone: The Collapse and Revival of American Community,* New York: Touchstone.

36. Ron Fournier and Sophie Quinton (2012), "In Nothing We Trust," *National Journal,* April 26, www.nationaljournal.com/features/restoration-calls/in-nothing -we-trust-20120419; George Packer (2013), *The Unwinding: An Inner History of the New America,* New York: Farrar, Straus and Giroux.

37. William D. Cohan, "How We Got the Crash Wrong," *The Atlantic,* June 2012.

38. David McLaughlin and Chris Dolmetsch (2013), "Goldman Sachs Wins Dismissal of Abacus CDO Suit on Appeal," *Bloomberg,* May 14, www.bloomberg .com/news/2013-05-14/goldman-sachs-wins-dismissal-of-abacus-cdo-suit -on-appeal.html; Beat Balzli (2010), "Greek Debt Crisis: How Goldman Sachs Helped Greece to Mask Its True Debt," *Spiegel Online International,* February 8, www.spiegel.de/international/europe/greek-debt-crisis-how-goldman-sachs -helped-greece-to-mask-its-true-debt-a-676634.html; Michael Lewis (2013), "The Trouble with Wall Street: The Shocking News That Goldman Sachs Is Greedy," *New Republic,* February 4, www.newrepublic.com/article/112209/mich ael-lewis-goldman-sachs.

CHAPTER 6

1. On Lampert, see Gregory Zuckerman (2012), "A Sears Wager Stings at Goldman," *Wall Street Journal,* January 23. Sears's stock fell 57 percent in 2011. On Ackman, see Shira Ovide (2011), "Bill Ackman Throws in the Towel on Target," *Wall Street Journal,* May 16, blogs.wsj.com/deals/2011/05/16/bill-ackman-throws-in-the-towel -on-target/. SRM, the largest hedge fund launch in European history at the time in 2006, lost almost all of its investors' money in less than three years after its portfolio manager, Jon Wood, made massive and mistaken bets on Motorola, Northern Rock, and Countrywide. On SRM, see FINalternatives (2011), "Battered SRM Rebrands, Offers New Fund," *FINalternatives,* January 24, www.finalternatives.com /node/15289 and Paul Murphy, "Wood-en Returns—Hedge Fund SRM All but Evaporates," *FTAlphaville,* August 15, http://ftalphaville.ft.com/2008/08/15/151 15/wood-en-returns-hedge-fund-srm-all-but-evaporates/.

2. On the squabble, see Tom Lauricella (2010), "Einhorn vs. Berkowitz: The Rumble over St. Joe," *Wall Street Journal,* October 10, http://blogs.wsj.com /marketbeat/2010/10/18/einhorn-vs-berkowitz-the-rumble-over-st-joe/. Also see Steve Shaefer (2010), "Berkowitz, Einhorn Square Off in St Joe Spat," *Forbes,* October 10, http://www.forbes.com/sites/steveschaefer/2010/10/19/berkowitz- einhorn-square-off-in-st-joe-spat/.

3. An even more recent "battle of the billionaires," as CNBC has labeled it, is over diet shake and energy bar maker Herbalife. Pershing Square's Bill Ackman thinks the company is a Ponzi scheme while Carl Icahn has been buying massive blocks of the stock. Jim Fink (2013), "Herbalife Is a Battle Royale between Hedge Funds," *Investing Daily,* January 11, www.investingdaily.com/16074/herbalife-is-a -battle-royale-between-hedge-funds.

4. On "activeness," see Beverly Goodman (2012), "Active Funds Come Out of the Closet," *Barron's,* November 17.

5. Steven Goldstein (2008), "Volkswagen Shares Skyrocket on Porsche Move," *MarketWatch,* October 27.

6. James Montier (2012), "The Flaws of Finance," *GMO White Paper,* May.

7. Quoted in Matt Levine (2013), "Senate Subcommittee Feasting on Whale Today," *Dealbreaker,* March 15, www.dealbreaker.com/2013/03/senate-subcommittee -feasting-on-whale-today/.

8. www.wintoncapital.com, home page.

9. Roger Lowenstein (2000), *When Genius Failed: The Rise and Fall of Long-Term Capital Management,* New York: Random House.

10. Satyajit Das (2006), *Traders, Guns and Money: Knowns and Unknowns in the Dazzling World of Derivatives,* New York: Financial Times Prentice Hall.

11. Ludwig B. Chincarini (2007), "The Amaranth Debacle: Failure of Risk Measures or Failure of Risk Management," *Journal of Alternative Investments,* 10 (3), 91–104.

CHAPTER 7

1. Jack L. Treynor (1966), "How to Rate Management Investment Funds," *Harvard Business Review,* 43 (1), 63–75; William F. Sharpe (1966), "Mutual Fund Performance," *Journal of Business,* 39 (1), 119–138; Jonathon B. Berk and Richard C. Green (2004), "Mutual Fund Flows and Performance in Rational Markets," *Journal of Political Economy,* 112 (6), 1269–1295; Eugene Fama and Kenneth French (1993), "Common Risk Factors in the Returns on Stocks and Bonds," *Journal of Financial Economics,* 33, 3–56; Mark M. Carhart (1997), "On Persistence in

Mutual Fund Performance," *Journal of Finance*, 52 (1), 57–82; Eugene F. Fama and Kenneth R. French (2010), "Luck versus Skill in the Cross Section of Mutual Fund Returns," *Journal of Finance*, 65 (5), 1915–1947.

2. Sharpe (1966), "Mutual Fund Performance"; Treynor (1966), "How to Rate Management Investment Funds"; Michael C. Jensen (1967), "The Performance of Mutual Funds in the Period 1945–1964," *Journal of Finance*, 23 (2), 389–416.

3. For example, one study of mutual fund performance from 1975 to 2002 finds positive alphas among the top 10 percent of funds, net of fees, which cannot be attributed only to luck. These managers showed stock-picking skill persistently. Robert Kosowski, Allan Timmermann, Russ Wermers, and Hal White (2006), "Can Mutual Fund 'Stars' Really Pick Stocks? New Evidence from a Bootstrap Analysis," *Journal of Finance*, 61 (6), 2551–2595.

4. Using survivorship bias-free data, Busse, Goyal, and Wahal studied the performance of 4,617 active domestic equity institutional products between 1991 and 2008. Taking into account the factors delineated in the Fama-French and Carhart studies, they find that the overall alpha was statistically indistinguishable from zero. While comparative returns vary markedly at any moment in time, the authors do not find much, if any, persistence of outperformance. In other words, hot streaks exist, but they don't last long. Likewise, Cuthbertson, Nitzsche, and O'Sullivan examined a large cross section of US and UK actively managed equity and bond funds, finding that a vast majority of them demonstrate negligible skill. Just a tiny slice of funds (less than 5 percent) deliver value after fees. Fama and French continue to find that very few funds perform well enough to justify their costs. Jeffrey A. Busse, Amit Goyal, and Sunil Wahal, "Performance and Persistence in Institutional Investment Management," *Journal of Finance*, 65 (2), 765–790; Keith Cuthbertson, Dirk Nitzsche, and Niall O'Sullivan (2010), "Mutual Fund Performance: Measurement and Evidence," *Financial Markets, Institutions, & Instruments*, 19 (2), 95–187; Fama and French (2010), "Luck versus Skill."

5. Because hedge fund databases are notoriously bias ridden, the authors corrected for both survivorship and look-back effects, thus rendering their overall findings "cleaner" and more robust. Roger G. Ibbotson, Peng Chen, and Kevin X. Zhu (2011), "The ABCs of Hedge Funds: Alphas, Betas, and Costs," *Financial Analysts Journal*, 67 (1), 15–25.

6. They also ran a more robust model building of the Fung-Hsieh seven-factor model (taking into account trend-following factors for bonds, currencies, and commodities; equity markets; size spread, bond market factor, and credit spread factor) and still arrived at statistically significant levels of alpha. Cf. William Fung and David A. Hsieh (2004), "Hedge Fund Benchmarks: A Risk-Based Approach," *Financial Analysts Journal*, 60 (5), 65–80.

7. Simon Lack (2012), *The Hedge Fund Mirage: The Illusion of Big Money and Why It's Too Good to Be True*, Hoboken, NJ: Wiley.

8. Ilia D. Dichev and Gwen Yu (2009), "Higher Risk, Lower Returns: What Hedge Fund Investors Really Earn," *Journal of Financial Economics*, July 1.

9. Doug Lennick and Kathleen Jordan (2010), *Financial Intelligence: How to Make Smart, Values-Based Decisions with Your Money and Your Life*, Denver, CO: FPA Press.

10. Michael J. Mauboussin (2012), *The Success Equation: Untangling Skill and Luck in Business, Sports, and Investing*, Boston: Harvard Business Review Press.

11. James Montier (2007), *Behavioural Investing: A Practitioners Guide to Applying Behavioural Finance*, New York: Wiley.

12. Galen Burghardt, Ryan Duncan, and Lianyan Liu (2007), "Superstars versus Teamwork," *Alternative Edge Research Note,* www.newedge2009.com/images_new edgegroup/aig/PDF/Superstars_Versus_Teamwork.pdf.

13. Paul Justice (2009), "Warning: Leveraged and Inverse ETFs Kill Portfolios," January 22, http://news.morningstar.com/articlenet/article.aspx?id=271892; Eric Oberg (2009), "The Perils of the ProShares UltraShorts," *The Street,* January 13; Joe Light (2012), "Beware 'Leveraged' ETFs," *Wall Street Journal,* May 11, http://online .wsj.com/article/SB10001424052702304543904577394261225920548.html.

14. US SEC, Office of Investor Education and Advocacy (2009), "Leveraged and Inverse ETFs: Specialized Products with Extra Risks for Buy-and-Hold Investors," US SEC, August 18, www.sec.gov/investor/pubs/leveragedetfs-alert.htm.

15. Jane Goodall (2010), *Through a Window: My Thirty Years with the Chimpanzees of Gombe,* Boston: Houghton Mifflin Harcourt, Kindle edition, location 243.

16. Paul E. Meehl, *Clinical versus Statistical Prediction: A Theoretical Analysis and a Review of the Evidence,* Brattleboro, VT: Echo Point Books and Media; Daniel Kahneman (2011), *Thinking, Fast and Slow,* New York: Farrar, Straus, and Giroux, 225.

17. Quoted in Floyd Norris (2013), "Masked by Gibberish, the Risks Run Amok," *New York Times,* March 21, www.nytimes.com/2013/03/22/business/behind-the -derivatives-gibberish-risks-run-amok.html?ref=business&pagewanted=print.

18. Kathryn Schulz (2010), *Being Wrong: Adventures in the Margin of Error,* New York: Ecco.

CHAPTER 8

1. Towers Watson, *Global Pension Assets Study 2013,* www.towerswatson.com/en /Insights/IC-Types/Survey-Research-Results/2013/01/Global-Pensions-Asset -Study-2013; cf. Jason Zweig (2012), "Are Pension Forecasts Way Too Sunny?" *Wall Street Journal,* January 28.

2. Arleen Jacobius (2013), "'Go Big' in Alternatives, Conference Attendees Urged," *Pensions & Investments,* April 23. Public pension plans from California to Texas to Florida have all made increasingly large allocations to hedge funds. For example, the North Carolina Retirement System recently pushed to up its allocation to alternatives to 40 percent, up from the already high figure of 34 percent. See Hazel Bradford (2013), "North Carolina Senate OKs Hike in Alternative Investments for State Pension Fund," *Pensions & Investments,* May 7.

3. Sam Forgione (2012), "Cash-Strapped US Pension Funds Ditch Stocks for Alternatives," Reuters, August 16.

4. Citi Prime Finance (2013), The Rise of Liquid Alternatives & the Changing Dynamics of Alternative Product Manufacturing and Distribution, http://icg.citi .com/icg/global_markets/prime_finance/index.jsp.

INDEX

absolute return paradigm, 67, 69, 71, 85, 106, 157, 161, 213
access, 130–1, 134, 137–8, 142–3
Ackman, Bill, 159
adaptation, 43–7
adaptive investing, 104–13
Ainslie, Lee, 75
alignable assortments, 24
allocation, 172–3
Alpern, Sol, 130
alternative investments, 32–3, 64, 69–70, 72, 85–6, 117–18, 142, 163, 188, 210, 217
Amaranth, 117, 177–9
American Century, 62
American Funds (Capital Group), 60, 62
arbitrage, 117–20, 172–3, 176–7, 223n34
Arden Asset Management, 93
Arendt, Hannah, 183
Arrow, Kenneth J., 219n4
Asness, Cliff, 98
availability bias, 39–40
Avellino, Frank, 130

Bacon, Francis, 41
Baupost, 116, 156
Bear Stearns, 83, 149
Berkowitz, Bruce, 159–60, 190
Berlin, Isaiah, 28, 43–5. See also hedgehogs and foxes
Bernanke, Ben, 30–1, 58
Bernard L. Madoff Investment Securities LLC (BLMIS), 129–31
Bernstein, Peter, 57, 226n11
Berra, Yogi, 25
Bienes, Michael, 130
Blackstone Group, 79, 141

Blue Bay, 150
BlueCrest, 79, 140
Bogle, John C. "Jack," 61, 73, 103, 188
Bohr, Neils, 1
bounded rationality, 52
Brevan Howard, 21, 106, 140
Bridgewater, 3, 20, 106, 156
Buffett, Warren, xii, 173
Burry, Michael, 84
Bush, George W., 125, 139, 144

calendar spread, 178
CalPERS, 146, 216
Campbell, Joseph, 97
Cantillon, 78
Canyon, 116, 163
Capital Asset Pricing Model (CAPM), 62
Capital Group, 60, 62
capital structure arbitrage, 172
Carhart, Mark, 186
Carlson, 75, 116
Carlyle Group, 141
Chamberlain, Neville, 42
Chancellor, Edward, 97–8
Chartered Financial Analyst (CFA) certification, 7
Chen, Peng, 186
Chiasson, Anthony, 147
choice regimes, 16–19
Citadel, 20, 83, 116, 140, 178
Clifford Street (London), 1–4, 41, 201–5
Cohan, William, 152
Cohn, Maurice "Sonny," 131
Cold War, 28–30, 45, 139
Columbo (television series), 204–5
complexity, 170–4
concentration, 156–8

confirmation bias, 40–2
convergence, era of, 7–8, 56–7, 92, 104, 123
convexity, 69
Countrywide Financial, 84, 160
Cowboys and Geniuses, 174–9, 192, 211, 214
Credit Suisse, 79, 213
cult of equity, 64
custom, 101–2

Dalio, Ray, 156
Dangerfield, Rodney, 108
Davis, Miles, 114, 116
Dawes, Robyn, 34
DB Zwirn, 117
DE Shaw, 79, 150
De Vita, Michael, 135
decision making, factors that influence, 34–45
Deutsche Bank, 79
Dewaele, Benoit, 33
Diamondback, 147, 156
Dichev, Ilia, 189
directionality, 156–7, 162–5
diversification, 22, 64, 66, 77, 192. *See also* false diversification
Do the Right Thing (film), 148
dollar-weighted returns, 189
Dow Jones Industrial Average, 25–8, 36, 57
Dreman, David, 31
Drew, Ina, 170–1
Dunning, David, 35

Einhorn, David, 159–60
Einstein, Albert, 155, 209
Eisman, Steve, 84
Elliot Associates, 64, 116, 156, 172
Ellis, Charles D., 61
emerging markets (EMs), 83–4
Emerson, Ralph Waldo, 134
endowment effect, 112
Endowment Model, xi–xii, 76–7
Enron, 73
errors of commission/omission, 212
Evans, Bill, 114
event-driven funds, 190–1
exchange-traded funds (ETFs), 7, 9, 19–21, 56, 81–2, 92–3, 105, 162, 189, 193–4, 220n14

experts, 1, 4, 7–10, 24–36, 42–8, 128, 170–3, 184–5, 205, 210. *See also* foxes and hedgehogs

Fairfield Greenwich Group (FGG), 131–4, 136
Fairholme, 159–60, 190
false diversification, 64, 166
Fama, Eugene, 19, 62, 68, 186
Farallon Capital, 79, 150
feedback loop, 23, 47–50
Feynman, Richard, 101, 104
Fidelity, 3, 21, 60–1, 64, 73, 93, 140, 143
Field of Dreams (film), 205
financial crisis of 2008, 4, 30–1, 53, 56, 71–2, 77, 82–7, 142–3, 148–50, 168, 170–2, 196–7, 212–14
Fortress Investment Group, 3, 20, 79, 141, 150
Fournier, Ron, 152
foxes and hedgehogs, 44–7, 50, 92, 107–8, 119–20, 122, 144–6, 170, 191–4, 197–8, 203
Franklin Templeton, 62, 140
Freedman, David H., 221
French, Kenneth, 62, 68, 186
FrontPoint Partners, 84, 147, 156
fundamental law of active management (FLAM), 22

Gambler's Fallacy, 37–8
Geniuses and Cowboys, 174–9, 192, 211, 214
Gladwell, Malcolm, 27, 48, 224n42
Glassman, James, 25–7, 36
Global Crossing, 73
Goldman Sachs, 78–9, 141, 152
Gomez, Lefty, 191
Goodall, Jane, 199–200
Gordon, Robert, 88–9
great contraction, 87–91
Great Moderation, 56–72, 77, 86–7
Greenlight Capital, 159–60
Greenspan, Alan, 31, 58
Gross, Bill, 64, 91
Growth Fund of America, 73
Gruss, 75, 118

Halcyon, 20, 118
Haley, Todd, 42
Hallinan, Joseph T., 27

happiness, 50–1
Harvest, 118
Hassett, Kevin, 25–7, 36
HBK, 20, 75, 116
hedge funds, definition of, 66–70
hedgehogs and foxes, 44–7, 50, 92, 107–8,
    119–20, 122, 145–6, 170, 191–4,
    197–8, 203
Herbalife, 159, 231n3
Highbridge, 20, 79, 173
hindsight bias, 42–3
Hitler, Adolf, 42
Hohn, Chris, 159
Hume, David, 100–2
Hunter, Brian, 178

Ibbotson, Roger, 186
Icahn, Carl, 159
Iksil, Bruno, 170–1
illiquidity, 59, 66, 77, 156, 168–70,
    175–81, 215
improvisation, 113–17
index funds, 20, 32, 60–1, 63, 73, 91, 186,
    188
inference, 100–4, 120
information mismanagement, 39–43
innovation, 173–4
Invesco, 73
investment management, modern era
    phases
    Great Moderation (1982–2000),
        56–72, 77, 86–7
    Lost Decade (2000–2009), 56, 72–86
    New Normal (2009-forward), 56,
        86–93, 116, 215
investor's paradox, definition of, 5, 18
Iyengar, Sheena, 14–15, 26, 97

Janus, 5, 73, 226n13
jazz, 114, 116
Jensen, Michael, 186
Johnson III, Edward C. "Ned," 60–1
JPMorgan, 3, 79, 141, 152, 170–1, 178

Kahneman, Daniel, 27, 37–8, 43, 48, 97,
    219n4
Keillor, Garrison, 183
Kellner DiLeo, 118
KKR, 141
Klarman, Seth, 156
Klein, Gary, 114–15, 224n42

Kohn, Sonja, 131
Kruger, Justin, 35
Krugman, Paul, 215
Kuhn, Thomas, 55, 70, 93

Lack, Simon, 71, 189–90
Lake Wobegon effect, 183
Lampert, Edward, 79, 159
law of small numbers, 37
Leakey, Louis, 199
Lee, Spike, 148
Leeson, Nick, 204
Legg Mason Value Trust, 73, 141
Lehman Brothers, 150
Level Global, 147
leverage, 156–8, 165–7, 175–6
Lewis, Michael, 98, 108
Lichtenstein, Warren, 159
Lipper, 63, 140
Lipstick Building, 129–34, 137
liquidity, 156–8, 164, 167–70, 175–6
Lo, Andrew, 83
Loeb, Dan, 159
London Whale, 152, 170
Long-Term Capital Management
    (LTCM), 64–5, 71, 76, 176
loss aversion, 38–9, 69, 112, 155
Lost Decade (2000–2009), 56, 72–86
Lowenstein, Roger, 64, 98, 180
Lynch, Peter, 60

Mackay, Charles, 97–8
Madoff, Bernie, 10, 42, 98, 121, 125–6,
    129–45
Magellan Fund (Fidelity), 60, 73
Malkiel, Burton, 61
manager selection, xii, 4, 7, 57, 86, 91
Mandel, Steve, 75
Maounis, Nick, 177
Markopolos, Harry, 133–4, 137
Marsalis, Wynton, 114
Martin, Steve, 112
Maurer, David, 125–7, 130, 134, 137
Meehl, Paul, 33–4
Meriwether, John, 176–7
Merkin, Ezra, 131
Merrill Lynch, 62, 79
Merton, Robert, 176
Meyer, Jack, 78
Millennium, 116
Mindich, Eric, 79

mistakes vs. bad outcomes, 212–15
modern portfolio theory (MPT), 22, 66
Montier, James, 91
Moore, 64, 116
Morgan Stanley, 79
Morningstar, 5–8, 18, 120–1, 123, 140,
    159, 212–13
Morningstar Style Box, 56, 62–3, 68–9,
    73–4, 161, 190
mortgage-backed securities (MBS), 83–4
Most Interesting Manager in the World,
    156, 174, 181
Motorola, 159
multi-strategy funds, 79, 105–6, 119–20,
    172–3, 177
mutual funds, 57, 59, 61, 67–8, 81–4,
    141–2, 146, 162–6, 169, 186, 190,
    232n3

NASDAQ, 25, 29, 66, 73, 129
NASDAQ Composite, 66, 73
nested forms of skill, 183–5
New Normal (2009-forward), 56, 86–93,
    116, 216
Newman, Todd, 147
Noel, Walter, 131
Northern Rock, 160

Och, Dan, 79
Och-Ziff Capital Management, 21, 75,
    79, 116, 118, 141, 173
operational due diligence (ODD), 142
optimism bias, 35–7, 216
ORN, 118
overconfidence, 35–7, 216

Packer, George, 152
paradigm shifts, 70–1, 74
paradigm, definition of, 70
paradox of choice, 16, 19, 23
path dependence, 101
pattern seeking, 36–8
Patterson, Scott, 98
Paulson, John, 84, 98, 106, 115–16, 118
Paulson Capital, 75, 84
Pearson, Karl, 99
Pelligrini, Paolo, 115
Peloton, 117
Perry, Richard, 79
PIMCO, 64, 86
Pine River, 140

Polygon, 150
Ponzi schemes, 130–3, 135
Pope, Alexander, 51
Powell, Colin, 111
prediction error, 51
preference articulation, 23–4
prop desks, 78–9
Protégé Partners, xii
PSAM, 118
Putin, Vladimir, 125, 139, 144
Putnam, 5
Putnam, Robert, 151–2

Rajaratnam, Raj, 147
regret, 50–1
regulation, 17, 66–7, 93, 139, 144
Reinhart, Carmen, 87
relative return investing, 63–4, 68–9, 71
Renaissance, 156, 159
risk aversion, 38–9
risk prism, 10, 157–74, 179–80, 211,
    214–15
Robertson, Julian, 65, 67, 195
Roese, Neal, 50–1
Roethlisberger, Ben, 42
Rogoff, Kenneth, 87
Rubin, Robert, 79

"60/40" portfolio allocation model, 91
S&P 500 Index, 20, 65–6, 73, 81–2, 84,
    193–4, 196
S&P 500 SPDR, 193
sample bias, 98, 180
Samuelson, Paul, 61
satisficing, 50–2, 113, 184, 218
Scholes, Myron, 176
Schwartz, Barry, 13, 16. See also paradox
    of choice
Scion Capital, 84
Securities and Exchange Commission
    (SEC), 109–10, 131, 133–4, 144, 150,
    194, 201
selection bias, 98, 180
Sentry Fund (Fairfield), 131–4, 136
September 11, 2001, 42
shadow banking, 66
Sharpe Ratio, 69, 133
Sharpe, William, 186
Shiller, Robert, 90
Shiller's P/E, 90
Simon, Herbert, 51–2, 218

Simons, Jim, 156
Simran Pre-Event Driven Activist
    Opportunity Fund, 146
Singer, Paul, 156
Singh, Dinakar, 79
Skowron, Joseph, 147
Smith, Adam, 100
Sowood Capital, 83
Stark Investments, 75, 106, 117
Steyer, Tom, 79
Sting, The (film), 126–7
Stock, James, 58
stock pickers, 8, 19, 31–3, 38, 48–50,
    60–1, 73, 75, 82, 91, 128, 165, 185
style bets, 161
style box paradigm, 46, 56, 62–3, 68–9,
    72–4, 77, 82, 121, 161, 190
style drift, 107, 120
Swensen, David, xi-xii, 76–7
Szporluk, Roman, 28

T. Rowe Price, 21, 62
Taleb, Nassim Nicholas, 31
Tetlock, Philip, 28–30, 34, 36, 42–4, 186,
    205, 222n6
Tiger Cubs (Robertson's protégés), 65,
    75, 79
Tiger Management Company, 65, 67, 195
Time Warner, 117, 159
time-weighted returns, 189

Tolstoy, Leo, 43–5
transparency, 109–10, 140–3, 201, 206
Treynor, Jack, 186
Trivers, Robert, 36, 136, 138
trust, 138–45
Tudor, 64, 116, 150
Twain, Mark, 155

UBS, 79

Vanguard, 19–20, 60–1, 64, 110, 140
Volcker, Paul, 58
Von Mueffling, William, 78

Watson, Mark, 58
Weinstein, Boaz, 98
Wellington Fund (Vanguard), 61, 140
Wermers, Russ
Winton Capital, 173
WorldCom, 73

X-Files, The (television series), 127–8,
    136

Yale model (Endowment Model), xi-xii,
    76–7
Yeats, W. B., 224n46
York, 118

Zuckerman, Gregory, 98

ABOUT THE AUTHOR

BRIAN PORTNOY, PHD, CFA, HAS BEEN SUCCESSFULLY RESEARCHING, advising, and investing in hedge funds and mutual funds for the past fourteen years. He is currently the Head of Alternative Investments and Strategic Initiatives for Chicago Equity Partners, a $10 billion asset manager. Previously, Brian held senior roles at Mesirow Advanced Strategies, a multibillion-dollar fund of funds, where he was the Associate Head of Hedge Fund Research; and Morningstar, the world's premier research shop on mutual funds.

Brian is a recognized expert on hedge funds, mutual funds, and investment due diligence. He has spoken at numerous investing conferences across the United States, Europe, and Asia and has appeared frequently in major media outlets such as CNBC and the *Wall Street Journal.* At Morningstar, Brian published numerous investment research pieces.

Prior to his investing career, Brian pursued his research and teaching interests in political economy and markets at the University of Chicago, where he earned his PhD in 2000. Brian's research on globalization was supported by the MacArthur Foundation. He was also the recipient of the University of Chicago's prestigious Century Fellowship. Across the United States and Europe, Brian taught and lectured on numerous topics, ranging from classic political economy to the current challenges of globalization. He trained in advanced research methods at Chicago, Stanford University, and the University of Michigan. Brian is a CFA Charterholder and a member of the CFA Society of Chicago. He currently lives in Chicago with his wife and three children.